LET'S STU
1 CORINTHIANS

Series Editor: SINCLAIR B. FERGUSON

Let's Study

1 CORINTHIANS

David Jackman

THE BANNER OF TRUTH TRUST

THE BANNER OF TRUTH TRUST
3 Murrayfield Road, Edinburgh EH12 6EL, UK
P.O. Box 621, Carlisle, PA 17013, USA

*

© David Jackman 2004
First Published 2004
ISBN 0 85151 885 0

*

*

Typeset in 11/12.5 pt Ehrhardt MT by
Initial Typesetting Services,
Edinburgh

Printed in Great Britain by
Bell & Bain Ltd.,
Glasgow

Contents

Publisher's Preface

*L*et's Study 1 Corinthians is part of a series of books which explain and apply the message of Scripture. The series is designed to meet a specific and important need in the church. While not technical commentaries, the volumes comment on the text of a biblical book; and, without being merely lists of practical applications, they are concerned with the ways in which the teaching of Scripture can affect and transform our lives today. Understanding the Bible's message and applying its teaching are the aims.

Like other volumes in the series, *Let's Study 1 Corinthians* seeks to combine explanation and application. Its concern is to be helpful to ordinary Christian people by encouraging them to understand the message of the Bible and apply it to their own lives. The reader in view is not the person who is interested in all the detailed questions which fascinate the scholar, although behind the writing of each study lies an appreciation for careful and detailed scholarship. The aim is exposition of Scripture written in the language of a friend, seated alongside you with an open Bible.

Let's Study 1 Corinthians is designed to be used in various contexts. It can be used simply as an aid for individual Bible study. Some may find it helpful to use in their devotions with husband or wife, or to read in the context of the whole family.

In order to make these studies more useful, not only for individual use but also for group study in Sunday School classes and home, church or college, study guide material will be found on pp. 287–306. Sometimes we come away frustrated rather than helped by group discussions. Frequently that is because we have been encouraged to discuss a passage of Scripture which we do not understand very well in the first place. Understanding must always be the foundation for enriching discussion and for thoughtful, practical application. Thus, in addition to the exposition of Galatians, the additional material provides questions to encourage personal thought and study, or to be used as discussion starters. The Group Study Guide divides the material into thirteen sections and provides direction for leading and participating in group study and discussion.

Introduction

O ur first introduction to Corinth in the pages of the New
Testament occurs in Acts 18:1–18, during Paul's second
missionary journey. Travelling from Athens, where he had so
recently addressed the philosophers of the Areopagus and left
behind a small group of new believers, Paul now approached a
very different context. Had there been a tourist information
office for him to visit and pick up some introductory leaflets
about his new environment, he would probably have found a
considerable amount of civic pride and communal energy in its
self-image.

Situated on the narrow isthmus between the Aegean and the
Adriatic Seas, Corinth had become an important centre of trade
and commerce. Although the settlement was centuries old, it had
been destroyed by the Romans two hundred years before Paul
arrived and its inhabitants had been enslaved. But after a century
of desolation, Julius Caesar had founded New Corinth and
rebuilt the city, which then became the capital of Achaia and was
ruled by its own proconsul. Acts 18:12 tells us that Gallio
occupied that office during Paul's eighteen months in Corinth.
An independent inscription from Delphi enables historians to
date the church-planting visit to 51–52 AD.

By this time, Corinth had become a wealthy, cosmopolitan
sea-port, with a reputation for being at the cutting edge of
Mediterranean life and culture. It had been resettled with
discharged soldiers from all over the Roman Empire, so that it
now provided a rich mix of ethnicity and religion. As an
accessible travel centre, it would draw all the itinerant
philosophers and rhetoricians on the circuit – the media pundits

of the ancient world. Archaeological excavations have revealed many evidences of a city life-style devoted to entertainment and self-indulgence, as can still be found in any great city today. It is hardly speculation to suggest that status, kudos, popularity, money, success and pleasure were the idols at the heart of Corinth, concealed in the outward pursuit of the good life with its aggressive and pervasive paganism. As citizens of the 21st century we would have found much that was instantly familiar had we been with Paul in Corinth, when he began to preach 'Jesus Christ and him crucified' (*1 Cor.* 2:2).

As usual, Paul began in the synagogue, with the Jews and Gentile proselytes or 'God-fearers': ' . . . he reasoned in the synagogue every Sabbath, and tried to persuade Jews and Greeks . . . testifying to the Jews that the Christ was Jesus' (*Acts* 18:4-5). He lodged with his fellow tentmakers, Aquila and Priscilla, also Jews, recently expelled from Rome, and worked alongside them, while he waited for Silas and Timothy to join him from Macedonia. In spite of fierce opposition and abuse, it was a mission owned by God and resulted in the conversion of the synagogue ruler, Crispus, and many of the Corinthian citizens (*Acts* 18:8). Indeed, so fruitful was it to continue to be that the Lord personally strengthened Paul in a night vision, encouraging him to continue and promising protection from harm, 'for I have many in this city who are my people' (*Acts* 18:9). The church seems to have been centred initially on the house of Titius Justus next to the synagogue (*Acts* 18:7), but in all probability rapidly outgrew this location. Those whom Paul addresses in the letter would therefore have been a mixture of Jews and Gentiles, from both monotheistic and pagan backgrounds, and from the little evidence we have it is likely that they would have represented a wide social range.

When we consider all these different factors, it is hardly surprising that the church faced many problems and appears to have drifted into several potentially disastrous errors, so early in its life. It is a fact that the church in any location and generation is far more likely to be conformed to the pattern of this world than is usually recognized or admitted. Certainly, in 1 Corinthians there are many evidences of the cultural 'squeeze' which had the potential to suffocate the young church. From their pagan background, many of the new converts would still have been attached to the phenomena of their old religion, including ecstatic speech and cult-prostitution. Pagan temples were at the heart of Corinthian social life, functioning as meeting places, markets and restaurants. D. R. de Lacey comments in his article on Corinth in the *New Bible Dictionary* (IVP, 1980, p. 316), 'As well as the emotional and cultic elements, Hellenistic religions also appealed to the intellect . . . Many of these religions developed a strongly dualistic outlook, for which matter was illusory and evil, whereas only the objects of thought, in the realm of the soul, were concrete and good. This easily led to a premium on knowledge; to a belief (also found in Hellenistic Judaism) in the immortality of the soul rather than the resurrection of the body.' In terms of behaviour and life-style, such views might lead either to ascetic legalism, with its rejection of the physical, or, paradoxically, to a libertinism which regarded the body as worthless, so that its activities were of no significance. There are evidences in the letter of all these forces at work.

Looking purely at the internal evidence of the letter itself, it becomes clear that certain key concepts are the focal points of the controversies besetting the Corinthian congregation. The opening chapter establishes the reality of the Corinthians' profession of saving faith in Christ. They are true believers, set apart and called to be holy, united with all other Christians. They are also a gifted congregation, enriched by God's grace in every area of their corporate life and ministry and eagerly awaiting Christ's return. But they are divided. As the first part of the letter unfolds, it becomes clear that there are four areas of controversy, which are encapsulated by particular 'buzz' words. The first is '*knowledge*' which the Corinthians wanted to elevate to the primary position, but which Paul wants to reduce in its importance compared with love (see *1 Cor.* 1:5; 8:1,7,10–11; 12:8; 13:2,8; 14:6). The second is '*wisdom*' around which most of the first two chapters rotate. Paul's argument is that their concept of wisdom is culturally conditioned and driven by the values of this world, whereas God's wisdom is located in the 'foolishness' of the Cross (*1 Cor.* 1:17,19–24,30; 2:1,4–7,13; 3:19; 12:8). '*Power*' is the next issue under discussion, as the Corinthian emphasis is so much on external excitement in the demonstration of the supernatural. Here the apostle's correction is to show that the greatest evidence of divine power is in the saving grace of God, generated by Christ's death (*1 Cor.* 1:18–24; 2:4–5; 4:19-20; 5:4; 6:14; 12:10,28–29; 14:11; 15:24,43,56). Lastly, Paul focuses on the vexed question of what it means to be '*spiritual*', with his strong shift from impressive external displays of gifts or ecstasy, to the humble service of love which is the heart-beat of the gospel (*1 Cor.* 2:13–15; 3:1; 9:11; 10:3–4; 12:1; 14:1,37; 15:44, 46).

Claims were being made for themselves, which effectively marked out the Corinthian church as an elite group. They canvassed their spiritual wisdom as superior to that of their apostle and claimed a greater degree of maturity, which he has to refute in the most direct and unflattering way (*1 Cor.* 3:1–4). This was probably associated with other claims that they were already living above the normal, material experience of Christians in this present world and had somehow already entered into the blessings of the eternal kingdom, making the future resurrection of the body irrelevant and redundant (*1 Cor.* 15:12). This over-realized eschatology which tried to bring all the blessings of the 'not yet' into the 'now' was attractive and exciting at first, but would ultimately lead to disillusionment and decline as its expectations could never be fulfilled in this world. For these and other reasons, quarrels were developing in the church, as they divided over different human leaders (*1 Cor.* 1:10–12; 3:3–9,21; 4:1–2), to whom Paul was definitely considered inferior by some. They were in danger of producing a boastful, 'puffed up' church, which was in danger of losing the gospel of Christ crucified altogether (*1 Cor.* 1:29–31; 3:21; 4:6–7,18–19; 8:1).

This, then, is why there was a battle taking place for the heart of the Corinthian church. But as we study the masterly teaching and application of the truth of the gospel by the apostle to the Gentiles, and its relevance to all of these (and many other) issues, the centuries roll away and we hear this same word addressing the very similar issues, which beset and divide churches and Christians in our own day. Not only does this letter challenge our contemporary eccentricities and inconsistencies, but it also teaches us a better way, 'a still more excellent way' of love and its powerful, penetrating message delineates the nature of a true spirituality which can emanate only from the gospel of the crucified Saviour. Once we have understood its melodic line, the letter will both provide the necessary teaching and generate the motivation for us to heed and practise its final exhortation. 'Be watchful, stand firm in the faith, act like men, be strong. Let all that you do be done in love' (*1 Cor.* 16:13–14). May God help us to be those who both hear the Word of God and put it into practice!

I

Their Lord and Ours

¹Paul, called by the will of God to be an apostle of Christ Jesus, and our brother Sosthenes,
²To the church of God that is in Corinth, to those sanctified in Christ Jesus, called to be saints together with all those who in every place call upon the name of our Lord Jesus Christ, both their Lord and ours: ³Grace to you and peace from God our Father and the Lord Jesus Christ (1 Cor. 1:1–3).

Like any other Greek letter from the first-century world, this first letter of Paul to the church at Corinth begins with a conventional enough form. The writer is introduced, the recipients are identified, and greetings are given. It is all rather like our 'Dear . . . ', 'Yours sincerely,' and the addressing of the envelope. And yet there is so much more to it than that. Paul's opening sentences are packed full of significance for the content and purpose of what is to follow.

THE WRITER (verse 1)

While Paul's identity was, of course, well known to his readers, since it was through his ministry that God had brought the church in Corinth into existence, the interest lies in Paul's self-description, which immediately carries with it a strong note of authority. An *apostle* is one who is sent with all the authority of the one who commissions his agent. In this case, it is none other than *Christ Jesus*. The emphasis is on the anointed one, who is the Saviour precisely because he is the Lord. Moreover, *the will of God* is the active initiator of this call, so that neither chance nor Paul's own choosing had any

[1]

part to play in his mission. It was God's will that he came to Corinth, in that it was by that will that the members of the church responded with faith to God's grace in the gospel, and it was in that same will that this letter was now being written to them.

THE RECIPIENTS (verse 2)

Defined as *the church of God that is in Corinth*, Paul again reminds his readers that their very existence as a community of believers is due to God's work alone. However, he wants to go further and to describe the characteristics of such an assembly, both in terms of what they have become and of what they must be, in practice. There are three distinctives which are always characteristic of the church of God, wherever it is found and at whatever time in history.

i.   Christians are *sanctified in Christ Jesus*. The participle is a past tense indicating that from the point of their initial union with Christ, by faith, they have been set apart as his own particular possession. They do not belong to anyone else but Christ, so they must not ally themselves to any merely human leader (verse 12). Sanctification is, at root, one of the great blessings of the gospel, received through faith in the atoning work of Christ on the cross. Its outworking in developing godliness is a daily experience in the life of the believer, but our being 'set apart' to God's own use is implicit in the new birth.

ii.   Christians are therefore *called to be saints*, or more literally 'set-apart ones'. While 'to be' does not occur in the original, the translators have usually included it, from the AV onwards, because the clear implication is that holiness of life must be cultivated in daily discipleship. We must be what we are. If we are 'in Christ Jesus', then we must grow more like him in every aspect of our living. This will have profound implications for ethical behaviour, as Paul demonstrates later in the letter.

iii.   Christians are united to one another by a common faith in Jesus as Lord. One of Paul's emphases in the letter is that the congregation at Corinth belongs to the universal church and is not at liberty therefore to choose its own path. They are *together with all those* [Christians] . . . *in every place.* Note the total inclusiveness of this description. God has no lone-rangers. What binds believers together is nothing less than a common faith. They *call upon the name of our Lord Jesus Christ.* Here the tense is present. It describes their ongoing experience, since their conversion. His 'name' is of course indicative of his nature, and here Paul uses the full title of Jesus, the rescuer, who is God's anointed king (Messiah or Christ) and therefore Lord of all. There is no other Lord, whoever and wherever his people may be. He is *their Lord and ours.*

Being part of a larger reality than merely our own congregation is something we also need to be reminded of. How we behave as individuals has implications for the local church of which we are members. Equally, how our congregation behaves has implications for the wider church. We are not islands. Gospel people, whose lives are characterized by calling on Christ, for his saving and empowering grace, will want to demonstrate their true unity, in Christ and the gospel, as widely as they possibly can. Denominationalism pursued for its own sake will always tend towards the sort of quarrels that were disfiguring the Corinthian church and divert us from the real work of the gospel. While the truth of the grace of Christ in the gospel can never be compromised (*Gal.* 1:6–9), it can only be a cause of profound sadness that those who share allegiance to the same Lord, in deed and in truth, seem so easily and so readily to separate from one another. Paul will return to this theme often in the letter.

THE GREETING (verse 3)

This is more conventional, *grace* being the characteristic New Testament greeting, paralleled by *peace*, the Old Testament greeting (shalom). The one flows from the other, but both come only from *God* himself, *our Father.* Note again the emphasis on unity, since we all have only one Father. And both are mediated to us solely through the person and work of *the Lord Jesus Christ.* Indeed, the repeated emphasis of his full title reminds us that he is the undisputed focus of these opening verses. Four times in the three verses the Lord Jesus is referred to, so that there is no doubt where Paul wants his readers to direct their attention. Everything centres in Christ. But, unfortunately, this is not the current state of affairs at Corinth, as we shall soon discover. The next seven verses (4–10) will reiterate the point of Christ's centrality over and over again, until it becomes inescapably clear that Paul's concern is to restore the unique and sovereign authority of Christ over a church that is in danger of losing its central reason for existence.

2

Enriched in Every Way

⁴I give thanks to my God always for you because of the grace of God that was given you in Christ Jesus, ⁵that in every way you were enriched in him in all speech and all knowledge – ⁶even as the testimony about Christ was confirmed among you – ⁷so that you are not lacking in any spiritual gift, as you wait for the revealing of our Lord Jesus Christ, ⁸who will sustain you to the end, guiltless in the day of our Lord Jesus Christ. ⁹God is faithful, by whom you were called into the fellowship of his Son, Jesus Christ our Lord (1 Cor. 1:4–9).

E ven though this was going to be a tough letter for Paul to write and a hard one for the Corinthians to receive, the apostle begins, characteristically, with thanksgiving. He is always giving thanks to God *for you*, for the very fact that they exist as Christian believers, in a city like Corinth, that was such a by-word for everything that was opposed to the Christian faith. But Paul wants them to realize immediately that this is entirely and only *because of the grace of God that was given you in Christ Jesus* (verse 4). There is no explanation for the existence of the church in Corinth other than that God's grace had been given to them. It had been given to them in the person of the Lord Jesus and in all that he had accomplished for them, and in the work of his Spirit convicting them of sin and granting them the gifts of repentance and faith, when they heard the message. Over the next few paragraphs, Paul will remind the Corinthian believers of his first visit and of the founding of the church (especially 1:26–2:5), but because they are in danger of elevating human instruments, he begins by underlining the only true source of their existence, namely, grace, which is in Christ alone, and which can only be received as God's gift.

PRESENT THANKSGIVING

Verses 4–8 form one long sentence in the original, through which Paul ranges, reflecting on what it means to be a recipient of God's Christ-centred grace. Halfway through the sentence, however, the focus shifts from the present to the future (verse 7b), so that the discussion is lifted from the perspective of what is currently going on in the Corinthian church to the universal and eternal dimensions of God's greater plans and purposes. The current issues are real and important (as they are in every congregation) but they have to be seen and evaluated in the light of the coming *day of our Lord Jesus Christ* (verse 8).

Already, Paul has given thanks for their existence, but the church in Corinth has much more than that, for which to praise God. Grace always 'filled the hungry with good things' (*Luke* 1:53) because whenever God's favour touches a life all of God's bounty and goodness that we could never have deserved of ourselves begins to flow in. Grace gives us what we do not deserve and mercy shields us from what we do deserve. So, we receive forgiveness in the place of condemnation, and righteousness instead of wrath. Outcasts are brought into God's family. Rebels become sons and daughters, who are dearly loved. *In every way you were enriched in him.*

However, Paul goes on to indicate the evidence for this claim in the present experience of the church, as he refers to what they had received, not only in the matter of salvation but *in all speech and in all knowledge.* These are terms that are going to recur many times in the course of the letter. In all probability they reflect the areas of church life and experience with which the Corinthians were especially concerned and of which they may have become inordinately proud (see 4:18 and 5:2). Corinth was a city whose culture thrived on rhetoric (fine speech) and knowledge, so it was hardly surprising that God would enrich his church in this way. In verse 6, Paul sees this as confirmation that *the testimony about Christ was confirmed among you.* The danger lies not in God's undisputed provision, but in the Corinthians' wrong attitudes.

Verse 7a states the point very clearly when Paul affirms *you are not lacking in any spiritual gift*. The term he uses is the familiar '*charismata*', usually translated 'spiritual gift' but better translated literally as 'grace gift'. This relates the 'gifting' to the gospel of grace, with which Paul began his thanksgiving in verses 4–5a. In that sense, these gifts are the proof that the Corinthians have indeed received and believed the testimony about Christ, which Paul had passed on to them as he preached the gospel (verse 6). As always, God has done this with overflowing generosity, so that Paul can affirm that they are not wanting in any endowment of grace. This is a very gifted church and Paul does not want to deny that fact, nor question it, for one moment. But he *is* concerned that they should attribute all of this to God's grace alone and not to human agents or to their own imagined worthiness. It is a trap that we can all readily fall into, as soon as we forget our total dependence on God's grace in Christ for everything we have and are.

FUTURE PERSPECTIVE

Paul's perspective, therefore, shifts to the future, which is also defined in terms of Christ. Christians *wait for the revealing of our Lord Jesus Christ* (verse 7), but Paul reminds his readers that this will be a time of assessment. The phrase *the day of our Lord Jesus Christ* (verse 8) echoes other biblical references to the day of the Lord as the day of judgement. The link between the two sections of his thanksgiving is perhaps best brought out by the term used in verses 6 and 8, where the same root is translated *confirmed* and *will sustain*. Just as the testimony about Christ was confirmed in the grace gifts given to the church, so the believers will be confirmed *blameless* when Christ returns. Both are the fruits of his grace alone. This explains why Christians await that great day eagerly and not with apprehension. The grace that saves is the grace that keeps, to the very end of the road, so that every one of his redeemed people will be presented guiltless in his presence, on that day (see also Jude, verse 4). But the apostle is concerned that the Corinthians keep that end point firmly in view. There is a danger that they may become so obsessed with their present experiences of enrichment that they will be tempted to imagine that already they are enjoying all the blessings of heaven, already they are living as super-conquerors, already they are triumphant over all their enemies. This will be addressed by Paul at some length in chapter 4, and again in chapter 15.

A clear future focus is essential for healthy Christian living in the present. Such a focus means not only that present decisions are made in the light of the ultimate big picture of God's purposes for our future, but also reminds us that we are constantly dependent on his grace today to keep us on track and to bring us finally to his glorious tomorrow. Grace 'now' is the guarantee of grace 'then', when Christ is revealed and we shall need to be *guiltless* before him. So, verse 9 provides the assurance that this is absolutely central to God's purposes and the certainty that it will be accomplished. Paul now returns to the idea of God's call, mentioned in verse 2. 'Saints' are called *into the fellowship of his Son Jesus Christ our Lord*, we now learn. Again, the full title is used to impress upon us the immense privilege and the supreme certainty of God's grace. We are shareholders in the same concern, members of the same family business, partners with Christ in his work in this world. Even more than that, we are called into a deep, personal relationship with him, by which each individual believer is united to Christ by faith. We live *in Christ*, and he in us, by his indwelling Spirit. So all who belong to Christ, personally and individually, must logically belong to one another, through him. This fellowship does not only exist between Christ and me, but between all God's holy people everywhere. Clearly, the appeal of verse 10 is already in view as Paul pens these words.

The emphasis, however, is on the first word of this new sentence (verse 9); the word, *faithful*. *God is faithful* is the key to every assurance the believer enjoys. It echoes down the centuries from the very first revelation that God gave of himself to the Old Testament believers as the covenant God who makes and keeps his promises. He fulfilled his word to Israel, calling his people out of Egypt, and bringing them first to Mount Sinai, where he revealed his character in his law, and then into the land of the promise, flowing with milk and honey; he can be trusted also by New Testament believers to fulfil his every word. His very name confirms it. That ancient revelation to Moses at the bush that I AM WHO I AM (*Exod.* 3:13–15), the name of Jehovah, or Yahweh, always translated in our English versions as the LORD, speaks of covenant faithfulness. He is the present-tense God, always the same, never changing, immutable and utterly dependable throughout all time and into eternity. What he says he will do, he does. His promises are always faithfully fulfilled, and the incarnation of the Lord Jesus is itself the greatest proof in history of that reality. *God is faithful.* If he has called us to be holy, he will present us blameless.

It is that quality of assured conviction that produces godly living in the present. If this is to be our goal, then what sort of people ought we to be now (see *2 Pet.* 3:11,14)? The realization of how utterly dependent upon grace we shall be on the last day will enable us to live all our days in the meantime in faithful dependence on our utterly faithful God.

3

Is Christ Divided?

¹⁰I appeal to you, brothers, by the name of our Lord Jesus Christ, that all of you agree and that there be no divisions among you, but that you be united in the same mind and the same judgment. ¹¹For it has been reported to me by Chloe's people that there is quarrelling among you, my brothers. ¹²What I mean is that each one of you says, "I follow Paul," or "I follow Apollos," or "I follow Cephas," or "I follow Christ." ¹³Is Christ divided? Was Paul crucified for you? Or were you baptized in the name of Paul? ¹⁴I thank God that I baptized none of you except Crispus and Gaius, ¹⁵so that no one may say that you were baptized in my name. ¹⁶I did baptize also the household of Stephanas. Beyond that, I do not know whether I baptized anyone else. ¹⁷For Christ did not send me to baptize but to preach the gospel, and not with words of eloquent wisdom, lest the cross of Christ be emptied of its power (1 Cor. 1:10–17).

The letter's opening section has referred to the Lord Jesus Christ in every one of the first nine verses, and verse 10 is no exception. In many ways it is a bridge verse between the greetings and thanksgiving section and the main business of the letter, to which Paul now turns. Central to its contents is *the name of our Lord Jesus Christ* (the eleventh mention), by which Paul beseeches his Christian *brothers* to unite. The whole argument is a strong personal plea on the ground of the fellowship that God's grace had already created between them, through the gospel (verses 4, 9). *I appeal to you, brothers.* The gospel has brought them into God's family and their responsibility is to demonstrate the family likeness, in so far as fallen people are able to reflect the perfect unity of the Trinity.

Verse 10 explains in considerable detail the nature of the unity for which Paul is pleading, and there is a strong emotional content to the verb. Here is the founder of the church of God in Corinth imploring his brothers in Christ, on whom the future of the gospel cause in the region depends:

i.   *That all of you agree.* The literal meaning is, 'that the same thing may be said by you all'. Divisions will inevitably surface in public sooner or later. What is true of political parties or multi-national companies is equally true of church denominations and local congregations. Where there are differences internally they will always become evident by contradictory public statements. Paul, therefore, starts with the outward symptoms, but by the end of verse 10 he has focused onto the internal causes.

ii.   *That you be united in the same mind and the same judgement.* The idea is that of being thoroughly knit together – no chinks or gaps appearing in their oneness. This can only be the case when there is genuine unity of thinking and opinion. In these days of 'spin-doctoring' we are only too familiar with the creation of an external image to cover up a much less impressive reality, or even a vacuum. But Paul knows that such unity is tissue thin; it can disappear like the morning mist. Only when God's people think alike – about God himself, about Christ and the gospel, and, consequently, about themselves and the church – can real unity be demonstrated. All true Christian unity is in God's revealed truth alone and any attempt to create 'unity' by side-tracking God's word, or by-passing the mind will, in the end, be shown up as spurious nonsense. In addition, for fear that the concept of unity of thought and speech might be too general a description of the unity that Paul longs to see at Corinth, the middle of verse 10 informs us as to when such a state exists and what it looks like.

iii.   *That there be no divisions among you.* No '*schismata*' – no rents or tears in the fellowship – is the evidence of the deep unity of heart and mind for which Paul is working. But sadly, the reality in Corinth was rather different, as indeed it is in many congregations today. The unity for which Paul is pleading is not an optional extra. His plea in the name of Jesus is certainly grounded in the teaching of Jesus: 'By this all people will know that you are my disciples, if you have love for one another' (*John* 13:35). Moreover, the same plea is found in the prayer of the Lord Jesus for those who will believe in him through the apostolic preaching, 'that they may all be one, just as you, Father, are in me and I in you . . . that they may become perfectly one, so that the world may know that you sent me and loved them even as you loved me' (*John* 17:20–23). It is a matter of great importance.

THE ROOTS OF THE PROBLEM (verses 11–12)

We do not know who *Chloe* and her *people* were, but they had brought Paul the news *that there is quarrelling among you*. Whoever they were, Paul clearly respected their judgement and believed their report. But it could be argued that it is just this sort of behaviour that causes divisions and schisms in churches – individuals going behind people's backs and passing on gossip and tittle-tattle. While that is undoubtedly true, we need, however, to notice the differences here. This household of Chloe was probably not from within the church at Corinth, but were presumably visitors who had become very concerned about what they had observed at Corinth and were determined that Paul should be informed. What they said was out in the open and they themselves were identified. Any insistence on anonymity would put an immediate question mark upon their motives. If we are not prepared to say things openly and put our name to them, we ought not to say them at all. That rule would certainly kill gossip.

However, divisions did exist in the church and such problems cannot be solved without examining their causes; these are listed by Paul in verse 12. The most frequently used word in the verse is, 'I', in stark contrast to the frequent use of the names and titles of Christ in verses 1–10. The focus in the Corinthian congregation has shifted from Christ to 'me', and this was the root of the problem. The method Paul uses as he starts to tackle this difficulty is as helpful as the actual content of what he says.

He begins with his own supporters. *What I mean is that each one of you says, 'I follow Paul'*. These were probably those who had responded to the gospel when Paul first arrived in Corinth, and he might even have baptized some of them (see verses 14, 16). Doubtless they had often defended Paul's ministry when it was under attack, but Paul does not commend them for this 'loyalty'. Acts 18:18 tells us that Paul stayed on in Corinth for some time but eventually left for Syria, accompanied by Priscilla and Aquila. He left them in Ephesus, promising to return later, and pressed on to Antioch and from there he visited the disciples in Galatia and Phrygia. 'Now a Jew named Apollos, a native of Alexandria, came to Ephesus. He was an eloquent man, competent in the Scriptures' (*Acts* 18:24). Luke tells us that he was 'fervent in spirit' but needed to be instructed in the way of God 'more accurately' as he 'knew only the baptism of John' (see *Acts* 18:25–26). Apollos travelled on to Corinth (*Acts* 19:1) carrying a letter from the Ephesian brothers encouraging the Corinthians to welcome him, and 'when he arrived, he greatly helped those who through grace had believed, for he powerfully refuted the Jews in public, showing by the Scriptures that the Christ was Jesus,' (*Acts* 18:27–28).

Some at Corinth were now claiming, *I follow Apollos*. Apparently Peter had also visited the Corinthian congregation. (Paul later speaks of Cephas, Peter's name in Aramaic, as having 'the right to take along a believing wife' with him on his ministry travels (9:5).) One can imagine those of more Jewish inclinations rejoicing at making him their champion and claiming, *I follow Cephas*. While Peter and Paul had their differences (*Gal.* 2:11–21) yet they always remained at one. But it would not be surprising if some of the followers proved to be more sectarian and divisive than their mentors. The phenomenon still exists of immature 'disciples' lining up behind a 'great man'!

Lastly, there were those whose claim distanced themselves from these squabbles. *I follow Christ* was their watchword, dissociating them from all those unworthy rivalries. Of course everyone professed to follow Christ, but this group's appropriation of the Master's name to their cause reduced his status to that of his servants and reduced themselves to just another clique. Perhaps they saw themselves as the really 'spiritual' party.

Paul's concern is that the whole controversy is wrong, because at root it is all about glorying in individuals, who are just human agents. Paul does not regard Apollos as a threat. In chapter 3, he will go out of his way to put him on the same level as himself, but both are only servants (3:5). If some of the Corinthians value Apollos more because of his rhetorical abilities, they are building on the wrong foundation. So are those who favour Paul because he was the original messenger, or Peter, because of his stronger Jerusalem connections. And no one should 'corner' the name of Christ for his own party, for how can Christ be divided? The gospel is not to be used to build personality cults, for no individual is to be set up in the place of Christ, as the focus of loyalty and faith. No one has the right to usurp his authority and his sovereign rule.

But how hard it is for us to learn the lesson! While Paul rejoiced in the '*charismata*' (1:7) that God had poured on these Christians, the tragedy is that these very gifts had been used to strengthen the '*schismata*' outlined here. The problem with gifts is that they can so easily divert attention to the gifted person and away from the giver. The recipient can easily become proud and ambitious. Others grow resentful and jealous, or they may attach themselves to the gifted person in an exaggerated way in order to share something of the limelight. They become Christian 'groupies', following the gifted person around, directing their loyalty towards him rather than to Christ. In this way, personality cults develop and grow into splinter groups that divide local congregations and wider church connections. Quarrels persist and at their root is found the dominant note, 'I', the tell-tale sign of the uncrucified ego. God's gifts of grace, even, have then been subordinated to bolster self rather than to serve him.

THE REPROACH IT CAUSED (verses 13–16)

Paul's tactic is to recall the divided church in Corinth to its senses, by posing three questions. *Is Christ divided? Was Paul crucified for you? Or were you baptized in the name of Paul?* The answer to each, of course, is 'No'. Anything else would be unthinkable. So, why then are they tolerating and even propagating the nonsense of such divisions? If Christ cannot be parcelled out, so that each little clique has a part of him, then how can his body be divided? To continue in this way would be to cut themselves off from Christ. Indeed, there was a sense in which their behaviour was actually tearing the body of Christ apart, at least in Corinth. If there is only one Christ then it is trivial, in comparison, to define oneself by attachment to any human leader, or party, or denomination. Conversely, no human labels can ever compensate for not being united to Christ by faith. For there is no other means of salvation, nor ever can be. No one else has been crucified for us, and there is no other baptismal confession, for there is no other Lord.

In verses 14–16, Paul reflects on his baptismal activity at Corinth. He seems personally to have baptized very few of the converts from his mission. *Crispus* is mentioned in Acts 18:8 as 'the ruler of the synagogue', who 'believed in the Lord together with his entire household'. Luke also tells us that 'many of the Corinthians hearing Paul believed and were baptized', but not apparently by Paul, other than *Gaius*, about whom we know nothing more, and then, as a late memory, *the household of Stephanas.* The really significant comment comes at the end of verse 16. *I do not know whether I baptized anyone else.* He obviously did not keep records, or lists, both because baptism was not his primary calling (verse 17) and also because of the danger of individuals assuming baptism by the apostle to be in some way superior and so shifting their focus from Christ to Paul (verse 15). The fewer he baptized personally, the less the danger. Baptism confesses submission to Jesus Christ as Lord, a submission that can never be owed to any mere man. So to make any human leader, who is only a channel of God's grace, your reference point, is a reproach to the name of the Lord Jesus Christ and, by the same token, a reproach to his servant.

THE REMEDY NEEDED (verse 17)

For Christ did not send me to baptize but to preach the gospel. This was Paul's great commission from which he would never be deflected. His call was to go and make disciples; others could, and did, baptize. But the whole thrust of the apostle's ministry was to exalt Christ, who is the good news, and to minimize himself. Whatever the church in Corinth may be thinking of Paul, and he was undoubtedly the butt of a good deal of criticism, he wants them to know that he was sent by Christ (remember verse 1). That is the essence of his apostleship and subsequent authority (see also 9:1–2). The Lord, who commissioned Paul as his agent, also dictated the job description. He was called 'to preach the gospel', not to be a public speaker, an orator or rhetorician, of which the first-century Graeco-Roman world had so many, but (literally) 'to evangelize'.

In the rest of the verse, Paul explains more fully what he means, in a negative way – *not with words of eloquent wisdom*. Tellingly, he adds, *lest the cross of Christ be emptied of its power*. It seems as though Paul had made a definite choice not to attempt to persuade his hearers to believe by eloquence and rhetorical skills, which were the currency of the pagan philosophers. Rather, he would proclaim the cross of Christ, in the assured knowledge and conviction that this was where God's power lay. 'If men are persuaded by eloquence, they are not persuaded by Christ crucified' (C. K. Barrett). The two are mutually exclusive. Paul will develop this argument all through the next few paragraphs, with his final explanation (in 2:5): 'that your faith might not rest in the wisdom of men but in the power of God.'

We shall follow that argument through in more detail, but at this point we need to underline why the conviction of verse 17 is so essential for authentic gospel work and true Christian unity. To rely on 'eloquent wisdom' (literally 'wisdom of speech') is to put one's confidence in man, which is precisely the Corinthian problem that Paul was addressing. By contrast, the message of the cross is totally humbling. Confidence in human skills of communication and argument tends to minister to the sort of ambition and self-glory which was proving so schismatic in Corinth. It draws attention to the messenger and to his method, rather than the message. Indeed, these things will come between the hearers and the gospel, so that they cannot see the cross. Whenever we rely on the preacher, or he on his communication methods, especially in situations where entertainment dominates, we shall empty the message of the power of the cross.

But these alternatives will always be more popular, because the means of our salvation is still despised and contemptible in the world's eyes. As soon as the world is allowed to write the agenda for the church's mission, the cross will be relegated in favour of something much more culturally in tune and acceptable. The current cult of 'spirituality' in which any and every sort of content (including no content at all) is equally acceptable, is eloquent testimony to this truth. But it will not save anybody. Only the cross of Christ can achieve that great work. Weak and unimpressive by human measurements, the simplicity of the apostolic message of 'Jesus Christ and him crucified' (2:2) is still the only locus of God's saving power. If that message is distorted the efficacy of the Holy Spirit's work will vanish, for God will not share his glory in Christ's finished work with any mere mortal. He does not need human eloquence or wisdom, nor does he acknowledge it, as the next few verses will show.

The remedy for the schisms developing at Corinth, therefore, was to return to the gospel of the cross, which is God's wisdom and God's power. Humbled at the foot of the cross, Christians recognize one another as sinners saved by grace, sisters and brothers, in God's family. Submitting to the one Lord, we are bound together in his one body, and we must express that unity in thought and speech. But the ground of that unity is in the truth of the gospel – the message of the cross – and the mark of embracing that message will be seen in the life-style of the cross, as we submit to Christ in love and live together in harmony. 'For he who does not love his brother whom he has seen cannot love God whom he has not seen. And this commandment we have from him: whoever loves God must also love his brother' (*1 John* 4:20–21).

If the gospel is going to make the headway that we long for in the Corinths of the twenty-first century, then here is the priority to which we must return.

4

The Word of the Cross

¹⁸For the word of the cross is folly to those who are perishing, but to us who are being saved it is the power of God. ¹⁹For it is written,

> *"I will destroy the wisdom of the wise,
> and the discernment of the discerning I will thwart."*

²⁰Where is the one who is wise? Where is the scribe? Where is the debater of this age? Has not God made foolish the wisdom of the world? ²¹For since, in the wisdom of God, the world did not know God through wisdom, it pleased God through the folly of what we preach to save those who believe. ²²For Jews demand signs and Greeks seek wisdom, ²³but we preach Christ crucified, a stumbling block to Jews and folly to Gentiles, ²⁴but to those who are called, both Jews and Greeks, Christ the power of God and the wisdom of God. ²⁵For the foolishness of God is wiser than men, and the weakness of God is stronger than men (1 Cor. 1:18–25).

Although we are beginning a new section at verse 18 in order to break up the text into manageable portions, we should not assume any break in Paul's argument, but follow the flow straight through. This is made plain by the contrast that is drawn between the 'word of wisdom' (verse 17) and the 'word of the cross' (verse 18). *For the word of the cross is folly to those who are perishing.* The cross seems to be the polar opposite of human wisdom. It is sometimes hard for us to realize just how offensive the cross was within first-century culture. Such a shameful and barbaric form of death was suitable only for the lowest strata of humanity, so that any association with a victim of crucifixion was socially completely unacceptable. To suggest that such a reject could be a divine person was absurd, and to attempt to found a new religion based on such a belief was utter foolishness. Evidence of this attitude has come down to us from excavations in first-century Rome. A rough cartoon scratched into the wall shows a man kneeling in worship before a deity. The god is hanging on a cross, and while he has the body of a man, the head is that of a donkey. The legend, by way of explanation, reads 'Alexamenos worships his god'. That was what the sophisticated, cosmopolitan population of Corinth would have thought about the Christians and their new-found faith. Who can possibly worship a god who becomes man and dies that sort of death on a cross? You might as well worship a donkey.

But Paul's point is that such an attitude simply reveals the spiritual state of those who adopt it. They are *perishing*. They must be, since they are blatantly rejecting the only means of salvation that is available to lost human beings. For the other side of the coin, clearly stated in the second part of verse 18, is that *to us who are being saved it is the power of God*. A double contrast begins to play around the meaning of the cross. On the one side there is the rejection of the message as folly and weakness, while on the other hand, that same message, when it is understood and received, is proved to be the wisdom and power of God. Clearly these were key issues, current buzz-words, in the Corinthian congregation, and Paul now takes some time to work through the complexities of the issue in verse 18. It is clear that the gospel he was sent by Christ to preach (verse 17) was the message of the cross (verse 18), and everything that had happened in Corinth had resulted from that message.

THE WISDOM OF THE WORLD (verses 19–21)

To describe human wisdom apart from divine revelation, Paul uses the virtually synonymous terms *the debater of this age* and *the wisdom of the world* (verse 20). Contained in these categories is everything that human beings experience and know through their God-given senses – all of the material universe that we call reality. It is rooted in this '*aeon*' (age) and in this world of time and sense, and such wisdom regards those who believe that there is something beyond this world – something 'other worldly' – with more than a hint of cynicism and sometimes with a dollop of pity. However, Paul's use of the term '*aeon*' implies that the material world is but a passing show, and its wisdom will pass with it. The two 'words' (of wisdom and of the cross) actually lead to two 'worlds' – two totally opposite views of reality.

It is important to understand Paul's argument here, because some have assumed that the quotation from Isaiah 29:14, which makes up verse 19, is a declaration of war by God on all human intelligence, opening the way for the dismissal of education and reason, and elevating ignorance and irrationality. A moment's thought will show that this cannot be so, because the very intelligence which marks out humankind from the beasts is itself a gift from God. It reflects his own nature and is made in his own image. We are not to suppose that the gospel extinguishes human intelligence and will lead to a retreat to a new Dark Age. Paganism will certainly do that, but it was the very re-discovery of the biblical gospel at the time of the Reformation that encouraged the increase of learning and scientific experimentation and discovery. These, in their turn, have produced the immense developments of the modern world. Biblically instructed Christians have never retreated from the created order, but have revelled in thinking God's thoughts after him and discovering the amazing properties of this world, provided by its Creator. 'Great are the works of the LORD; studied by all who delight in them' (*Psa.* 111:2). This is therefore no retreat into thoughtless ignorance.

The quotation of verse 19 has a context in Isaiah, where it is a pronouncement of God's judgement on the hypocrisy of Israel. Although they honoured God with their lips, their declarations were empty words and their worship came not from the heart, but was merely an adherence to a set of rules that others had drawn up (*Isa.* 29:13). They were totally committed to this world and its wisdom. God therefore announced that he must punish this worldliness by depriving them of the wisdom and intelligence they thought they had and bringing them into a situation of chaos, with which they would be unable to cope. In this way, their wisdom was 'made foolish' (as verse 20 expresses it). This context helps us to understand how to interpret verse 21. *In the wisdom of God, the world did not know God through wisdom.* The folly of human wisdom is that it thinks that it can come to right judgements about God by its own unaided intellect, with no need of revelation. But God's wisdom, which controls the whole world, has seen to it that human beings can never find their own way to him. Years ago, when the first Soviet astronaut, Yuri Gagarin, returned from space, one of his well-known comments was, 'I didn't see God up there', affirming, in his atheistic wisdom, that therefore God did not exist. But that is the essence of folly. Any so-called 'God' whom we could reach by our own thought processes, could observe and analyse, or run through our computers like so much data, would, by definition, cease to be God. The moment finite human wisdom thinks it has comprehended God, then that 'God' has ceased to be infinite, and therefore ceased to be God.

Worldly wisdom will never be able to explain the world, let alone the nature of God and the world to come. That is why science must be forever content with asking and answering the question 'How?' but can never project beyond that to the question 'Why?'. If ever we are to know anything about the infinite Creator it must be by his self-revelation, and that is precisely Paul's point in verse 21. *It pleased God through the folly of what we preach to save those who believe.* Notice how the whole focus changes, from knowing to believing and from wisdom to salvation. This was always God's plan of wisdom. Faith in the God who became man in the person of Jesus Christ, and who voluntarily gave himself up on the cross as the atoning sacrifice for our sins – that has always been God's great plan to rescue lost humanity. Foolish it may appear to human, man-centred wisdom, but because it is God's wisdom, the gospel of Christ crucified is the only power to save.

Paul has already equated 'those who believe' (verse 21) with 'us who are being saved' (verse 18). He is not therefore appealing to some abstract theory, but to the Corinthians' own experience. They knew the powerful dynamic of the cross that had transformed their lives, as do all real believers. So the apostle invites them to see the greatest demonstration of God's power in their own salvation, resulting in changed lives, and in doing this he is responding to their great desire to see spiritual power at work. Paul has no problem with that. He recognizes that all ministry needs to be exercised in the power of

God, for as he will later state, 'The kingdom of God does not consist in talk but in power,' (4:20). But while the Corinthians may have had plenty to say about such power, the real issue, as Paul sees it, is not the nature of the bold and extravagant claims that may be made, but the actual transforming of lives. God's power in the gospel of the cross is the only explanation for such transformations. Nothing else could ever have produced a church in Corinth in the first place.

THE DYNAMIC OF THE GOSPEL (verses 22–24)

There is no greater demonstration of divine power, then, than the changed lives of truly regenerate people. But because we live in a culture which is so opposed to the word of the cross and which wants to organize itself in rebellion against God's right to rule his world, there is always going to be a demand for a different message, and even Christians can be affected by this. *For Jews demand signs and Greeks seek wisdom* is how Paul focuses the issue in his cultural context (verse 22). The descendants of these Jews and Gentiles are still with us, in that so many of our contemporaries reject the Christian message for identical reasons – lack of material evidences or lack of intellectual acceptability. In the first century, the Jews were always looking for God to appear in splendour, for Messiah to demonstrate himself in signs of great power and authority, to 'zap' the world into submission. They had their own view of how it should work and so, by imposing their conditions on God, they effectively blinded themselves to Christ when he came to them. For the Greeks, a new idea and a clever argument was everything. If it was put across with all the logic and rhetorical skills that constituted the epitome of a liberal education, it was worthy of consideration, but if it was not witty, clever and sophisticated then it was nothing. That was what the first century demanded, and the great danger, Paul senses, is that the church at Corinth wanted to meet those demands.

It is certainly not hard to travel twenty centuries in time and see our own contemporary equivalents. The spiritual marketplace is still very open to miraculous signs and esoteric wisdom and still very closed to a message two millennia old about a crucified Saviour. There is so much on offer that seems so much more impressive than the cross, that Christians are constantly tempted to adapt the message to the demands of the culture. But the church is never in greater danger than when her leaders are demand-led. It was the challenge in Corinth and it is the challenge today. We begin to imagine that the only way to make an impact upon our culture is to mimic it, to meet its demands, follow its patterns, and package Christianity in a thoroughly culture-friendly, non-confrontational way. The perils of 'Corinthianism' are all around us still.

In every generation, the church is always much more influenced and infected by its cultural environment than we care to admit, and we take on the world's norms and colouring without even being aware of it. In a celebrity-focused culture like ours, we are tempted to think that Christians in the media, or celebrities who are Christians, are what we most need. We invest in training spokespeople to appear on TV, to deal with the press, to market the gospel, to produce superior websites, and so on. None of these things may be wrong in themselves, but the issue is whether we are putting our confidence in them, and if so, why. Similarly, in an entertainment culture, Christians can easily start to imagine that if it isn't fun, it won't communicate. This certainly seems to lie at the root of much contemporary Christian youth work, which is strong on excitement and bereft of gospel content. 'Young people don't want to read, so we don't do Bible study any more,' is a mantra that I have heard repeated many times. 'They don't want to sit and listen and they hate being preached at, so we've given up on talks, we just mingle with them and try to be the presence of Jesus with them.' The age range of youth work continually shrinks and teenagers continue to haemorrhage from the churches by their hundreds every week. In an image-obsessed culture, where spin and political correctness rule, where 'coolness' is the criteria of value, we shouldn't be surprised to find the uniqueness of Christ downgraded, the realities of judgement and hell hardly mentioned, and the need for repentance and holiness of life constantly undersold. When we are led by the culture's demands, we shall quickly become Corinthian.

At first, it may look exciting and attractive. All sorts of events and programmes can draw a crowd, at least for a time, especially when they seem to speak a very contemporary language. But what they do, in reality, is to focus the church not on its ministry of proclamation of what God has done in the cross of Christ, but on a ministry of performance, where the interest is in what God might be doing now or about to do in the near future, through some very impressive people. The presentation can be highly professional, clearly attractive and superbly entertaining, but if it is not the 'word of the cross', no one will be saved. It will simply be this world's wisdom in a suit of 'Christian' clothing.

Of course, this is no excuse for rutted traditionalism or obscurantism, still less for presenting the gospel in a way that seems irrelevant or boring. We can be all those things, and sometimes cantankerously proud of ourselves into the bargain. But Paul was not like that, nor would he have condoned such an attitude (see for example 9:19–23). He knows that the cross will appear *a stumbling block to Jews and folly to Gentiles* (verse 23) when they first hear the message, but that does not deter him for a moment. This is how the cross had first appeared to him, but look how God had turned his life around! For Paul, the chief ingredient in his reckoning is an unseen power that operates whenever *we preach Christ crucified*. He expresses this dominating conviction in verse 24, in the phrase *but to those who are called*. That is what makes all the difference. It is a power that the secular rhetorician can know nothing of at all, however skilled he may be. The best presentation will not be able to call on this divine power, for it is centred only in *Christ the power of God and the wisdom of God*. Everything depends on the content of the message, not on the methods of the messenger. For the content of the message determines whether or not God will own it and use it to call men and women, Jews and Greeks, to believe and be saved (verse 21).

Once again, Paul has shifted the whole argument. The world wants to know; but God wants to save. We are not therefore discussing power encounters or philosophical theory, but witnessing God on a rescue mission. That is the greatest need of humanity and it explains why the word of the cross is the only expression of the wisdom and the power of God. The tables are completely turned. Human wisdom, that considers the cross to be foolishness, is now itself demonstrated to be total folly, in that it rejects the one means of salvation. Human power, so ready to deride the weakness of a crucified King, is now revealed to be utterly ineffectual in rescuing anyone from God's wrath. Only the cross of Christ has such limitless power (verse 25).

THE CONTINUING CHALLENGE

At this early stage in his letter, Paul wants to impress upon his readers the importance of the decisions that they are making, and making them almost without realizing how far-reaching their implications will be. To the unbeliever, then and now, there *is* a folly about the gospel, and this must never surprise or unnerve us. The paradoxes of God's self-revelation in Christ are profound; they can even appear unbelievable on first hearing. To be taught that God became man; that his perfect life was subjected to death; that the only righteous One was made sin for us; that the immortal died; that all our blessings flow from his being cursed; and that this is the only means by which sinful human beings can be redeemed from eternal destruction and become partakers of eternal life – all this could never be reached by human reasoning. It had to be revealed by God.

But the implications of this revelation impact every area of the believer's life. The gospel demonstrates that the God who rules his world does so by suffering, dying love. That is the reality at the heart of the cosmos, and it means that the only way for me to live in a world that belongs to such a God is for me to humble myself, to receive his reconciling grace, to take up my cross and follow him. In such a world, fulfilment will be found only in self-giving love, for that is the nature of the Creator in whose image we are made. The challenge is whether we believe our doctrine sufficiently for us to allow its truth to mould our life-style.

The more the Corinthians hankered for human wisdom and power in the life of the church, the more they displayed their capitulation to the cultural norms of their city. This is the 'worldliness' that Paul will expose in chapter 3. Eventually it kills the life of a church, because its values belong to the world that is in rebellion against God's right to rule. In reality, the world has been made to respond to self-giving, compassionate love. The more the Corinthians looked for the marks of impressiveness and success, the more they demanded that God should lift them out of life's suffering and problems in order to live super-triumphantly, the further they drifted from Christ. For the God of the gospel was not delivered from the cross; he suffered and bled and died.

So whenever Christians look for influence or power in this world, or security, comfort and a quiet life, they are in danger of forgetting that they follow a crucified Lord, who calls them to be a suffering, servant community. Such thinking cuts right across the wisdom of this world, but it means that those who embrace it can never be exterminated. It reduces the power structures of this world to rubble, and it proclaims a victory over all the hostile forces ranged against humanity, that is total and eternal. An innocent Messiah, hanging on a cross, is the direct contradiction of all human ideas of wisdom and power. Yet this act of God has achieved what the sum total of human abilities never could achieve. Such wisdom is, in the end, inscrutable; but its power to save from sin and death and hell is invincible. The challenge is whether, we like Alexamenos, will be found worshipping our crucified King and living the life-style of the cross, not only in our creedal confessions, but in our church fellowship and activity, in all our personal relationships, and in the hidden depths of our own hearts.

5

Boast in the Lord

26 For consider your calling, brothers: not many of you were wise according to worldly standards, not many were powerful, not many were of noble birth. 27 But God chose what is foolish in the world to shame the wise; God chose what is weak in the world to shame the strong; 28 God chose what is low and despised in the world, even things that are not, to bring to nothing things that are, 29 so that no human being might boast in the presence of God. 30 He is the source of your life in Christ Jesus, whom God made our wisdom and our righteousness and sanctification and redemption. 31 Therefore, as it is written, "Let the one who boasts, boast in the Lord."

1 And I, when I came to you, brothers, did not come proclaiming to you the testimony of God with lofty speech or wisdom. 2 For I decided to know nothing among you except Jesus Christ and him crucified. 3 And I was with you in weakness and in fear and much trembling, 4 and my speech and my message were not in plausible words of wisdom, but in demonstration of the Spirit and of power, 5 that your faith might not rest in the wisdom of men but in the power of God (1 Cor. 1:26 – 2:5).

In this section, Paul continues to fight for the life of the church at Corinth, because if the word of the cross is moved out of the central place, then everything else ultimately will be lost with it. It is no accident that he describes his own ministry in terms of the proclamation of that word, for that is where God's power is demonstrated still. What makes the death of Christ powerful in the contemporary world is not the priest performing the mass, nor the personality persuading people to buy into his spirituality, but the preacher whose simple message is *Jesus Christ and him crucified* (2:2). Once the church moves from that, a different message and ministry will inevitably follow. The gap will have to be filled by something – signs and wonders, healings, prophecy, ecstatic utterances, music and worship, theatre, sacramentalism, philosophical speculations – the list is endless. What they all have in common is their focus on human beings and their performance now, rather than on God and his work at the cross and in the resurrection. The ministry becomes one of performance rather than proclamation, and in the end it will empty the churches. Already, the dissatisfactions were beginning to surface in Corinth.

THE WRONG SORT OF PEOPLE? (verses 26–31)

Looking around the congregation seems to have been a pretty depressing experience for many of the Christians at Corinth. How would they ever be able to influence such a contemporary, sophisticated city as theirs with such an unimpressive group of believers? Where were the movers and the shakers, the people with flair and power? Not, apparently, in the church. This is not pessimism, but realism, according to Paul. *Not many of you were wise according to worldly standards, not many were powerful, not many were noble* (verse 26). Certainly he doesn't say 'none', but the inference is clear. The large majority of the Christian community would not be admired, or even known, in Corinthian society, and this is regarded as a great defect. The inference seems to have been that this was due to the message Paul preached and to his own performance as the messenger (see 2:1–5). His message was 'weak' since it centred on that shameful death of Christ on the cross, and his technique was unimpressive compared to the travelling philosophers and public orators Corinth was used to. So, all in all, it was this wrong man with the wrong message, which had produced such a disappointing and unimpressive congregation. Change was therefore urgently needed.

In answering this erroneous reasoning, Paul takes his readers back to an emphasis that we have already noted – the call of God. At the start of the letter he introduced himself in these terms (1:1) and in 1:24 he stressed that it was this factor which turned the foolish, weak message of the cross into divine wisdom and power. So, picking up that thread, he writes, *For consider your calling, brothers.* It is only because of God's call that they are brothers, or Christians, at all. If then, they are having problems with the unimpressive composition of the congregation, Paul argues, it is no good laying the blame at his door, as the apostolic messenger. They must blame God. Three times he makes the point. *God chose what is foolish ... God c hose what is weak . . . God chose what is low and despised in the world, even things that are not* (verses 27–28). God did the choosing, so you are blaming him.

This, too, is paradoxical, like so much of what we have already learned of God's wisdom and power. Far from it being any kind of mistake or oversight on God's part, it is central to God's plan to choose to call to himself those whom worldly wisdom would never select. The reason is not simply that he overturns the self-centred rebellious will of a world at war with himself and his values, but *so that no human being might boast in the presence of God* (verse 29). The glory of the gospel is that God does not need human wisdom, strength or status to establish his kingdom. In this new community, the systems and values of the rebellious world are an irrelevance. God therefore deliberately chooses to make the living stones of his church from foolish, weak and lowly people – ordinary people who count as nothing in the eyes of the world's powerful elites – for his purpose is *to bring to nothing things that are* (verse 28b).

This is a profoundly important truth to grasp. Verse 19 reminded us that God frustrates mere human intelligence and destroys mere human wisdom, because it is set up in opposition to his own sovereign rule. The message, throughout the Bible, to all who rebel against God is that their days are numbered. Human beings are mortal; they, and their systems, rise but they must also fall. In Isaiah's memorable imagery, 'All flesh is grass, and all its beauty is like the flower of the field. The grass withers, the flower fades' (*Isa.* 40:6–7). The existence of a new community of ordinary people, called by God to a relationship with himself that is eternal life, is a statement, in time, of what will be throughout eternity. By this master plan, God shames the wisdom and strength of the rebellious world and demonstrates that all its schemes will come to nothing. The church at Corinth is the outcrop, in time and space, of the eternal kingdom of glory. That is why it cannot contain those who glory in themselves, but only those who, called by God, have been humbled in the dust before the cross and now live the life-style of the crucified Lord. This policy removes all possibility of self-glory from every one of God's people. *He is the source of your life in Christ Jesus* (verse 30a); he alone, *so that no human being* is in any position to *boast in the presence of the Lord.*

At this point, Paul rather surprisingly returns to the theme of wisdom, asserting that it is *Christ Jesus whom God made our wisdom.* God is, of course, supremely wise, as he is supremely powerful, and now we are shown how that wisdom is operative in the lives of those whom he has called. He is making this world's 'nothings' into the likeness of his Son. This is the divine wisdom in which the Corinthians should be rejoicing, rather than seeking out some already bankrupt cultural alternative. The root of our understanding of this verse lies in our recognition that we are 'in Christ', because of God's gracious call in the gospel. It is his initiative ('he chose') that we are united to his Son by faith, and therefore have access to all the riches of his grace, described as wisdom from God and spelt out in terms of *our righteousness and sanctification and redemption* (verse 30). This has the second implication that if we are 'in Christ', we must not be surprised to discover that the world will treat us as it treated him. That is why we need to understand the resources that are available to us in our weakness.

The word of wisdom (of the cross) has brought about a right standing before God, because Christ's *righteousness* has become ours. Jesus carried the just punishment of our sins, atoned for our guilt and paid the ransom price for our deliverance through his death on the cross, and so his righteousness is credited to our account. In his second letter to these very Christians, Paul will expand on this thought, as he describes the great exchange: 'For our sake he made him to be sin who knew no sin, so that in him we might become the righteousness of God' (*2 Cor.* 5:21).

Jesus has also become our *sanctification* (an echo of 1:2). Here the emphasis is not so much on our status, as on the process that God is working in our lives as we become more like the one to whom we are united, in character and in behaviour. The life of Christ, planted by his grace, through faith, within our souls will produce its own fruit, because the Holy Spirit dwells within. And the Spirit's great work is to make us more and more like Jesus (*2 Cor.* 3:18). Finally, Jesus has become our *redemption*. The chains of our captivity to Satan and sin were broken at the cross and we are no longer enslaved. Furthermore, in the eternal kingdom we shall be totally free from our fallenness: 'We shall be like him, because we shall see him as he is,' (*1 John* 3:2).

This, then, is our wisdom from God. It is to be brought, by grace, into a right relationship and an accepted standing with God, to have a true knowledge of him and to share in the life of God as his consecrated, treasured possession. He is the source, and the wisdom that he gives is new, eternal life in his Son, Christ Jesus. Therefore the distinctive mark of the church in Corinth, or anywhere else in the world, is the divine life within her, now and for ever. No wonder that all human boasting is excluded. *Therefore, as it is written, 'Let the one who boasts, boast in the Lord,'* (verse 31).

The context of this quotation from Jeremiah 9:24 is very illuminating. The preceding verse has been taken up with the very issues Paul is debating here. 'Let not the wise man boast in his wisdom, let not the mighty man boast in his might, let not the rich man boast in his riches.' We already know why, because these things are all uncertain and temporal. 'But,' Jeremiah continues, 'let him who boasts boast in this, that he understands and knows me, that I am the LORD, who practises steadfast love, justice and righteousness in the earth. For in these I delight, declares the LORD.' The Lord delights in these manifestations of his character, that have become ours in Christ Jesus, and if he rejoices in them, so should we. Perhaps an indication of the reality of our relationship with the Lord is provided by how much we boast in him, and in all that he has called us to share of his wisdom and power.

Rather than being the wrong people, therefore, the Christians at Corinth were chosen by God and demonstrate the reality of a relationship with him. They delight in God for who he is, as well as for what he has done. But it required the wisdom and power of God in the cross of Christ, to see and recognize that reality then, and exactly the same is true today. When people say that they have 'moved on' from the simple gospel of the cross, or that they value their evangelical roots but have grown far beyond them now, I want to ask what it is they have moved on to. The only place to go on to, beyond the cross, is the resurrection body and the life of the world to come! What they call moving on is actually missing the plot, being diverted from the real gospel into a spurious, but culturally attractive, alternative. True Christians delight in Christ. He is the centre and focus of their boasting. Perhaps, like the Corinthians, our danger is to talk and think about Christianity rather than about Christ, and about the failings of the church rather than the glories of the King. We need to remember that the people of wisdom and power are those whom God has chosen to be 'in Christ'.

THE WRONG SORT OF PREACHER? (2:1–5)

In this paragraph, Paul tackles head-on some of the criticisms of himself and his ministry that the rival groups seem to have been propagating in Corinth. Just as the unimpressive make-up of the congregation must be put down to the choice of God's wisdom, so the aspects of Paul's ministry that disappointed some are now shown to be the apostle's deliberate choices, based on the very same premise, namely, the nature of the gospel. He invites them to remember his arrival in Corinth (verse 1), calling them *brothers*, once again. This is both a mark of his genuine affection and oneness with them, and also a reminder that they would not be in this sort of relationship with one another, if it were not for the power of God at work in the gospel that he had preached. The fact is beyond dispute. *And I . . . did not come . . . with lofty speech and wisdom* (verse 1). They knew that this was the case, and so did Paul. In this sense he was totally unlike the travelling teachers of his day. They relied precisely upon the skills of rhetoric and philosophical argument in order to produce an impressive performance, develop popularity, and, no doubt, line their pockets.

Verse 2 shows that this difference was intentional ('*I decided*') and the reason is not hard to find. Paul came announcing *the testimony of God*. His message depended on God, both for its origin and content. He came as a commissioned messenger and the message had to be authenticated in the ambassador. To those Corinthians who had been criticizing his unimpressive style and presence and who were looking for new leaders to give them more intellectual fireworks or exciting power displays, Paul says, in effect, 'Can't you see why it had to be this way?' Messengers of a crucified Saviour are not impressive people seeking to draw attention to themselves. Indeed, to try to clothe the message of the cross in eloquence or intellectual brilliance would be to undermine its very essence and nature. This is why Paul affirms *I decided to know nothing among you except Jesus Christ and him crucified* (verse 2).

In the first-century world, the people who were thought to have real influence were the rhetoricians who went from town to town with their impressive array of technical skills and speaking abilities. All sorts of new ideas were disseminating from these powerful, impressive teachers. But Paul's confidence was entirely different. He knew he had a message that, in spite of its apparent weakness, was far more powerful than any form of human rhetoric ever could be. He knew that in that message, the very power of God was demonstrated. When people understood that Jesus died on the cross for them, and when they put their faith in him personally, finding in him their rescuer and ruler, their lives were turned around. All sorts of other 'Christs' might be preached, but the authentic Christ is the crucified Christ; the real gospel has the cross at its very centre. It was therefore entirely appropriate that he should have come to them as a weak messenger. Whether he meant by this that he was nervous, or that his health was not good, or that he was just over-awed by the task, or a combination of all these things, we cannot be sure, but it produced in him the responses described in verse 3 – *in weakness and in fear and much trembling*. He certainly did not cut an impressive figure. They were not lining up to interview him on the news programme that evening on Corinthian television! His powers of speech must have been unimpressive compared to the standards of the day. *My speech and my message were not in plausible words of wisdom* (verse 4). He deliberately chose not to take that route. He would not use all the tricks of the trade of the salesman or the peddler. He deliberately refused to adopt the media methodology of his day. Instead, he preached the cross of Christ, and God worked by his words, so that there was now a church in Corinth. It was a church that was enriched in many ways, in all sorts of spiritual gifts and in knowledge, but a church that had been established only because the message of the cross was proclaimed in that city.

This should make us stop and think. Ours is an age of 'super-star' celebrities, and the great danger is that the Christian church might be tempted to follow the same pattern as the world and grant its preachers and communicators, its worship leaders and youth workers, a similar celebrity status. Every minister will find that some people will want to put him on a pedestal and that part of him will want to allow it. We all love to have our heroes in our churches. We like to imitate the world in the way we run things, to have our super-stars and to give allegiance to human leaders, and Paul is saying to us, 'That is absurd. The only real power within the Christian faith is the power of God at work in a crucified Christ'. Why do we try to mimic 'glitzy' Corinth if we are following a Jesus who was reviled and rejected, spat upon and beaten, and eventually nailed up to that most agonizing and humiliating death on the cross? How can we go the way of Corinth and try to re-create in the church a Christianised version of a pagan culture? This is where the challenge of the passage really impacts upon us. Do we really believe still that it is the power of the cross of Jesus Christ, and that power alone, which will transform people's lives? Or are we into some sort of cultured version of Christianity, which actually builds on human power, human wisdom, and human personality?

It is striking how in this paragraph Paul brings together the Word and the Spirit. *My speech and my message were not in plausible words of wisdom, but in demonstration of the Spirit and in power* (verse 4). The Spirit's power, then, is seen in the preaching of the cross, because that is the only message that can save, transform people's lives, and make them new in Christ. The apostolic gospel is not about Jesus bringing me that little bit extra in life, to make me feel good always. It is about humbling myself before a Christ who died for me in order to rescue me from hell, and about submitting my life to him in gratitude, because he gave himself up for me on the cross. This is where the Spirit's power is seen. When God produces that change in an individual's life, his grace works in time in a way that lasts for eternity, and these two ingredients, Word and Spirit, can never be divorced in biblical Christianity. And just as we can never separate the Word from the Spirit, so we must never separate truth from experience. They belong together.

Many of our problems in the contemporary church stem from our failure to believe this. This is why Christians look for other authorities and other methodologies, and why the church in the West during the last century has been involved in an increasingly desperate search, trying to find what it is that will really impact our culture. But all the time, the answer is staring us in the face. It is Jesus Christ and him crucified, God's power in human weakness.

As we sum up and apply the important themes of these opening paragraphs, we see that they both warn and encourage. The warning is against a 'Corinthianism', which imagines that the only way to impact the world is to become like it, to become personality-led, to become entertainment-led, to become image-focused as churches and as Christians. If we go that way, we may have a certain amount of superficial success. We shall reflect the culture back to itself, there will be some impressive performances, and it will produce a 'feel-good' religion. What it will not produce is New Testament Christians who stand in a day of persecution and who, when the going gets tough, remain faithful to the gospel and continue trusting the Lord. It is only those who know what the cross is about in their lives who have that sort of lifestyle. This is not an excuse for obscurantism or mere traditionalism, nor for being boring and irrelevant – Paul was none of those things. But the lure of Corinth is very strong in contemporary Christian practice, and it is highly dangerous.

It is operating whenever we feel pressure on us to pull the heavenly glories of the future into the present. If only we had enough faith, we might experience glory and triumph now. Yet beneath the surface of everybody's life, there is an ache that will not go away. We may ignore it, pretend it does not exist, or attempt to bury it under a mountain of activity, but it will not disappear. For the fact is that we were designed to enjoy a better world than this, and until that better world comes along, we will groan for what we do not have. An aching soul is evidence, not of neurosis, but of spiritual realism. To understand that is to begin to understand what the cross is all about. The cross spells the answer to that ache, but only in a measure now. The full answer will only be given in the presence of the Christ who died and rose and ascended, before whom we will stand on that last day, made perfect and complete in him. The great danger is that because we are not prepared to wait for this, we dilute our faith, re-focus it or adapt it to our culture, and we leave the whole purpose and scandal of the cross behind. In effect, we nullify it.

[35]

But there is always this great encouragement that the word of the cross is still the power and wisdom of God. It is still the only way that lives can be transformed on a daily basis. It is only when I am crucified with Christ and when Jesus is enthroned as Lord in my life that the message of the cross starts to meet the deepest aches and needs of my heart. What an encouragement to know that that is the very reason why God planned the cross. What an encouragement also to know that God still uses ordinary Christians, who live by this faith, to bring to nothing the proud, pagan empires of this world. His love and his truth are still the most radical and subversive means of collapsing Satan's strongholds. But the divine power is always clothed in human weakness, so *that your faith might not rest in the wisdom of men but in the power of God.*

6

God's Secret Wisdom

⁶Yet among the mature we do impart wisdom, although it is not a wisdom of this age or of the rulers of this age, who are doomed to pass away. ⁷But we impart a secret and hidden wisdom of God, which God decreed before the ages for our glory. ⁸None of the rulers of this age understood this, for if they had, they would not have crucified the Lord of glory. ⁹But, as it is written,
> *"What no eye has seen, nor ear heard,*
> *nor the heart of man imagined,*
> *what God has prepared for those who love him" –*
¹⁰these things God has revealed to us through the Spirit. For the Spirit searches everything, even the depths of God (1 Cor. 2:6–10).

From verse 6 to the end of chapter 2, Paul turns back to the theme of wisdom, and provides a much more positive assessment of its function. He is keen to correct any misunderstandings the Corinthians may have. He is not against wisdom in itself, but that autonomous human wisdom which stands in arrogant independence of the cross and is even opposed to its message. By contrast, God's cross-centred wisdom is recognised and valued *among the mature*. This terminology introduces a set of contrasts that will be developed later in chapter 3. There, Paul contrasts the mature with 'infants' (3:1) – a contrast that reflects his distinction in the same verse between 'spiritual' and 'worldly'. However, far from gathering a spiritual elite around him, the pronoun *we*, used throughout this section, applies to all who are wise enough to submit to the gospel of Christ crucified and who are therefore true believers.

The verses that follow provide a set of criteria by which we can assess whether or not we are demonstrating that sort of spiritual maturity. Paul's method is to develop a series of contrasts by which he defines the nature of mature, biblical spirituality, as he compares divine and human wisdoms in their different manifestations. In this section, we will consider the first two.

HUMAN WISDOM ORIGINATES IN MAN AND IS TIME-BOUND (verse 6)

This is the first great disadvantage and Paul wants to emphasize the negative in order to woo his readers away from their false confidence. You cannot learn God's wisdom in the world or from the world, because the world, in its rebellion against its Creator, will always rule love and reverence for God out of the equation. Worldly wisdom is always about living for self and living in the present. 'Look out for number one.' 'There is no such thing as a free lunch.' 'Never trust anybody.' Cynical and hard-nosed, worldly wisdom has learned the reality of human depravity in the hard-knocks school of experience. *This age* and *the rulers of this age* are however *doomed to pass away*. They have no ultimate future. Those who marry the spirit of the age are very soon widowed.

This is a sobering thought whenever we are tempted to be impressed by contemporary, secular values. Empires rise and fall. Fashions flow and ebb. Experts come and go. Nothing makes the point more clearly than the media personality, pop star, sports hero, culture in which we live. The fall of such idols is often as meteoric as their rise, and the ideas and values they promote are as thin and transient as themselves. Shakespeare was right when he wrote that, 'Gilded boys and girls all must, like chimney-sweepers, come to dust'. There is only one eternal kingdom, one city that remains, and it is built on a totally different set of values.

DIVINE WISDOM IS REVEALED BY GOD AND IS ETERNAL (verse 7)

God's *secret wisdom* does not originate in the thought of man at all. Because it has been *hidden . . . before the ages*, there would be no way in which we could even have begun to understand it, had it not been revealed to us. But that is very humbling. All the religions of the world are shaped by man's desire to reach up to the ultimate by his own unaided efforts, to climb whatever ladders he has erected in order to reach his heaven. It is fashionable to see man's religious quest as a noble expression of the human spirit, but the Bible's consistent message is that we are not really looking for God at all (*Rom.* 3:10–12). In fact, God has come down the ladder to us, to reveal his gracious rescue plan in and through his Son, Jesus Christ. God has disclosed his great mystery, *decreed . . . for our glory*, and for the most part we have regarded it as folly and walked away from his mercy, because we find it too humbling.

We would know nothing of God if he had not condescended to make himself known to us. We find the supreme revelation of this knowledge in 'Jesus Christ and him crucified'. Yet this mystery, revealed in time through Christ's birth and life, death and resurrection, was no emergency plan. It originated before time began and was destined to bring his people into his eternal glory, world without end. What a contrast Paul draws! The rulers of this age and those who follow them will lose their glory and come to nothing because of their rebellion against God and rejection of his Son. But the Lord Jesus has gained everlasting glory by his acceptance of his Father's will, his obedience even to death on the cross, and we share in that glory as we are united to him by faith. We are thus led on to Paul's second set of contrasts.

HUMAN WISDOM IS IGNORANT OF GOD'S GREAT PLAN (verse 8)

It is a fact of history that *none of the rulers of this age understood this*. Pontius Pilate, Herod, Annas, and Caiaphas, all stand condemned in the gospel narratives of Christ's passion as ignorant, blind and foolish, in spite of all their natural cunning, political skill, authority and pomp. They conspired together to do away with the Son of God and so they *crucified the Lord of glory*. Had they known who he was, they would not have dared to carry out such a heinous action. But they did not understand precisely because they were '*of this age*'. While this does not make them innocent (see *Acts* 2:23, 4:27–28), it does explain the bitterness of their opposition. They had no understanding of God's great rescue plan that was being worked out even as they hounded Jesus to his unjust and early death.

DIVINE WISDOM CENTRES GOD'S GREAT PLAN IN CHRIST'S SELF-GIVING LOVE (verses 9–10)

The quotation from Isaiah 64:4 is included in order to contrast what the human senses can perceive with the hidden realities of God's provision in heaven, for the knowledge of which we are entirely dependent on spiritual revelation. Wisdom is not the product of a knowledge acquired by the senses of sight or hearing, or reached by intellectual effort. Heaven is impenetrable to such human assaults. Its realities are not given as a reward for knowledge but as the fulfilment of love. This is because love for God is the only touchstone of Christian reality and maturity.

We have already noted how impressed the Corinthian church was by knowledge; its own (1:5) and that of others, but there seems to have been very little emphasis given to love. In chapter 8:1 we shall find Paul reminding his readers that 'knowledge puffs up, but love builds up.' By the time we reach chapter 13, we will be only too pain-fully aware of the jealousies, pride, litigation, greed and exploitation that seem to deny this gospel priority. It is no surprise, then, that the apostle, even at this early point in his letter, wants to stress the difference that a cross-centred spirituality makes in terms of outward-going love and sacrifice for others. No human being in his natural self-centredness would ever think that way, but *these things God has revealed to us* (that is, every believer) *through the Spirit*. This explains too why Paul was so concerned that his ministry at Corinth should be 'with a demonstration of the Spirit and of power' (2:4), for that alone turns the 'folly' of the cross into a message of salvation, received by faith.

By way of explanation Paul teaches that *the Spirit searches everything, even the depths of God*. Only the Spirit can reveal the hidden secrets of God because only he knows the unique intimacy of the Holy Trinity in which he lives, with the Father and the Son. The Spirit does not have to grasp an idea or a revelation and attempt to pass it on accurately, in the way that human teachers do. He is the very agent of revelation, so that what he discloses in his Word is the very truth of God. Furthermore, it is the Spirit's work to dive deep, as to the bottom of the sea, and to bring up treasures of revelation that would otherwise never be disclosed to human beings. He brings them to the surface in order to reveal their glory to all who are humble and willing to learn – to those who are truly mature and wise.

7

The Mind of Christ

[11] For who knows a person's thoughts except the spirit of that person, which is in him? So also no one comprehends the thoughts of God except the Spirit of God. [12] Now we have received not the spirit of the world, but the Spirit who is from God, that we might understand the things freely given us by God. [13] And we impart this in words not taught by human wisdom but taught by the Spirit, interpreting spiritual truths to those who are spiritual.

[14] The natural person does not accept the things of the Spirit of God, for they are folly to him, and he is not able to understand them because they are spiritually discerned. [15] The spiritual person judges all things, but is himself to be judged by no one. [16] "For who has understood the mind of the Lord so as to instruct him?" But we have the mind of Christ (1 Cor. 2:11–16).

A s he continues his series of contrasts between divine and human wisdom, Paul argues for the necessity of the direct ministry of the Holy Spirit in revealing God's truth, by making use of a parallel line of human experience. Perhaps we can best grasp the important teaching of this paragraph by dividing it into three sections, with the heading of each section being one of the three great assertions made here about what it means to be a Christian. The '*we*' who are referred to throughout the verses clearly stands for every believer.

(i) WE HAVE RECEIVED THE SPIRIT (verses 11–12)

Individual human wisdom is derived from an individual's thought processes of enquiry and reflection. We all have an inner thought life that is unknown, even to our nearest and dearest, to every one in fact, except God! One of the marks of love and trust in human relationships is that we opt to reveal more and more of those inner thoughts to others. But always we remain in control of that 'revelation' and unless we choose to open the door to others, they cannot know our thoughts. Exactly the same must be true of God, but on an infinitely greater scale (verse 11b). How could we ever begin to know God's thoughts or understand his wisdom?

Paul's answer in verse 12 is that we have received *the Spirit who is from God*. He has already established that *the spirit of the world* is quite useless in such matters, since it is a spirit that depends on human thought and perception, and spiritual realities that have to do with God are beyond its range. This is a powerful reminder of our total dependence on the activity of the Spirit in the work of evangelism. We shall not find people understanding the hidden wisdom of the cross if our efforts at reaching them are conditioned by the world's methods. All we shall succeed in doing is to enrol them in a religious, but worldly, club.

Take, for example, the 'prosperity gospel' teaching which is so popular and so devastating to real Christian faith, in so many parts of the world. The spirit of the world encourages us all to pursue wealth as if it were the greatest goal of our lives in this world. If we accept this view, we will regard God as being the ultimate provider of wealth, health and happiness. When we come into possession of such things we will believe that it is a sign of his love for us and his approval of our lives. When we do not, we will believe that something is wrong and we need to appease God or to appeal to him, so that he will relent and be gracious. It is essentially a type of works religion, where God's blessing has to be earned by our efforts. What we are left with is a worldly version of Christianity or rather, more accurately, a basically worldly mind-set, covered by a thin veneer of piety.

But this is not the work of the Holy Spirit, whom we received when first we trusted Christ as our Saviour and submitted our lives to him as Lord. His ministry in the believer is *that we might understand the things freely given us by God* (verse 12b). Acts 2:38 teaches us that the only way to receive the Holy Spirit is to repent and to receive forgiveness for our sins in the name of Jesus Christ. This promise is for all people, in every generation. Indeed, no one can become a Christian without receiving the Spirit of Christ (*Rom.* 8:9) and all who have received God's Spirit belong to him. Therefore, if we are to know God, he must open our minds so that we see Jesus for who he is, and for what he has done for us through his death and resurrection. Such blessings of forgiveness, reconciliation and enlightened understanding are the fruit of his work, and the sure mark of the Spirit's activity is that we acknowledge them to be God's free gifts and not something we can ever deserve or earn.

(ii) WE UNDERSTAND THE SPIRIT'S LANGUAGE (verses 13–14)

We impart this, takes us back to what God has freely given us in the gospel. In all probability Paul is referring again to his strategy when he first evangelised Corinth. The language he then used was not the rhetoric of the contemporary philosophers, with its persuasive techniques and verbal fireworks. That would have been *words . . . taught us by human wisdom*, and the response of the Corinthians would not then have been from real faith and would not have had any lasting significance (2:4–5). So the apostolic method was to avoid such compromise deliberately and instead to use *words . . . taught by the Spirit, interpreting spiritual truths to those who are spiritual* (verse 13). It is as though the Spirit gives to us a whole new vocabulary to understand freshly revealed spiritual realities in human words and to convey them to fellow-believers (literally, to 'spirituals').

Once again, Paul is introducing a theme early on in the letter to which he intends returning in much greater detail later (see chapter 12 following). But who are these 'spirituals'? It was a key issue in Corinth and remains so today, when we hear a great deal about different 'spiritualities', and when being 'spiritual' seems to have as many variant forms as one chooses to imagine. What is of primary importance here, however, is to note that the only spirituality Paul is interested in is that generated by the Holy Spirit and taught by him. Any other type of spirituality would come under his category of human wisdom since it would owe more to human ingenuity and invention than to divine revelation.

[44]

As a contrast, Paul introduces us to the opposite category of human being: the man without the Spirit, called here, *the natural man*. This individual's main characteristic is negativity towards every aspect of the Holy Spirit's ministry. He *does not accept the things of the Spirit of God . . . he is not able to understand them because they are spiritually discerned*. This process is probably best understood in reverse order. Because he lacks spiritual discernment, which is the gift of the Spirit, the natural man cannot understand and so does not accept spiritual revelation. All he has are the human faculties of eye, ear and intellect, and without illumination he is unable to grasp the truth of the gospel. He judges the world by what he sees. He explains everything by the use of his sensory perceptions and his reason, because he believes that the world's discernment is able to explain the world. But the 'spiritual man' knows that the only way to explain the world is by God's Word (see *Heb.* 11:3) and that only divine wisdom can reveal to us our true purpose and significance in time and in eternity. Of course the gospel seems foolish without the Spirit's work, since it inverts all of the natural man's values and systems. It literally turns the world upside down or, rather, right side up, with its secret wisdom of the crucified Lord of glory. The cross is emphatically the ultimate test of all 'spirituality', a test at which all new age, triumphalist and legalistic spiritualities alike stumble and fall.

(iii) WE HAVE THE MIND OF CHRIST (verses 15–16)

In this closing paragraph, Paul again returns to his methodology of contrast. Human wisdom is incapable of making judgements on spiritual matters, but divine wisdom has the mind of Christ. *The spiritual man* is not an elite super-saint, but any humble believer who lives in the power and wisdom of the cross. He *judges all things*. As God provides discernment for understanding his revelation, Christians are able to come to right and good judgements about all things. Because we have divinely revealed principles and standards, we can know right from wrong, wisdom from folly – and all from God's perspective. Clearly, this does not make Christians infallible, but it is a promise of God's direction and guidance if we are dependent on his revealed wisdom in Scripture, and on the Holy Spirit as our teacher.

A Christian is not therefore to be gullible or naïve, nor is he to switch off his mind and pretend that rationality is the enemy of spirituality. We can be truly wise with the wisdom of God, because we have a solid foundation of unchanging truth and reality in the gospel, on the basis of which we can come to active conclusions. This will help us to see through the travesties of the world's wisdom, to balance the realities of our smallness before God with the reality of the divine destiny of glory given to all who believe the gospel, and above all to assess everything by the Christ-centred spirituality of the cross.

But is himself to be judged by no one. In other words, the truth of the gospel liberates us from living under the judgement of other people's opinions of us. Of course, the natural man will make his own judgements about the gospel and those who believe it and will often not be in the least reticent about expressing them very freely. But his judgements have no authority in these areas and Christian people are not subject to them. I remember that on leaving my school-teaching career to work with university students in Christian Unions my headmaster told me frankly that he thought I was very foolish and warned me not to come asking for my job back in six months' time. He expressed his natural, unspiritual judgement, but I was not subject to it – nor did I return! The spiritual man is resigned to the fact that the world will not understand what his faith is all about, *for who has understood the mind of the Lord so as to instruct him?* (verse 16a, quoting *Isa.* 40:13).

Spiritual things can only be spiritually discerned. The spiritually mature will not be thrown by unbelief, nor will they compromise their message to fit in with the prejudices of the current political correctness of their culture. So when we are told, 'I cannot accept a God who . . . or who does not . . . ' followed by some fashionable protest against God's self-revelation in Scripture, we should not be in the least surprised. It is all a matter of revelation, for the spiritually mature are those who accept and live by God's revealed secrets as found in the apostolic gospel. The gracious and loving response must surely be to point out that the issue is not whether we can accept God, but whether he will accept us.

Such divine acceptance will only be through the gospel and it is the gospel that has made all the difference. The miracle of the new covenant is that *we have the mind of Christ*. We can know his revealed thoughts and share his wisdom. This is the honour that God confers on those whom the world will always despise, those who have knelt at the cross and submitted to God's foolish wisdom.

8

God's Fellow-Workers

*¹But I, brothers, could not address you as spiritual people, but
as people of the flesh, as infants in Christ. ²I fed you with milk,
not solid food, for you were not ready for it. And even now you
are not yet ready, ³for you are still of the flesh. For while there
is jealousy and strife among you, are you not of the flesh and
behaving only in a human way? ⁴For when one says, "I follow
Paul," and another, "I follow Apollos," are you not being merely
human?*

*⁵What then is Apollos? What is Paul? Servants through whom
you believed, as the Lord assigned to each. ⁶I planted, Apollos
watered, but God gave the growth. ⁷So neither he who plants nor
he who waters is anything, but only God who gives the growth.
⁸He who plants and he who waters are one, and each will receive
his wages according to his labour. ⁹For we are God's fellow workers.
You are God's field, God's building* (1 Cor. 3:1–9).

The first four chapters of this letter are devoted to dealing with
the divisions that were such a threat to the work of the gospel
in Corinth. We have seen Paul's tactic for exposing the first of two
foundational mistakes that his opponents and detractors were
making. They were in danger of rejecting the gospel of the cross in
favour of a human wisdom, which seemed so much more successful,
attractive and, in particular, Corinthian. Now Paul turns to their
second mistake as he begins to show them how they have misunder-
stood the unique nature of the church and its leadership. The root
of the problem is the same. They are adopting the cultural norms of
their own situation in Corinth, and seeking to apply those to the

church. Once human wisdom and power have displaced the gospel of 'Jesus Christ and him crucified', in a church setting, then the spotlight will inevitably fall upon the church leaders. If the message is so unimpressive, then the messengers must compensate for it by their wisdom, spirituality and charisma. As chapter 3 opens, Paul's tactic is to expose the immaturity and worldliness of such a view.

THE SPIRITUALITY OF THE CROSS EXPOSES WORLDLINESS (verses 1–4)

The opening of the chapter is full of irony. The very people who were setting themselves up as 'spiritual' and elevating the claims of their heroes over against the apostle, were indicating, by this very action, that they were still only 'babies'. Two devastating phrases sum them up. They are *infants in Christ* (verse 1) and *still of the flesh* (verse 3). It is important to recognize that Paul has no doubts as to whether these misguided members of the church in Corinth are in fact true Christian believers. He calls them *brothers* (verse 1) and affirms that they are *in Christ* (verse 1b). But having stated, at the end of chapter 2, that 'we have the mind of Christ', he now, at the beginning of chapter 3, tells the believers at Corinth that they were not using their Christian minds. They are certainly 'spiritual' in the technical sense of chapter 2, i.e. they are not any longer the 'natural' men that they once were. However, their behaviour is totally inconsistent with their new status. Being spiritual separates them from those without the Spirit, just as the church is separate from the world. But their mistake is to see the gift of the Spirit as leading to an elite status for some within the church, and from this springs all their jealousy and quarrelling – the evidence of their worldly condition.

Paul's devastating analysis continues. Not only does he say that they were unweaned infants, but that they were still *not ready* for *solid food* (verse 2). Literally, they were 'not able to deal' with it. It is possible, therefore, for real believers to be stunted in their development and for a whole congregation to be affected by this problem. There is plenty of activity and exercise of spiritual gifts, but the church is characterized by childishness. The story of Peter Pan, the boy who never grew up, is still a great favourite, but in the real world it is an unmitigated tragedy. Arrested development is a sign that

[49]

something is seriously wrong. In the spiritual context, we must never remain content with childishness. To be so is, for Paul, synonymous with 'worldliness' or (more literally) 'the flesh'. It is to drift back to the old way of living, to the world's outlook and value-systems, *behaving only in a human way* (verse 3), in other words, being a 'natural man' (2:14).

The indisputable evidence of this is their elevation of favourite teachers to the position of party leaders, and a consequent lining up behind them as rival parties. That is *behaving only in a human way*, adopting the world's lifestyle. This jealousy of what others have, and what others can do, automatically leads to rivalry and strife. At such a point, the church becomes indistinguishable from the world. But Paul's point is that this worldliness illustrates that they have not yet come to grips with the message of the cross. They are not able to learn anything more, because this fundamental lesson has been forgotten. The reason is very clear. To bow before a crucified Saviour is to acknowledge ones wretchedness and abject need, to cast oneself on the rich mercy of God, as a rebellious sinner, who deserves nothing but God's wrath and an eternity of separation from him. It is to recognize that we have nothing to bring before him. Clearly, that spells the end of all human pride and self-seeking, and therefore of jealousy, quarrelling, factions and divisions. It is the first lesson in the school of spiritual maturity. So the factions developing in the Corinthian congregation illustrate that they have not yet grasped the need to be crucified with Christ.

Sadly, such immaturity is all too prevalent in our own lives. How often do we compare ourselves with others and fret because God seems to have blessed them more than he has blessed us. We look for our favourite leaders behind whom we line up in jealousy or resentfulness, in criticism and a quarrelsome spirit towards others. It is all very self-centred and what lies behind it is a presumption that God is not gracious and loving, and that he cannot be relied upon to do what is best in our lives and in our churches. In fact, it is childish behaviour, where we think we know better than he does and want to be at the centre of our world. Of course, mature Christians will not always agree together about everything, but the way in which we handle our differences reveals whether we are still worldly, still trapped in the spiritual crèche, or not. It is certainly true that all party spirit in the church of Christ belongs to the nursery, and while this might be excused in a new-born babe, it demonstrates a terrible disfigurement of Christ's Body when it is exercised amongst more mature Christians, and even amongst leaders who should know better.

THE SPIRITUALITY OF THE CROSS MODELS SERVANTHOOD (verses 5–9)

Paul continues to build his argument on the example of Christ crucified. There seems little doubt that the Corinthians saw their community as inferior (1:26). Paul has already addressed this attitude and reminded them that God was responsible for their situation. The church is as it is because God himself has chosen it to be that way. It is never his intention for the church, as a human institution, to sparkle in this world. The church is a divine activity, but it is made up of citizens of heaven who, while on earth, are called to live the life of faith. Their maturity is seen in their belief in God's promises, their obedience to his commands, and their focus on the future reward. But this worldly church longed for leaders on this earth and for the glories of the kingdom to be demonstrated in the present. They therefore demanded that their leadership become god-like, a substitute lord in the place of Jesus Christ (1:13). Once the cross becomes an unacceptable message, then the focus will be on the present, both for reward and for recognition. And once the focus is on the present, rivalry will inevitably arise between different Christian groups.

In verse 5, Paul attacks this wrong thinking, by asserting that he and Apollos, and anyone else working in the church, were only *servants*. They are not creators of a new philosophy or lifestyle, but the messengers of a given revelation. Moreover, it is required that the message be confirmed by the lifestyle of the messenger. The cross is a paradigm of the gospel, and for that reason it is also the model of all gospel ministry. Servants must not become masters to worship and follow; they are the Lord's agents *through whom you believed*. Paul might well have added: 'not *in* whom'. They were not converted to him or Apollos, or anyone else, and therefore human agencies, however gifted, must be kept in perspective. A servant simply takes his orders from his master: *as the Lord assigned to each* (verse 5). Perhaps Paul is also making the comment that the church has no right to tell him how his apostolic ministry is to be conducted.

Paul's point is made with great simplicity and clarity in verse 6, where the tenses help us to understand the thrust of what he is saying. *I planted, Apollos watered.* The aorist tense here indicates an action that happened at a point in time, but the tense of the verb of which God is the subject, *but God gave the growth,* is an imperfect tense, which refers to a continuing work over a period of time. We might render it, 'God kept on making the seed grow'. Paul's point is that it is God who is doing the real work through his servants, for he is the only one who can give life to the seed. Without that miracle, the planting and watering would be in vain. Although Paul and Apollos have different tasks, they are on an equal footing before their Lord – they are simply servants. The Corinthians' perspective of them is far too high. They have no independent importance or inherent significance in and of themselves. Their only value lies in their function as servants. Indeed, if it were not for God's activity there would be no church at all. The Christians must therefore stop treating their leaders as rulers and see them as workers, following in the footsteps of a crucified Saviour. This is a powerful counterbalance to any possessive thinking about local congregations and Christian service. So often we think of *my* church, *my* pulpit, *my* people or *my* small group, but they all belong to Christ. No labourer is indispensable and any of us can be moved at any time in his harvest field. Rightly understood, this spells the end of all the competitiveness between Christians, which is the cause of so much bitterness and hurt and which undermines so much gospel work. Instead of such divisions, gospel spirituality stresses the essential unity of all service truly offered to Christ and representative of his example.

The text makes the same point very powerfully in verse 8, which reads, literally, 'the planting and the watering are one'. Here the word 'one' is neuter, meaning one unit or one entity. Although Paul is talking about individual human beings, his stress is that they are not in competition with one another as preachers, leaders, or even as Christian servants. They are not rivals, because they are working for the same master and involved in the same grand project. God gives us all different tasks, and different opportunities, and we have distinctive gifts and contributions, so that every piece of service matters. We shall not be compared and contrasted with one another for *each will receive his wages according to his labour* (verse 8). Again, the focus is on the future reward, and Paul sees mature spirituality in terms of responding to the grace of God in the gospel by serving in God's field or on his building site (verse 9).

It is wonderfully liberating to realize these things. God is not going to judge one Christian against another, unlike so many of the judgements of our culture. In Paul's day, the travelling philosophers graded their disciples into beginners, those making progress, and the mature. It seems as though the Corinthians had taken those secular categories into their thinking about spiritual growth and ministry. But the Lord Jesus does not set up tables of merit. He loves to reward, and his criterion is faithful labour – hard work done for his glory. That is something we can all aspire to and live by. We shall therefore have diverse tasks, according to our differing gifts, but with one purpose and with rewards for every faithful servant. In the summary of verse 9, the word 'God' comes first three times in the three sentences of the verse and each time it is a statement about possession.

Speaking on behalf of those who have served the church in Corinth, Paul says that they belong to God, as his *fellow workers*. The emphasis is on labouring together, not alongside God, who is the supreme Lord and Master, but alongside one another. God is the owner; we are the work-force. But the church itself is the field that God owns and in which he sets his labourers to work. So then every Christian is a part of *God's field*, and *God's building*. This last verse summarizes the thrust of the paragraph. We *all* belong *only* to God. Leaders do not own the church, whether it is local, national or universal. Nor do the members own the church. However many years they have been part of a local congregation, however much time, money and energy they may have poured into it, members have to remember that it is *God's* field and *God's* building. He produces the crop. He raises the edifice. He selects the labourers and he allots the tasks. He will reward the faithful. To realize this is not to abdicate from proper leadership, but to realize that the spirituality of the cross requires servanthood as its fundamental distinguishing mark. Do we really know and believe that 'only God makes things grow'? (verse 7).

9

A Skilled Master Builder

¹⁰According to the grace of God given to me, like a skilled master builder I laid a foundation, and someone else is building upon it. Let each one take care how he builds upon it. ¹¹For no one can lay a foundation other than that which is laid, which is Jesus Christ. ¹²Now if anyone builds on the foundation with gold, silver, precious stones, wood, hay, straw – ¹³each one's work will become manifest, for the Day will disclose it, because it will be revealed by fire, and the fire will test what sort of work each one has done. ¹⁴If the work that anyone has built on the foundation survives, he will receive a reward. ¹⁵If anyone's work is burned up, he will suffer loss, though he himself will be saved, but only as through fire (1 Cor. 3:10–15).

We know, from the end of verse 9 that this paragraph is not primarily about building our own spiritual lives, but about building the church. It therefore has a major application to all who have responsibilities within local congregations and especially to those whose ministry is in evangelism and teaching. Of course it is true that how we build our own lives, in obedience to God's Word, has a profound impact on the health, or otherwise, of the local church, but the focus is not on the individual here. All of the uses of the pronoun 'you' are plural and the application is therefore corporate. When we get to verse 17, we shall see that building is identified as 'God's temple'.

THE RIGHT OF FOUNDATION (verse 10–11)

Paul begins by reminding them that he is not an empire builder but a church builder. He describes himself as *a skilled master builder*, or 'wise masterbuilder' as in the AV, a reference, perhaps, to the 'wisdom' that seemed to have excited so much interest in Corinth. If they were looking for someone who demonstrated wisdom, then his method of building should give them excellent evidence. But such wisdom was the result of God's grace in calling him to the apostolic ministry and commissioning him to the work among the Gentiles. Once again Paul is reminding them of his own initial ministry at Corinth in order to underline the principles on which he acted and to illustrate that he had not shifted from them. His role then was to lay the foundation, and others, including the current leaders in the church, were now building upon it. The metaphor is well chosen because building, especially the building of a temple, is a long, slow process, costly in man–hours, energy and finance. One generation might lay the foundation, the second might build upon it, and a third complete it, as with many medieval cathedrals. But Paul's primary concern is that their discontent might lead them to imagine that they can build something different from that which the foundations dictate. His stress, in verse 11, is that if the Corinthians were going to build a church, then there could be only one true foundation, and he had already laid that in the gospel of Christ crucified. That foundation determined the shape of the whole superstructure. If the church was to be Christ-like, it had to be built on Christ alone. There can be no true Christianity without Christ. You cannot have Christian ethics without Christ. You cannot have a meeting place between God and man (the purpose of the temple) without the cross of Christ.

If Christ is not the basis of whatever sort of moral life a person may try to live, it is not the Christian life, and if he is not the basis of whatever sort of community men may try to build, that community is not the Christian church. Clearly, Paul's fear is that they will subtly change the foundation, thinking that they are not replacing Christ but supplementing him with a fuller and richer spirituality. If that happens, then the end product will not be a Christian church. The sufficiency of the gospel of Christ is the issue that is at stake here, and Paul is again fighting against the Corinthian view that the apostolic gospel is somehow inadequate and needs to be supplemented with a form of supernatural triumphalism.

QUALITY MATERIALS (verses 12–15)

The wise builder not only lays the right foundation, he also builds with quality materials, and he does so realizing that his work will be tested in the future. In this section, Paul explains his own motivation as a Christian teacher, and relates it also to the work that is going on in the building of the church in Corinth. The big question is not whether it looks impressive now, but whether it will last the test of time and especially the test, or the day, of God's judgement. The potential tragedy is that having started with the right foundation they are now building with rubbish. It is clearly inappropriate to build a temple with *wood, hay, straw* (verse 12). These are inferior materials to use if the purpose of the construction is to be a meeting place between God and man.

Any normal human builder would want to use the very best materials for such a noble purpose. The list in verse 12, beginning with *gold, silver, precious stones*, seems to be chosen not so much to make the point of decreasing value, as of increasing flammability. When God's day of judgement brings to light the quality of each man's work, *it will be revealed with fire* (verse 13). The fire will test the quality of each man's work and then the materials that have been used will be revealed for what they are. This is not a judgement about the eternal salvation of the builder, and there is certainly nothing here that remotely points to the idea of purgatory, or of being refined by fire. That is an idea totally without any biblical warrant. In fact, verse 15 makes it abundantly clear that the builder with hay or straw will himself be saved, even though his life's work may go up in flames. The picture is of someone escaping with his life from a building engulfed in fire, and about to be totally destroyed.

Applying this to the Corinthians' situation, Paul's meaning is that the fundamental weaknesses of the church may cause it to be built in a way that will not last. They were looking for a perfect church that would make an impression on the glitzy culture of Corinth, and would seem to reflect the values of the community in which they lived. Paul wants to sober them into recognizing that actually they need to be building a church that will stand on the Day of Judgement and that the victory of the church will be experienced in the eternal perspective, and not necessarily in the context of its present work and ministry. The more they relied on the wisdom of the world with its impressive rhetoric and powerful leaders, the more they sought displays of supernatural power, all the more would they be building with that which was perishable. The danger was that they would become obsessed with the gifts such as prophecy, tongues and knowledge, not realizing that all these were passing and perishable. They are bound by time and will not be needed in eternity. So the churches that are built with such materials rather than with the gospel of Christ crucified and the love that it produces, may be in danger of neglecting the one true foundation and constructing an edifice made of perishable materials.

These are challenges that we need to apply to our own current situation. Will the churches that are founded upon the biblical gospel continue in that tradition and continue to build with the finest materials? Wisdom, power and spiritual gifts are *not* the foundation of the New Testament church. The true foundation is 'Jesus Christ and him crucified'. We need to regain that understanding as the fundamental, non-negotiable reality of church life and growth. It is, however, exactly in this area that we are tempted to drift in every generation. We are told that people do not want to hear the message of the cross, because it is humbling and demanding, and quite unacceptable to the wise man of this age. But when have things ever been any different? Gospel work *is* hard and always has been. People are resistant; the opposition is strong. But we need to have the conviction that it is the quality of each man's work that God is concerned with, not its apparent outward success. Our problem is that we do not always find it easy to discern the subtle, quick-fix methods to which we are so often tempted, but which actually deny the gospel of the cross. Certainly some of the model 'churches' that are on offer today seem almost the polar opposite of the apostle's teaching.

Today we are offered the church as an entertainment centre, where the congregation gathers in order to evaluate and appreciate the efforts of the professionals 'up front'. In such a situation there is always a buzz of excitement, frequent visiting celebrities and stars, and the participants go out on a high, longing for the next inspiration, but seldom sobered by the cross. Or, we have the church as a university lecture room, where knowledge is the most important ingredient and where the more involved and complex the understanding, the greater the temptation to believe that we have the keys to an elite wisdom of which ordinary Christians are ignorant. Such gatherings are never humbled by the cross and never repentant of their arrogance and judgementalism. Perhaps the most popular form of all is the church as health farm, where the feel-good factor is at its greatest, with generous helpings of personal charm, affirmation, positive thinking and therapeutic counselling. What is lacking, however, is the recognition of the total sufficiency of Christ crucified to bear my sin and guilt and to make me truly accepted by God. Where that is lacking, there can be no real growth in Christ-likeness, in love for God or for my neighbour. The servant heart has been replaced by the consumer mentality. Paul's teaching reminds us that whenever we put our gurus on a pedestal and start to follow human leaders; whenever we allow gifts and experiences to be the focus of the church; whenever power, wisdom and knowledge are our goals, rather than love for God; we cease to build wisely. Indeed, as the next paragraph will show us, we may even turn into careless wreckers.

No More Boasting!

¹⁶Do you not know that you are God's temple and that God's Spirit dwells in you? ¹⁷If anyone destroys God's temple, God will destroy him. For God's temple is holy, and you are that temple. ¹⁸Let no one deceive himself. If anyone among you thinks that he is wise in this age, let him become a fool that he may become wise. ¹⁹For the wisdom of this world is folly with God. For it is written, "He catches the wise in their craftiness," ²⁰and again, "The Lord knows the thoughts of the wise, that they are futile." ²¹So let no one boast in men. For all things are yours, ²²whether Paul or Apollos or Cephas or the world or life or death or the present or the future – all are yours, ²³and you are Christ's, and Christ is God's (1 Cor. 3:16–23).

As his application becomes more pressing, Paul's style becomes more direct. These are very sobering verses, expressing as they do the real nub of the Corinthian crisis. With the introduction of the image of the temple, Paul reminds us that the purpose of the temple in the Old Testament was to be the meeting place between God and his people. God's temple is his dwelling place, inhabited by his Spirit. In 6:19, we shall see Paul referring that imagery to the individual believer, when he writes, 'Do you not know that your body is a temple of the Holy Spirit within you, whom you have from God?' However, here in this section the application is plural and corporate. It is to the whole church at Corinth, not just a special group, or an inner ring, that the apostle is referring. Those who prided themselves on their super-spirituality may well have thought about themselves in this way, but that is why the disastrous divisions had appeared. It is therefore probably true that Paul is thinking about them, when he contemplates the possibility of the church being destroyed (verse 17). He may well mean that internal wrangling was in danger of tearing out the very heart of the church. Or, as some others have suggested, the reference may be to the church's inability to function any longer as a viable alternative to the pagan culture of Corinth, if it was so infected by Corinthian thinking and ways. If the Christian believers were not holding onto the foundation of Christ, with faith, hope and love, then neither the nature nor the fruit of the gospel would be seen in Corinth and there would be nothing to challenge the city's idolatry and immorality. Either way, those who were called to be church builders, might turn into reckless destroyers.

DO NOT BE IGNORANT (verses 16–17)

At verse 16, Paul uses a phrase to which he will return ten times in the course of the letter – *Do you not know?* A survey of the way in which he uses it shows that he wants to shock his readers out of their complacency. What makes the Corinthian congregation a temple, or an inner shrine, of God, was the glory of God dwelling in his people by the Holy Spirit. That is what makes the church *holy*, set apart as God's special possession. It is the one place where God can be met in Corinth, in the fellowship of his people. This is why the health and effectiveness of the church was so important. It is God's demonstration, in time, of the transforming power of the cross and the resurrection. His alternative society is designed to make the world hungry in its empty frustration of life without God. To move away from that radical gospel to a culture that is a pale shadow of paganism is a tragedy of the first degree. Indeed, Paul wants to label it sabotage, or even suicide. No one will be rescued on the Last Day by a spirituality that has taken its colour from the surrounding culture. All that will happen is that the church will become increasingly ashamed of the cross, will give up the preaching of the cross, and as a result there will be no lasting work done for eternity. Nobody will be saved because there is no other gospel. When that happens, a local congregation always degenerates into a religious club in one generation, and a ruined, destroyed building in the next. There are many ways of destroying a local church. In the first half of the twentieth century, when anti-supernaturalism reigned, it was hardly surprising that people gave up attending church when there was no divine Christ being proclaimed. The irony is that in the current situation where super-supernaturalism seems to be in the ascendancy, the same criterion of unbelievability may deter the new generation from seriously considering the gospel. Factionalism; empire building; adding to Scripture; all these can achieve the same destructive goal, but the chilling note at the end of verse 17 reminds us that this is not a matter of insignificance or neutrality with God. *If anyone destroys God's temple, God will destroy him.* It is sobering to think that a ministry can be enthusiastic and sincere, but ultimately destructive. Paul therefore develops his argument further.

DO NOT BE DELUDED (verses 18–20)

'Let no one delude themselves,' is a more literal translation of verse 18a. It is particularly pertinent to the Corinthian situation. They thought that they were 'wise', but what Paul has exposed is that their wisdom was of this world and of this present age, and therefore had absolutely no credentials with God. It was in reality folly (1:20) because it was human in origin and could not bring anyone to a true knowledge of God. His appeal, then, is for them to be 'Christian fools' rather than worldly fools, by coming back to the true wisdom that is only to be found in the gospel of the cross. What that would mean, in practical terms, would be to refuse to put their confidence in the securities of the contemporary pagan society all around them. It would mean recognizing that its value systems were totally wrong and futile (verse 19a). Wealth and prestige, impressive leaders and rhetoricians, secret knowledge and supernatural powers, elite in-groups and envious outsiders: confidence in any of these is considered folly by God. All of these will be removed in a moment. Quoting from Job 5:13, *'He catches the wise in their craftiness'*, Paul perhaps means us to complete the verse for ourselves. It continues: ' ... and the schemes of the wily are brought to a quick end.' There is a constant reminder in Scripture that man can never outmanoeuvre God. He alone is the giver of life and breath, and he also can remove them whenever he chooses. In the same way, the second Old Testament quotation, from Psalm 94:11, reveals him as the God who avenges, who vindicates his people, who sees and hears and knows, and who disciplines and punishes foolish rebels. In the light of such knowledge no one would want to be a self-deluded fool; Paul therefore makes this strong appeal to the Corinthians to think things through clearly and to act accordingly.

DO NOT BE BOASTFUL (verses 21–23)

It is characteristic of the natural man that he will be boasting about himself and others, because these are all that he has in which to put his confidence. But that is not the Christian way and the second half of verse 21 explains why. It contains the linking word '*For*', leading on to Paul's great statement, *All things are yours*. Here is the antidote to boasting and the reason why gospel spirituality is never man-centred. The irony is that we know that some of the Corinthians were in fact boasting in men – 'I am of Paul, I follow Apollos'. What they should have boasted of was the great certainty with which the chapter ends, *You are Christ's, and Christ is God's* (verse 23). Rather than belonging to any human leader, they should have rejoiced that they belonged to God and that the human leaders whom God had given them, along with all his other blessings in this world, belonged to them. While it may be very natural to find self-esteem by associating with leaders whom one admires, such practice nearly always leads to narrowness and inhibition. They failed to take into account the much bigger picture that is involved when belonging to Christ. On that reckoning, *the world or life or death or the present or the future – all are yours* (verse 22).

If Paul and Apollos were only 'servants', then they belong to God. So also do the Corinthians; they do not belong to their leaders. This world belongs to God, as does the gift of life, and the great enemy death is under the sovereign rule of the Lord Jesus, for the risen Christ holds the keys of death and of Hades (*Rev.* 1:18). The present and the future are in his omnipotent hands, and in that his people are also held in those hands, all things belong to them. This is the challenge with which Paul wants to leave his readers at the end of this section. If all the greatest realities are ours, through Christ, why become the slave of a party leader or a gifted guru? Why allow one's natural preferences to be hardened and narrowed into exclusive prejudice? Why limit the freedom we have in Christ by signing up to a small, elite group who think they have got everything just right? Usually, the answer to such questions is because we want to be accepted. But if we have once understood that through faith in Christ crucified we are fully accepted and belong to God, that the local church is his special delight, and that he raises up a variety of gifted leaders to enrich the church but not to rule it, then we have truly entered into the freedom of the gospel of Christ. Believers with such convictions will always be wise builders, not careless wreckers.

I I

Faithful Stewardship

¹This is how one should regard us, as servants of Christ and stewards of the mysteries of God. ²Moreover, it is required of stewards that they be found trustworthy. ³But with me it is a very small thing that I should be judged by you or by any human court. In fact, I do not even judge myself. ⁴I am not aware of anything against myself, but I am not thereby acquitted. It is the Lord who judges me. ⁵Therefore do not pronounce judgment before the time, before the Lord comes, who will bring to light the things now hidden in darkness and will disclose the purposes of the heart. Then each one will receive his commendation from God (1 Cor. 4:1–5).

A s this new chapter opens, Paul is still concerned with the question of leadership. It has been occupying his mind since first he identified the divisions in the Corinthian church back in chapter 1:12. Corinthian Christianity was keen to put the spotlight on its leaders, and because they regarded themselves as a spiritually superior congregation, they obviously needed superior leaders. Paul just did not seem to measure up to this standard. However, as we saw in the last chapter, his concern is to trim these pretensions down to size. The Corinthian church is only what it is because of the grace of God in the gospel. It is clearly not part of God's intention that the human institution should be elevated in this world. What God is looking for, both in the church and in its leaders on earth, is faithfulness, as this short paragraph makes abundantly clear. Such faithfulness means being full of faith, living according to the unseen realities and allowing the priorities of the gospel to dominate our lifestyle. The alternative is to live by sight, rather than faith, and this is always a temptation to a church living in a sensory world. But whenever the church starts to follow the world's agenda and dance to its tunes, it inevitably begins to exalt men. One of the clearest exposures of this in the whole Bible is the teaching of the Lord Jesus in Matthew 23 as he confronts the worldliness of the Pharisees. They are given special titles and uniforms. They love the places of honour at banquets and the most important seats in the synagogue. They specialize in greetings in the marketplaces when they are accorded special titles – Teacher, Father, Rabbi. But Christ's devastating dismissal of all this is conveyed in the one sentence, 'They do all their deeds to be seen by others' (*Matt.* 23:5). The focus is all on their abilities as leaders and on the impressive nature of their performance, as viewed by the surrounding culture. Whenever such career-mindedness develops within a Christian community, it will inevitably bring with it criticism, rivalry and, ultimately, division.

A concern for leadership is still uppermost in Paul's mind as he now begins to consider the criticism that he has been receiving from the Corinthian church. Taking some key principles and applying them to himself and to Apollos, he provides for them and for us an analysis of how relationships in the church can so easily sour, particularly in the areas of leadership and ministry. To do this he makes use of a different metaphor, namely, the picture of a household, and of the responsibility of a steward within the household. The apostle indicates to his readers where they are going wrong in this whole process, and we discover that they are to blame in three particular areas.

(i) THE WRONG JUDGES

Verse 1 introduces two new terms that the apostle uses to describe not only himself but all his fellow ministers in the gospel. They are *servants of Christ* and *stewards of the mysteries of God* (verse 1). The first phrase means an attendant who is on hand to carry out the instruction of the master. The second describes a senior position in the household. In those days, the steward would hold the keys to his master's resources, and was the most senior and trusted of the servants. His responsibility involved the correct use of those resources to equip the master's people to do the master's work. The two terms would be very familiar to Paul's readers. But the emphasis in each phrase is on the other part of each description – *of Christ* and *of God*. The implication seems to be that gospel ministers are not firstly servants of the church, nor stewards of the church's reputation, which is what the Corinthians seemed to have forgotten. The force of this is very well expressed by Paul elsewhere when he asks, 'Who are you to pass judgement on the servant of another? It is before his own master that he stands or falls' (*Rom.* 14:4). It is totally inappropriate, therefore, for the Corinthians to be setting the examination paper for Paul. The one who has commissioned him to his service is the only one who is properly qualified to assess the degree of his faithfulness (verse 2). This is the background to the very liberating statement that Paul makes in the next verse when he affirms, *But with me it is a very small thing that I should be judged by you or by any human court.* This is strong language which might equally well be translated, 'For me, it could not matter less . . . ' We are not to consider this as bravado, much less stubborn refusal to listen to any criticism. What he wants to impress on his readers is that the church at Corinth had no right to judge him, as they were doing, and so he is not going to pay attention to their assessments, whatever they say. If they can come to see the truth and spiritual wisdom of this, they will save themselves a great deal of breath and avoid much trouble. The logic is that he is *Christ's* servant, not theirs. This is why he could never be judged by any human court (or, literally, 'day'). Clearly there is an echo here of chapter 3:13, where he spoke about *the* Day, meaning the day of the final judgement. Any human 'day', therefore, is ultimately irrelevant in comparison with eternity. But there is also a third judge whose judgement, together with that of the Corinthians, and of any human court, is not valid, and that is Paul himself (verse 3b). When he says that he does not judge himself, this is not evidence of spiritual arrogance but of spiritual realism. *I am not aware of anything against myself, but I am not thereby acquitted* (verse 4a). This is certainly not to be taken as meaning that Paul is never self-critical. That would be a particularly desperate state to be in, though some Christian leaders have been known to think that they are always right about everything! No, Paul is constantly examining himself to keep his conscience clear, but he knows that God may well see sins that are hidden, even from his own eyes, or be aware of ingrained evil in his life, of which he is personally unaware. So neither any other human being, nor even the servant himself, is qualified to judge his work. *It is the Lord who judges me* (verse 4b). He who commissioned and equipped is the only one capable of assessing and rewarding. Just as it is wrong, then, to boast about human leaders, so it is equally wrong to judge them. None of us is qualified to do that.

(ii) THE WRONG CRITERIA

If the first factor that disqualifies us from making judgements of our leaders is ignorance, then the second is our sinfulness. We know from the earlier chapters the criticisms of Paul that seemed to abound in the Corinthian church. His wisdom was not well enough developed to attract the pagan listeners. He himself seemed to have very little power. He was a weak and unimpressive messenger. His own life illustrated none of the higher spirituality that was to be found amongst the Corinthians. But all these criteria are this-worldly. They are part of the futility of human culture, which God is bringing to nothing. That is why Paul stressed in verse 2 that faithfulness to the gospel is the one qualification the steward must fulfil. Faithfulness to the master's message is faithfulness to his goals and, ultimately, faithfulness to the master himself, which is the standard by which all his servants will be judged. So, to be concerned about how one particular leader compares to others, to seek the approval of a denominational hierarchy, or to seek the popularity of the congregation, must all ultimately lead to *un*faithfulness. All such behaviour is a futile diversion and verse 5 makes plain why this is so. These criteria are based on what we see, what we feel, and what we like. But while man looks on the outward appearance, God *will disclose the purposes of the heart*. Gospel work requires gospel motives, but it should also stop us sitting in judgement on any other Christian, whose heart we cannot possibly know.

(iii) THE WRONG TIME

Verse 5 draws attention to another fault in the Corinthians' thinking. *Therefore*, says Paul, *do not pronounce judgement before the time, before the Lord comes*. Their context was always the present. They wanted

[68]

to have everything *now*, in a glorified super-church full of wisdom, power and impressive spirituality. Paul, however, has been relent-lessly underlining that the real test is not now but on the last day; what he calls here *the time*. That is the examination day, when the Lord Jesus returns and judges his servants. Christ is far more interested in the hidden motives than in the external signs. His criterion of judgement will not be outward success but godly faith-fulness. To judge his servants presently by our standards is a massive presumption and an usurpation of God's authority. Moreover, we are extremely likely to get it all completely wrong, because our judgement is sinful, tinged with jealousy and self-seeking, charac-terized by pride and prejudice. What an encouragement then it is to be told, in the last sentence of verse 5, that God loves to praise and reward his faithful servants. Whenever he sees the faithful service of a heart motivated by love, he is a kindlier judge than the hard-nosed critics in Corinth. These verses have a good deal to say to us in our contemporary context. Criticisms of those in the ministry, or of other congregations, abound in churches. Much of this is not only fruitless but dishonouring to the Lord, so we need to examine our own attitudes. Whether we are under criticism, or meting it out to others, the one thing needful is to examine our own faithfulness to Christ and our desire to please him above everything. It is because we are called to be pleasing only to him, that he alone has the right to judge his servants. Of course, this is no excuse for us to be undiscerning in matters of biblical doctrine, or practical behaviour. The rest of the letter will exhort the Corinthian church to right judgements, both in ethical issues and in practical lifestyle. But it is the writing off of Paul because Apollos is your guru, or the rubbish-ing of any servant of the Lord because his face does not quite fit, which is condemned. The sobering reality is that such attitudes have destroyed so many churches and still do; far better to heed Paul's warnings and to look to receive praise from God at the last day, rather than condemnation.

Fools for Christ

⁶I have applied all these things to myself and Apollos for your benefit, brothers, that you may learn by us not to go beyond what is written, that none of you may be puffed up in favour of one against another. ⁷For who sees anything different in you? What do you have that you did not receive? If then you received it, why do you boast as if you did not receive it?

⁸Already you have all you want! Already you have become rich! Without us you have become kings! And would that you did reign, so that we might share the rule with you! ⁹For I think that God has exhibited us apostles as last of all, like men sentenced to death, because we have become a spectacle to the world, to angels, and to men. ¹⁰We are fools for Christ's sake, but you are wise in Christ. We are weak, but you are strong. You are held in honour, but we in disrepute. ¹¹To the present hour we hunger and thirst, we are poorly dressed and buffeted and homeless, ¹²and we labour, working with our own hands. When reviled, we bless; when persecuted, we endure; ¹³when slandered, we entreat. We have become, and are still, like the scum of the world, the refuse of all things (1 Cor. 4:6–13).

Continuing his analysis of where the Corinthians were going wrong in their attitude to himself, Paul now turns their attention to the area of their motivation. He is not thinking of their hidden motives, which, of course, he is unable to judge, for the reasons given in the previous paragraph. His assessment is based on the external manifestations that he has seen in the way in which they have behaved towards him. The key to understanding why they were acting in this way is to be found at the end of verse 6. *That none of you may be puffed up in favour of one against another.* Pride or being 'puffed up', illustrates the wretched self-centredness that lay at the heart of the Corinthian problems. Inflated with a false sense of their own importance and their own achievements, they not only forgot the gospel of the cross but actually resented taking up their cross daily to follow in the steps of their Lord. Probably one of the great attractions of the alternative spirituality on offer in Corinth, was the avoidance of being crucified with Christ. By contrast, they wanted to be rich and to be kings (see verse 8). Nor can we stand back in judgement over them, because we are all very easily tempted in the same direction. When the evil one first ensnared Adam and Eve in the garden, *the* original sin was precisely of this sort. 'Your eyes will be opened, and you will be like God, knowing good and evil' (*Gen.* 3:5). The lure of divinity lies at the base of most of our capitulation to temptation. Every time we usurp God's role as judge, we bear testimony to our own sinful pride.

THE PERIL OF PRIDE (verses 6–7)

Paul wants them to understand how serious this is, by indicating two areas in which the audacity of pride is breathtakingly revealed. Firstly, he indicates that pride believes it knows the mind of God. This seems to be the thrust of the comment in verse 6, Do not '*go beyond what is written*', or as D. A. Carson paraphrases it, 'Keep your finger on the text.' The danger seems to be that the Corinthians thought they could read God's mind, because of their superior spirituality, and that they could therefore predict God's judgement. But we have already learned, in 2:11, that, 'No one comprehends the thoughts of God except the Spirit of God'. There is only one way that human beings could ever know his mind and that is by revelation from the Spirit. Paul's position is that the only certain locus of that revelation is what is written, that is, the Scriptures. If they are subtracted from or added to, then the mind of God revealed in his inspired Word is distorted. As soon as we imagine that we can begin to know his mind outside the teaching of Scripture, we shall be in danger of elevating our own inspiration and opinions to the same authority level as God's revelation. Once again, the results are bound to be pride, rivalry and dissension. That is why so-called 'extra-biblical revelation' is always so divisive in a local church community. It also explains why any sort of party spirit, pushing one leader's ideas in opposition to another's, is equally destructive. We have introduced the wrong criteria and we are the wrong judges. The spirituality of the cross, therefore, produces a culture of humility and submission to the Lord of glory, and an unwillingness to go beyond what he has revealed in his Word, as the ground of our authority. In this way, Paul provides apostolic authenticity for the Reformation cry of '*Sola Scriptura*'.

However, there is another feature of human pride to which verse 7 draws our attention. Pride also forgets how much it needs the grace of God. Here is the ultimate deathblow to all sinful judgementalism: *For who sees anything different in you?* Human beings are constantly seeking to present themselves as superior, in at least some area, to others. It may be in intelligence, status, possessions, personality, appearance, popularity, abilities, or moral virtues. In a multiplicity of ways, human nature seeks to elevate itself at the expense of others. But the gospel of Christ crucified spells the end of all such pride, which is why it is so resisted. In response to Paul's question the true Christian says, 'Anything I have and all that I have is God's gift of grace to me. If he has given me health and strength, opportunities to serve, abilities and skills, family and friends, they are all as much his gifts of grace, as is salvation itself. I have simply received them, totally undeservedly. So there is nothing to boast about in me; I will boast only in the Lord.' This is how we should respond, in the light of the two questions that Paul asks in verse 7. If, on the Last Day, God finds us worthy of any praise or reward, that will be due solely to his grace and therefore entirely for his glory. There is no need for us therefore to compare ourselves with others, but only to seek to live in a way that is pleasing to him. What a liberating perspective that is! Behind all our judgementalism lurks the monster pride, ignorant of humility, forgetful of grace. The only place where pride can be dealt with is at the cross of Christ. This again reminds us why it is the cross that is God's secret of wisdom and power. The way of the cross is the only path that liberates us to freedom and life, to unity and joy. What we need to remember is that it is by grace alone that such amazing blessings come to us in the gospel.

THE CONFUSION OF CORINTH (verses 8–13)

Verses 8–10 are full of biting irony, designed to warn the Corinthians of the perils they are facing, since they seem to be so ignorant of themselves and so wrong in their judgement of Paul. The thrust of verse 8 is in the repeated word *already*. Their claim, clearly, was that everything they needed was already in their possession, here and now. They were already wealthy and prosperous, already reigning, and already kings in supreme authority. In short, the blessings of heaven were already theirs. It is not too difficult to see how their thinking may have developed. In the gospel, God has already pronounced the verdict of the Last Day. We know that, 'There is therefore now no condemnation for those who are in Christ Jesus' (*Rom.* 8:1). Christ himself has taught us that, 'whoever hears my word and believes him who sent me has eternal life. He does not come into judgement, but has passed from death to life' (*John* 5:24). Building on the fact that the verdict had already been announced, the Corinthians it seems began to assume that all the other blessings of the full coming of the Kingdom were available to them in the present. What God had reserved for the end of time they were making their own already. Throughout chapters 3 and 4 we have seen that Paul's concern is to emphasize the Last Day, when the Lord will come and the fire reveal every man's work. But what Paul hopes for on that day, the Corinthians seemed to have been claiming was theirs already. Perhaps they used this argument to show just how superior they really were! They no longer had to hunger and thirst after righteousness; they were already glutted. They no longer needed to mourn over their spiritual poverty; they were rich. They were, in fact, claiming to be super-victorious, already embarked on their kingly reign, so they have no need to wait for eternity and no need to bother with Paul or the other inferior Christian messengers. All this makes the irony at the end of verse 8 devastatingly strong: *And would that you did reign, so that we might share the rule with you!*

For the apostle, however, the normal Christian life has proved to be something very different. In verse 9, Paul envisages the procession of triumph coming into the Roman arena. The emperor, or one of his returning generals, rides in great victory into the amphitheatre. Unlike some of our great occasions, when the most important person enters last, at the end of the Roman triumph came the captured prisoners who were about to be thrown to the wild beasts, or to fight for their lives with the gladiators for the general amusement of the public. Now, says Paul, that is what apostolic life seems to me to be like. It is marked by public humiliation and denigration, both before men and angels. There could hardly be a greater contrast than that between the life of an apostle and the triumphalism of the Corinthian church. This, then, is the focus of their confusion, and therefore the apostle puts to them this implied question, 'Which is the genuine article? Which is real Christianity?' Or, as implied in verse 10, 'Who looks more like Christ?' It is a very searching question but not one that is hard to answer. At the heart of verse 9 is the scandal, or the stumbling block, of the cross. Paul does not merely follow a crucified Lord, it is the very heart of his message, and therefore of their faith. He is committed to the folly of God's wisdom in the cross, to the weakness of his power and the dishonour of his glory in the death that Jesus died for sinners. Whereas the Corinthians are choosing wisdom, strength and honour in this world, Paul came with foolish wisdom, in weakness, fear and much trembling, as he preached to them the gospel of God. We are right back with the agenda of chapters 1 and 2. The point Paul is making here is that it will always be like that for a real Christian, doing real gospel work, in *this* world.

The two 'alreadys' of verse 8 are balanced by two other phrases in verse 11, *to the present hour*, and verse 13, *and are still*. Paul is purposefully talking about time, and not yet about eternity. But the contrast between verses 8 and 11 is immense. For the apostle, his present experience in the 'now' is one of brutal treatment and homelessness. This is hardly characteristic of someone who has come into the full inheritance of the children of God. He is serving in the era of the church militant and suffering here on earth. Whether then it is physical suffering (verse 11) or hard toil (verse 12), these are the twin characteristics of Paul's discipleship, focused as it was upon the cross. One suspects that the Corinthians were not really interested in either of these aspects. They were not going to buy in to being *reviled*, *persecuted* and *slandered* (verses 12–13). That is why they resisted the gospel of the cross and the sort of Christian life that flows from it. Paul's language becomes extreme in order to shock them into realizing the significance of their attitude. When he describes himself as *the scum of the world, the refuse of all things,* he wants them to see how far they have fallen from apostolic priorities. For the Corinthians, if following the cross meant being treated like the sweepings from the floor, the dirt removed from the body, or the contents of the dustcart, then they would rather be looking for an alternative spirituality. All of us know what this feels like, and the degree to which we identify with Corinth and resist the gospel of the cross is an indication of just how confused we are about the present world and the life to come.

One of the most important points this paragraph is making is that the miraculous wisdom and power of God are not seen in a popular church; the kind of church that is admired by the pagans, that carries all before it, is envied for its wealth and prestige, and puffed up by its own press releases. Rather, the power and wisdom of God is seen in those actions of response to the world's hostility, which characterized Paul's own life. *We bless . . . we endure . . . we entreat* (verses 12–13). When a man is seen to be responding like that, knowing at the same time that it will not change the attitude of the opposition one iota, there the power of God is being demonstrated. When the apostle goes on being Christ's fool, blessing others, enduring suffering, answering the most appalling cruelty with kindness, a miracle of immense proportions is taking place. But it will only happen when the whole life is focused on Christ crucified, when we see that being in the world, as Christ was, requires a genuine participation in his sufferings. We have to be realistic in recognising that *up to this moment* this is how it has been, and how it will be, but that we can be totally confident of the future because everything is in Christ's hands, and we belong to him (3:21b–23). Then will be the age of the church triumphant.

It is again good to reflect on the relevance of this paragraph to our contemporary confusion. So much energy goes into thinking about how we should 'market' the Christian faith in our generation. Often this is done by pretending that all the blessings of the age to come are available here and now, if only we could believe firmly enough. One day, we shall have everything we want – freedom from sin, sickness, and even death itself. Perfect wisdom, holiness and fullness of joy will be ours. But that is what Heaven is for! If we promise it on earth, we shall only breed disillusioned malcontents. We must not however go to the other extreme and forget that we are already members of that kingdom. It was the problem of the Thessalonian Christians that they were so focused on Christ's return and the eternal kingdom that some gave up working and started to live off the charity of other believers, and Paul had to rebuke them (*2 Thess.* 3:6–13). We are not to devalue our lives in this world, by minimizing the great joys and blessings that are already ours in Christ, as though there was nothing but doom and gloom in this life. There is much to enjoy and to revel in. We must never let our doctrine of redemption eclipse our doctrine of creation. Our human relationships, family and friends, the creative arts, practical skills, sport and exercise, music and literature, all have their place in the Christian's life. But they are all temporal, and they all belong to a fallen world. They are given us richly to be enjoyed (*1 Tim.* 6:17), but they must never be confused with the glories of heaven, the immeasurably greater riches of the world to come. The only way to live as Christ's fools is to be mastered by the gospel so that we give our lives to spreading and demonstrating its truth.

13

The Kingdom of Power

¹⁴I do not write these things to make you ashamed, but to admonish you as my beloved children. ¹⁵For though you have countless guides in Christ, you do not have many fathers. For I became your father in Christ Jesus through the gospel. ¹⁶I urge you, then, be imitators of me. ¹⁷That is why I sent you Timothy, my beloved and faithful child in the Lord, to remind you of my ways in Christ, as I teach them everywhere in every church. ¹⁸Some are arrogant, as though I were not coming to you. ¹⁹But I will come to you soon, if the Lord wills, and I will find out not the talk of these arrogant people but their power. ²⁰For the kingdom of God does not consist in talk but in power. ²¹What do you wish? Shall I come to you with a rod, or with love in a spirit of gentleness? (1 Cor. 4:14–21).

This concluding paragraph of the first part of Paul's argument in the letter, provides a wonderfully refreshing example of how to deal with a difficult situation in a godly way. For the final time in this section, Paul again changes the metaphor that he is employing in order to illustrate his life as a teacher. This time he refers to the relationship of a father with his child. The whole thrust of his argument depends upon the context of the loving, personal relationship that he has with the Corinthian Christians, created and experienced in and through the gospel. Here again, the power and wisdom of God are shown to be at work. The apostle addresses them as *my beloved children* (verse 14), revealing his warm, affectionate concern that gives the lie to any suggestion that his irony is written out of irritation or pique. Again, he reminds them, *I became your father in*

Christ Jesus through the gospel (verse 15), referring to the unique relationship established by God through their reception of the message. As Paul points out, you can only have *one* father. Timothy is coming to visit them as a brother, and is described in verse 17 as *my beloved and faithful child*. The whole thrust of the paragraph is relational, and its purpose is clearly restorative. At the beginning, in verse 14, Paul assures them that his purpose is to *admonish*, not to make them *ashamed*. There is no retaliation or destructiveness about his dealings with them. Their good is his only motivation. How could it be otherwise, if he is truly governed by the cross of a Saviour who gave himself up for us all. That was why the Father sent the Son into the world, and as the agent of the Lord Jesus, the apostle wants the very best for his children, even when they seem impossibly fractious and irritating, as the Corinthians undoubtedly were. This paragraph of apostolic realism brings before us the responses of a relational, fatherly love in Christ, towards fellow members of the kingdom.

LOVE WARNS (verses 14–15)

The whole paragraph is a fascinating example of apostolic ministry, based on the theology and spirituality of the cross. The meaning of the cross is not peace at any price, the sweeping of all difficulties under the carpet, and the pretence that they do not exist. Nor is it that other popular way out of the difficult situations that arise in many human conflicts, namely cutting off all communications and withdrawing entirely, because sorting things out is just too painful. The Lord Jesus succumbed to neither of these temptations. He knew that the reality of mankind's alienation from God could only be met by substituting himself as an atoning sacrifice for the sins of the world. The powers of evil could only be overcome by taking that punishment upon himself; by confronting them, and defeating them, in his act of propitiating God's righteous wrath. We must never forget that the example of his love is that of voluntary submission to do the Father's will. At any moment he could have withdrawn from the pathway that led to the cross but, out of love for his people, he resolutely persevered, setting his face to go to Jerusalem, enduring the cross and despising its shame. In setting this example he was revealing to us the heart of the Father and fulfilling the Father's will (see *Heb*. 10:5–10). The measure of Christ's love is his fulfilment of this responsibility, to the very limit. With Christ's work as an example, Paul is prepared to follow the same pathway, as the preceding paragraph has demonstrated. His strong warning stems from the strength of his demonstrable, fatherly love for them. They may have *countless guides*, innumerable pedagogues, countless teachers, who would help them on in the Christian faith, but they have only one spiritual father, and the apostle is not ashamed to draw on this special and unique relationship. Indeed, the warning is itself an expression of his love.

LOVE EXHORTS (verses 16–17)

I urge you then be imitators of me (verse 16). A father's love models a way of life for the children to follow. We often use the familiar phrase, 'like father, like son'. The Corinthians had been shown the nature of their spiritual father's life in verses 11–13, so how *could* they now continue to reject the way of the cross when he had demonstrated its essence and vitality? Here, in verse 17, the significant emphasis is added that this is not simply a matter of doctrine, or orthodox belief, but of daily lifestyle and consistent behaviour. Timothy (a much-loved son) is able to confirm to these other sons and daughters of Paul's ministry what the authentic gospel lifestyle consists of, and to testify that this has been Paul's constant behaviour and message, wherever he goes. Timothy had been with Paul on his journeys and had witnessed the founding of most of the New Testament churches. He is therefore in a unique position to vouch for the truth of Paul's description of his apostolic lifestyle, and he himself is also modelling it as a son who is a *faithful child in the Lord*. Because their teaching and lifestyles are one consistent whole, Timothy is to be welcomed and listened to, in his role as their founding father's personal emissary.

LOVE REBUKES (verses 18–21)

Paul is realistic enough to realize that although he is appealing to the church at Corinth, his letter may not succeed. Ultimately, in such a case, a father's love must be tough and so verses 18–21 both rebuke and threaten discipline to the Corinthian church should his warnings and exhortations be ignored. As the section ends, Paul zeros in on the small group (*'Some'*) who are the cause of all his trouble. They have become *arrogant*, or 'puffed up'. He uses the same word as that in verse 6, which at root has the idea of being self-inflated. Doubtless they had decided that they did not need a visit from Paul, but he affirms his intention to come very soon, unless God prevents him, and then the real situation in the Corinthian congregation would be exposed for what it was. *I will find out not the talk of these arrogant people but their power* (verse 19). Just as the Day of Judgement will test their works when Christ returns, so when the apostle came back to Corinth the proud claims and assertions of the triumphalists would be seen for what they really were. It is one thing to rubbish Paul behind his back, but another to meet him face to face. Therefore, though there is plenty of talk about 'power' within the Corinthian congregation, Paul is interested not in words but in the reality. Verse 20 is a very important principle to take on board. The kingdom of God *is* all about power, but about God's power, not man's. Words are cheap, and those who talk most about power do not necessarily demonstrate it at all. One of the problems at Corinth is that they were very impressed with words, but when all the argument and discussion was over and done, where was the power of God to be seen at work among them? Paul's answer is, by now, very familiar to us. The power of God is demonstrated in the message of Jesus Christ crucified, which alone saves people. That power is secondarily revealed in a reviled and persecuted apostle, cursed and slandered, but insisting on pursuing his gospel ministry. Day after day his life of self-sacrificing hard work for the sake of the gospel is proof of the power of God.

The same inference needs to be drawn with equal clarity in our contemporary context. The power of God's Spirit is not to be seen in some super-spirituality, existing in a never-never land of make-belief, preserved by conspiracy in order not to expose the true nature of the Emperor's clothes. Instead, the power of the Spirit is seen in the way he preserves frail gospel workers and weak Christian believers, through whose witness to Christ he brings others to eternal life. The lifestyle of the Christian messengers proves or disproves the reality of the Christian message. The rebuke concludes with a challenge in verse 21. *What do you wish?* Paul could come to them prepared to whip them into shape, or he could come (as he would prefer to do) as their spiritual father in love and gentleness. His response will depend upon how they themselves react to this letter. If they are willing to repent of their pride, their false triumphalism, their short-sightedness, premature judgements, and arrogant fault-finding, then they will find the apostle, like the God who welcomes sinners, more than willing to turn to them in forgiveness and mercy. His challenge is that they should take up the cross and become faithful stewards of the gospel, living the crucified lifestyle, until the Lord comes to reward and to bring to light the hidden motives of men's hearts. That is a challenge as relevant and pertinent to us today as it was to Paul's original readers. We need to pray for God's grace to enable us to face this challenge, to recognize where we are deficient, and to turn in renewed repentance and faith to the grace that flows from the cross of the Lord Jesus.

14

Cleanse Out the Old Leaven

¹It is actually reported that there is sexual immorality among you, and of a kind that is not tolerated even among pagans, for a man has his father's wife. ²And you are arrogant! Ought you not rather to mourn? Let him who has done this be removed from among you.

³For though absent in body, I am present in spirit; and as if present, I have already pronounced judgment on the one who did such a thing. ⁴When you are assembled in the name of the Lord Jesus and my spirit is present, with the power of our Lord Jesus, ⁵you are to deliver this man to Satan for the destruction of the flesh, so that his spirit may be saved in the day of the Lord.

⁶Your boasting is not good. Do you not know that a little leaven leavens the whole lump? ⁷Cleanse out the old leaven that you may be a new lump, as you really are unleavened. For Christ, our Passover lamb, has been sacrificed. ⁸Let us therefore celebrate the festival, not with the old leaven, the leaven of malice and evil, but with the unleavened bread of sincerity and truth (1 Cor. 5:1–8).

Here at chapter 5, the letter begins a new unit that runs through to the end of chapter 7. Much of the material is devoted to sexual behaviour within the Corinthian congregation, beginning with a case of incest, where the church has failed to discipline the 'evil person' (5:13). In discussing this case, Paul provides additional teaching on how Christian sex ethics, derived from and reflecting the gospel, are to be worked out. He then proceeds to apply these ethics to such issues as: the prevalence of prostitution in Corinth; marriage – between believers, and between a believer and an unbeliever; and the priorities of betrothed couples. There is other material in this section, notably about lawsuits among believers, but the unifying theme seems to be the nature of true Christian freedom. This will be seen in Christ-like behaviour, not in pagan licence. At 6:12, Paul picks up what seems to have been one of the catch-phrases of the Corinthians, 'All things are lawful for me', and the teaching of the three chapters revolves around his qualification of what that should mean in the practice of a godly life, shaped by the gospel of the cross.

There is here also, however, a strong connection with chapter 4. At the end of that chapter we saw the arrogant leaders of the separatist factions in Corinth denigrating Paul's authority and questioning his power. The apostle's response was to deny the validity of their judgement, and this he now further proves by demonstrating how totally inadequate is their response to the sexual immorality in their midst. Their actual weakness, spiritual poverty and foolish wisdom, which were exposed by the biting irony of 4:8–13, are now revealed much more clearly and straightforwardly, as Paul shames their compromising behaviour in these matters of sexual conduct. It is also a helpful reminder to us to keep the corporate context clear in our interpretation. We are so used to individualizing the ethical teaching of the New Testament, that we readily overlook the responsibility of the whole congregation for the right conduct of its individual members. This is even more the case in a society like ours that resists discipline, and wants to assert the rights of individuals to live as they please. But it is the church that Paul rebukes for not taking action against a flagrant case of immorality. It is the church that constitutes the fellowship of God's people, and that must remain true to the Lord in its witness before a pagan world. To do so involves upholding biblical standards and not being afraid to exercise discipline against unrepentant offenders. Such things are no more popular today than they were in Corinth, but that does not make them any less necessary.

THE CHURCH MUST BE DISCIPLINED (verses 1–5)

The case mentioned in verse 1 – *a man has his father's wife* – is regarded as incest in the law of God. Leviticus 18:8 could not be more clear and specific. It is condemned by pagans, even the pagans of a city such as Corinth that was notoriously loose in sexual matters. Why, then, does this seem to have been tolerated, and even justified, by the members of the church? Paul is horrified by the situation and implies that all right-thinking people would share his reaction. There must have been some spurious spiritual reasoning going on which effectively blinded the Corinthian Christians to the reality of the situation. Perhaps it was the combination of a wrong understanding of their freedom from the Old Testament law through the justifying grace of the gospel, together with something of their old Greek thinking about the dualism of soul and body. Later on in the letter, in chapter 15, we shall see that this second point certainly raised problems for them as they sought to understand the idea of a bodily resurrection. If the pure spirit was all that really mattered in eternal terms, then perhaps it was of no significance what was done in the body. We can see therefore how a combination of a wrong understanding of freedom from the Law and a wrong view of the importance of the body might have produced this careless attitude. Of course, there may well have been disagreement within the church over how to deal with the problem, but in fact nothing had been done, and so they were effectively turning a blind eye to a gross scandal against the name of Christ – and this is the church that boasted about its superior spirituality! No wonder Paul challenges them, *Ought you not rather to mourn?* (verse 2).

Paul is especially aware of the shame that such behaviour brings to the person of the Lord Jesus Christ. After all, the church is not just a collection of individuals; it is Christ's body. 'If one member suffers, all suffer together' (12:26). The reaction of those who are following a crucified Saviour should therefore be sorrow and then separation, if the offender shows no repentance. But in vain did Paul look for these two reactions within the Corinthian congregation. While it is true that the gross public nature of the sin is deeply concerning to Paul, it is good for us to be reminded that every sin committed by a Christian wounds the body. None of us stands alone, and the life of each one of us has an effect on our fellow believers. That is why the church has to exercise discipline over its membership.

Paul's remedy for the situation consists of one long sentence in the original. It runs from verse 3 to verse 5. He begins by affirming his involvement with them in this issue, even though he is not present in Corinth. There may have been some detractors who assumed that his absence meant that he was no longer interested in them, but the whole letter is a denial of that view. Secondly, he has no doubt about the guilt of the sinner. *I have already pronounced judgement on the one who did such a thing* (verse 3). All the specious arguments that may have been advanced are swept away immediately. Such behaviour is a sin against God and against man, and the apostle has already judged it as such. That is the responsibility of godly leadership in a local congregation. If asked, 'Who are you to condemn?' Paul's answer would surely be, 'I am a man whose conscience is captive to the Word of God.' In other words, he wants the Corinthians to realize what it means to live under the authority of God's Word. Its prohibitions are absolute and its definition of sin is final.

This is not a matter of personality differences, or of a power bid on behalf of the apostles, but of using Scripture to form a judgement – an action that the church had manifestly failed to perform. Verse 4 indicates the action that needed to be taken. The church must meet together, and could be assured not only of Paul's spiritual support but, more importantly, of the presence and power of the Lord Jesus with them. 'For where two or three are gathered in my name, there am I among them' (*Matt* 18:20). Although we are accustomed to applying this verse to times when the church meets for corporate prayer, the context in Matthew is clearly one of church discipline. The action that needs to be taken carries with it therefore the authority of the Lord himself and of his apostles. Verse 5 seems to indicate that what is required is expulsion from the church fellowship. The difficult phrase, *deliver this man to Satan* (verse 5), probably indicates that the realm outside the fellowship of the church is regarded as Satan's sphere, and the immoral man must be consigned to that by a solemn action of the congregation. His membership is forfeited. However, the second half of verse 5 indicates that the purpose is not punitive but restorative. In such a case, the flesh may suffer, but the spirit will be saved. The perspective by which the apostle views these events is again that of the *day of the Lord*. This is always a necessary counterbalance so as not to be overly impressed by present difficulties. In view of that day, is it not more loving to send this man out of the fellowship, that he might be brought to his senses, rather than to tolerate his sin and cause his eternal loss? The necessity of church discipline is therefore an act of love, since its aim is not to punish but to restore and to heal. In fact, when we come to Paul's second letter, we discover that this is exactly what happened. 'The punishment by the majority is enough, so you should rather turn to forgive and comfort him, or he may be overwhelmed by excessive sorrow,' (*2 Cor.* 2:6–7). But that would never have happened had not the discipline been exercised as Paul instructed. The reason for church discipline becomes even more obvious in the next three verses.

SIN MUST BE DEALT WITH (verses 6–8)

To bolster further his instruction, Paul sets out to show the church why failure in this area would be disastrous for their future. Reminding them that they have nothing to boast about, he uses an everyday illustration to make a powerful, spiritual point. *A little leaven leavens the whole lump.* In the same way, sin tolerated in one member may soon spread to others. Already they are sinning by boasting that they are so spiritual and yet tolerating this gross evil, and Paul is therefore deeply concerned that the whole church is beginning to be infected. There is only one remedy and it must be a drastic one. At this point, Paul links the imagery of yeast to the Old Testament picture of the Passover. Before the Passover feast, within the period called the seven days of unleavened bread, a Jewish household would search out and remove from the house every scrap of leaven. This symbolized, not only the speed of the exodus, but also the complete break with the life of Egypt. Unleavened bread was therefore a symbol of the new life of separation to God, into which God had brought his people. However, the dominant ingredient of the Exodus narrative concerned the sacrifice of the Passover lamb. God's people were only redeemed from his wrath through the substitution of the lamb, whose blood, sprinkled on the doorposts and the lintels of their houses, afforded protection against the destroying angel. When Paul therefore exhorts the Corinthians to *cleanse out the old leaven* in order that they may be what they really are, *a new lump ... unleav ened,* it is not surprising that he quickly links this to the Passover sacrifice of the Lord Jesus, the Lamb of God, 'who takes away the sin of the world' (*John* 1:29).

When we consider the identity of our Passover Lamb, compared with the animal sacrificed in Egypt, how much greater is our responsibility to put away sin! The Lord Jesus gave his life for us, not just so that our past sin might be forgiven, but to make us new creations in him. This is what we really are. Christians are therefore no longer to serve sin, but to become a purified and holy people. We are to keep the Festival by living Christian lives that are defined by *sincerity and truth* (verse 8). In this sense, the whole Christian life is one of 'unleavened bread'.

The implications of Paul's teaching in this paragraph are far-reaching. Although the primary focus is corporate, we must also look to our own consciences and wrestle with the ongoing sins in our own lives. Whenever sin attacks the church, it tests all the members. This may not be evidenced by a gross moral evil, like the incest of this chapter, but *the leaven of malice and evil* is always present with us and part of our Christian discipleship is the work of rooting it out constantly, admitting our guilt and returning to our Passover Lamb for his fresh forgiveness. Sin, tolerated in the church, remains one of the major hindrances to the spread of the gospel. Similarly, the greatest contribution that we can make to evangelism in our generation is to live lives of sincerity and truth that confirm and illustrate the reality of the message we speak.

15

Purge the Evil Person from among You

⁹I wrote to you in my letter not to associate with sexually immoral people – ¹⁰not at all meaning the sexually immoral of this world, or the greedy and swindlers, or idolaters, since then you would need to go out of the world. ¹¹But now I am writing to you not to associate with anyone who bears the name of brother if he is guilty of sexual immorality or greed, or is an idolater, reviler, drunkard, or swindler – not even to eat with such a one. ¹²For what have I to do with judging outsiders? Is it not those inside the church whom you are to judge? ¹³God judges those outside. "Purge the evil person from among you" (1 Cor. 5:9–13).

The relationship of the Christian to the world has often been a source of disagreement and contention within the church. The many centuries of Christian faith and practice have witnessed the swing of the pendulum between a policy of withdrawal from the world and the opposite practice of over-identification. Sometimes the church has been so aware of the wickedness of the culture around it and its unremitting hostility to the gospel that the only way forward has seemed to be to separate entirely from it and to concentrate on cultivating godliness in what was essentially an hermetically-sealed environment. At other times, by way of reaction, the cry has become that Christians are 'in it to win it' and the church's identification with its cultural environment has been almost total. This may involve 'baptizing' many of the cultural norms, or giving them a Christian veneer, so that in the name of evangelisation, 'sitting where they sit' has drifted into 'being what they are', and the church becomes indistinguishable from the world. Both extremes have proved to be equally damaging to the cause of the gospel.

JUDGING THE WORLD (verses 9–10)

Verse 9 might seem to imply that Paul is simply trying to clarify an ambiguity in a former (and now lost) letter that he had written. But it is more likely that his teaching on sexual ethics in that letter had been wrongly, and perhaps deliberately, interpreted. When he had instructed them *not to associate with sexually immoral people*, he was not advocating the setting up of a Christian ghetto in Corinth, which would have no point of contact with the pagan culture. Such a policy *has* sometimes been advocated by sincere, but misguided, Christians, but, as Paul bluntly says, *since then you would need to go out of the world* (verse 10). One thinks of some extreme groups who have tried to limit their human contacts exclusively to other Christians, and then, increasingly, only to those who agree with their views. The one common factor in all such groups is their constant division and ultimate disintegration. For, as Martin Luther once remarked, 'You can take the monk out of the world, but you can't take the world out of the monk.' All attempts to withdraw into an apparent sanctity by having nothing to do with sinners are doomed to failure, just because the sinners and their sins are within. Any Christian ghetto where the saints pride themselves on the avoidance of worldly behaviour is bound to fall victim to the sins of arrogance, jealousy, envy, gossip and judgementalism. It is an observable fact that these are often the most prevalent characteristics of churches which are turned in upon themselves. Such attitudes are more at home in Pharisaism than amongst the followers of a Christ who 'receives sinners and eats with them' (*Luke* 15:2).

Following the testimony of the Lord Jesus, we learn rather that God has other purposes for his people and that these involve their being in the world. 'I do not ask that you take them out of the world, but that you keep them from the evil one' (*John* 17:15). Any Christian who lives in the fallen world, as God intends, will inevitably rub shoulders with the *sexually immoral . . . or the greedy and swindlers, or idolaters* (verse 10). That is what the world is like, but God has not yet removed his church from it. On the contrary, because all authority belongs to the risen Christ, we are commanded to go into all the world (every people group as well as every geographical location) and make disciples, through the preaching of the gospel (*Matt.* 28:19). Our visual image of the church may be of a circle where every member is joined to all others, holding his neighbour's hand, and therefore being connected to all the rest. But if that is so, then it is important to remember that the circle must face outwards to the lost world, for which the Lord Jesus Christ was crucified. We are not to become moral hermits or, like the Pharisees, to separate ourselves from all others, in a sense of imagined spiritual superiority. Such an attitude reveals how little we have actually learned of the love that the cross exemplifies. God alone is the judge of the world (verse 13a) and we dare not usurp his sovereign authority. 'Shall not the Judge of all the earth do what is just?' (*Gen.* 18:25). The area of *our* responsibility lies within the believing community, and this is the other strand of teaching Paul that now develops.

JUDGING THE CHURCH (verses 11–13)

The nub of the argument is expressed in verse 11. You are not to *associate with anyone who bears the name of brother if he is guilty of sexual immorality or greed, or is an idolater, reviler, drunkard, or swindler.* This was what Paul had originally intended them to understand by his previous prohibition. We should expect the world to be characterized by unbridled sin, but not the church. Just because the Corinthian congregation had been planted in such a morally hostile context, the reality of the gospel's power could be supremely demonstrated when the believers lived radically different lives of purity and Christ-likeness. How could 'a brother' possibly behave in any of these worldly ways? Paul is not claiming that Christians never fall or fail, but the terminology refers to persistent and unrepentant behaviour, a way of sinful living that is becoming, or has become, habitual. They are *not even to eat with such a one.*

Is it not striking that, just like the Corinthians, we often ignore this duty of necessary separation but are prepared to pursue an unnecessary withdrawal from the world? However, Paul is so convinced of the hypocrisy that would lie behind such a life-style that he refers to any perpetrator as one *who bears the name of brother*;

suggesting that no one could possibly be a true child of God and still indulge their sinful appetites in such ways. The New Testament always places a large question mark over any profession of Christian faith that is belied by an unreformed life-style. Acknowledging Christ as Lord is incompatible with the behaviour described in verse 11. Action therefore must be taken. Then, as now, eating a meal together was a sign of friendship and acceptability, a mark of genuine fellowship. To refuse to eat with an unfaithful 'brother' would amount to a very powerful signal of the rejection of his sinful behaviour by his fellow believers. Indeed, if this was something on which the whole congregation was agreed, and which they acted upon together it would effectively separate the offender from his fellowship base and therefore from any meaningful involvement in the church.

Is it, however, consistent with Christ's command to his disciples to love one another? Church discipline is most often avoided or ignored today because it is construed as an unloving response to moral failure. Paul would completely disagree. The church has a responsibility to judge *those inside the church* (verse 12b). When the sin is clear and the sinner unrepentant, expulsion, by withdrawal of table-fellowship and other forms of social friendship, may be the most loving response that can be made, in view of the eternal dangers involved. There were plenty of precedents for such action in the Old Testament law code, with the refrain repeated several times in Deuteronomy, 'You shall purge the evil from your midst' (for example, *Deut.* 13:5; 22:21, 24). This is the inevitable conclusion of Paul's argument from the feast of unleavened bread and from the Passover meal, because the standards of the New Testament Israel, the church, cannot be any lower than those expounded in the 'Torah'. A serious view of sin that will not tolerate a compromised message, or a compromised church, is a clear demonstration of an underlying love for God and love for neighbour.

One concluding word of caution is that none of those who are responsible for exercising such discipline should imagine themselves to be 'above the law'. The potential for responding from a Pharisee-heart that imagines itself to be 'not like other men', lurks within us all (*Luke* 18:9–14). Sometimes it demonstrates itself in a hard and critical spirit, making no concession to human frailty and instigating unnecessary and ungodly 'witch-hunts', which ruin churches even more than the original targeted 'sins'. Sometimes it is seen in a worldly, dictatorial attitude, where no one is ever quite good enough and where discipline is exercised all too frequently, so that the members of the flock are continually being beaten by the shepherd's rod. But the mark of a godly under-shepherd is that he himself is first of all a humble and obedient sheep. While discipline will be needed at times, it must not be the first recourse and its exercise must always be patterned on the example of the Good Shepherd – that Good Shepherd who was also the Passover Lamb, who laid down his life for the sheep (*John* 10:14–15). Such considerations will ensure that an authentic gospel-spirituality is maintained, centred upon Christ and shaped by the cross.

16

Brothers at Law

¹When one of you has a grievance against another, does he dare go to law before the unrighteous instead of the saints? ²Or do you not know that the saints will judge the world? And if the world is to be judged by you, are you incompetent to try trivial cases? ³Do you not know that we are to judge angels? How much more, then, matters pertaining to this life! ⁴So if you have such cases, why do you lay them before those who have no standing in the church? ⁵I say this to your shame. Can it be that there is no one among you wise enough to settle a dispute between the brothers, ⁶but brother goes to law against brother, and that before unbelievers? ⁷To have lawsuits at all with one another is already a defeat for you. Why not rather suffer wrong? Why not rather be defrauded? ⁸But you yourselves wrong and defraud – even your own brothers!

⁹Do you not know that the unrighteous will not inherit the kingdom of God? Do not be deceived: neither the sexually immoral, nor idolaters, nor adulterers, nor men who practise homosexuality, ¹⁰nor thieves, nor the greedy, nor drunkards, nor revilers, nor swindlers will inherit the kingdom of God. ¹¹And such were some of you. But you were washed, you were sanctified, you were justified in the name of the Lord Jesus Christ and by the Spirit of our God (1 Cor. 6:1–11).

In his discussion of Christian freedom thus far, the apostle Paul has shown that we need structures of discipline within which true liberty can be experienced. A little reflection makes clear that this is a commonplace of everyday life. There could be no safety on our roads without a highway code. You can only play a game successfully if there are rules and a referee to apply them. Exactly the same pattern is true of living the Christian life. For this reason, God has given us his law, which defines right and wrong, calls sin by its proper name, and provides structures in which Christian freedom can be enjoyed. But what happens when Christians disagree about the rules? How should the church behave when disputes arise between believers? This occurred at Corinth and still does today. Sadly, Christian marriages break down, husbands and wives cannot agree, even though they both confess Christ as Lord; a Christian employee has a dispute with his Christian boss, or a Christian tenant with his Christian landlord; two Christian brothers disagree as to how to divide up their father's estate; or a Christian business partnership turns sour. What does Christian freedom look like when brothers are at variance with one another? Do they rush off to the lawyers and seek redress through the courts? Apparently, some were doing just that at Corinth, so Paul writes this corrective, continuing his practical teaching on what it means to live the lifestyle of the cross.

In chapter 5, we were taught not to judge those outside the church, since that is God's role. On the other hand, the ability to judge matters of legal disputes in cases within the church is a competence that Christians do possess and which Paul now explores.

HANDLING DISPUTES (verses 1–6)

Paul's basic position is that Christians should not be taking their disagreements to the secular courts, but should be able to settle them within the fellowship of the church. This does not mean that the apostle was writing off the secular courts of his day as useless. In Romans 13, the magistrate is seen as 'God's servant for your good'. He is also 'an avenger who carries out God's wrath on the wrongdoer' (*Rom.* 13:3–4). Part of God's good ordering of society is that he has provided for authority within government, and law and punishment are part of his means of ordering a fallen world. Nevertheless, in this context, Paul describes the secular judge as *unrighteous* (verse 1) because he is not committed to following the law of God but the law of the land, whatever that might be. In his own life he may be at variance with God's law in all sorts of ways. The wisdom that one can expect therefore from the secular law court is inevitably the wisdom of this world. Christians however belong to the community of God's people, referred to here as the *saints*. Of course, this is not a claim to any sort of perfection but simply to a relationship with God that God himself has brought about, bringing Christians into the sphere of fellowship with himself, through the gospel. The two groups of people, to whom Paul is referring, will follow, quite understandably, two different criteria of judgement. But the basic mistake that the Christians at Corinth seem to have been making was to view their disputes as a legal, rather than a spiritual, problem. Thus, in one stroke, they had divided their lives falsely into the secular and the sacred. These matters were worldly affairs, so what use was the church in that situation? It might bring peace to your soul, but surely it was not the means of bringing peace to quarrelling men. Would it not be better to keep the church out of the issue and get some justice through the secular courts? Paul's response is to say that they could not have been more wrong! *If the world is to be judged by you, are you incompetent to try trivial cases?* (verse 2).

At this point, we can pick up the link to chapter 5:12, where the apostle told the Corinthians not to be passing judgement on those outside the church. The role of the church in society is not to censure but to serve. Here, chapter 6:2, he makes the point by reminding his readers of the eschatological perspective which the Day of Judgement should bring to their thinking. The details may be somewhat difficult for us to imagine, but the drift of the argument is not hard to follow. There will be an ultimate day of God's judgement when his saints will be united with their Lord. They will be seated with him upon the throne of judgement, to which all created beings, including the angels (verse 3) will be summoned. This is an argument from the greater to the lesser. Paul's line of reasoning is that if saints are to exercise such jurisdiction in the last day, do they not have enough God-given wisdom now to deal with the comparatively trivial differences which they experience in their relationships in this world? After all, this was a church that boasted of its spiritual maturity and wisdom but, apparently, it could not solve its own internal disagreements. What was to be done?

Verses 4 and 5 provide Paul's answer. Firstly though, we must notice that there are two possible translations of verse 4. In the ESV it is translated as a question, '*So if you have such cases, why do you lay them before those who have no standing in the church?*' The men of no standing referred to here would probably then be pagan judges who were of little account in the church, not because of incompetence within their own field, but because they did not have the spiritual wisdom and discernment that chapter 2 has mentioned. If, however, the verse is translated as a command, as in the AV and NIV, '*Appoint as judges even men of little account*', then Paul is telling the Corinthians that it is better to have the least competent Christians settle the dispute rather than dragging the name of Christ into disrepute before a pagan judge. Verse 5 would certainly seem to support this view. On the other hand, we must not see this as an excuse for mediocrity. Wise people are certainly needed within every congregation, but the point of verse 6 is that there are in every church those who are qualified to deal with such problems without bringing the gospel of peace into disrepute by taking the disputes of Christians to pagan courts. For, at the end of time, 'the unrighteous' will be judged by God, so why should those who are his people go to the ungodly now for judgements in a temporal context?

FACING DEFEAT (verses 7–8)

Perhaps Paul's most trenchant comment is made here. A Christian has already lost his case by bringing it to the secular courts, whatever the verdict. It *is already a defeat for you* (verse 7). The reason is not difficult to see. By the time a dispute between believers reaches the court, the Christians concerned are already totally defeated as Christians. The fact that they have appealed to pagan judgement shows that their trust is no longer in God. Whether as plaintiff or defendant, attacking one's brother or defending oneself, they are immersed in a battle of wits and arguments in which God is automatically ignored and excluded. Such courts inevitably are governed by the wisdom of this world, which assumes that a man is justified in any expense in defending his own interests or in preserving his own rights. On such a basis, the typical consequences of such a court are inevitably divorces, damages, enmities, great expense and emotional stress for all concerned. In fact it could be convincingly argued that the only winner is the devil. The very existence of such quarrels between Christians is a defeat for the gospel and a calumny against Christ.

However, there is a still deeper reason why an application to the courts is a defeat for the Christian in such cases, and Paul draws attention to it at the end of verse 7. *Why not rather suffer wrong? Why not rather be defrauded?* In using these two verbs, Paul re-directs our thinking away from rights and winning cases to the One who carried our guilt through the sham of an unjust trial that cost him his life. The spirituality of the cross is as operative here, as in all the other issues that Paul discusses. The wisdom of God, centred in 'Jesus Christ and him crucified' is the most pertinent factor to apply to the situation. At the cross, what looked like utter defeat was actually total victory; the victory of an unquenchable love that not even death could destroy. The question is: Did that victory come about by the Lord Jesus standing on his rights, safeguarding his interests and insisting upon having his own way? The answer is, of course, a resounding 'No'. What does the cross teach but that sacrifice is the road to reconciliation and forgiveness. That is God's way, and the Corinthians seemed unwilling to tread that path. Disputes, such as these that they were taking to the pagan courts, arise primarily from pride, self-will, an insistence on one's rights and a defence of one's own interests. None of those things were exhibited in Jesus as he made his way to the cross for us. Christ's way therefore points us along a different route, although it may be hard to follow and difficult to understand. Nevertheless, if we do not tread it, we shall never know real peace. Although it may seem difficult for Christians to suffer, in terms of being wronged or cheated, it is actually much more difficult to fight on. And any hollow victory that the pagan courts might provide would in reality prove to be a total spiritual defeat.

There could be no doubt as to what was Christ's way. He himself taught, 'Do not resist the one who is evil. But if anyone slaps you on the right cheek, turn to him the other also. And if anyone would sue you and take your tunic, let him have your cloak as well. And if anyone forces you to go one mile, go with him two miles' (*Matt.* 5:39–41). If as Christians we ignore his words, we can only ultimately be defeated. That is exactly the trap the Corinthians had fallen into. *But you yourselves wrong and defraud – even your own brothers* (verse 8). That cannot be the way of victory. Such disputes are generated by pride, jealousy, greed or belligerence, so that to act like that towards my brother is to indicate that I am totally defeated. I am acting on the basis of sin, even if I am simply responding to his sin, and what I need to do is to repent, to ask for forgiveness, and to be restored to a real discipleship, being prepared to walk the way of the cross. At root, this is a commitment of our lives into the hands of God and a practical way of showing that we trust his perfect will and are prepared to entrust ourselves 'to him who judges justly'. (See *1 Pet.* 2:21–25 for a further explanation of this pattern of the Lord Jesus that we are called to follow.)

RECOGNIZING DECEPTION (verses 9–11)

The concluding paragraph of this section focuses once again upon the danger of self-deception, which, by its very nature, is so hard to discern. Verse 9 begins *Do you not know*, and, as usual when Paul uses this form of words, he wishes to alert his readers to something which they should know in theory, but which in practice they seem not to be applying to their discipleship. The fact to which he draws their attention in verse 9 is that *the unrighteous* (literally 'the wrong-doers') *will not inherit the kingdom of God*. The point is made more pertinent by his use of the same verb ('doing wrong') that he had used in verse 8 to describe the action of Christians. The point is therefore a very powerful one. In taking fellow-Christians to law they are no different from other wrongdoers who are outside the kingdom. It is a salutary reminder of the standards that kingdom-membership requires. While it is true that none of us will be in the kingdom of God apart from his free grace and mercy, yet it is equally true that nothing that defiles can enter that kingdom (see *Rev.* 21:27). On that basis, sin excludes every one of us from the heavenly city. By emphasising *do not be deceived*, Paul wants to stir up the Corinthian Christians to appreciate the compromise with which they have become so accustomed. The lists in verses 9 and 10 of those who are outside the kingdom focus on the two great false gods of Corinth, and of the twenty-first century: sex and money. The danger is that the Corinthian Christians were presuming on God's grace and were so familiar with the idea of his free forgiveness that they were failing to see sin as God sees it. It is impossible to combine membership of

God's kingdom with habitual sexual sin, or the love of money, but the great delusion is that this is not so, and so multitudes of people are self-deceived. The case of the Christian brother at war with another brother, or at law with him, is exactly the same. It is a sin that excludes from God's presence.

But the section ends with the most wonderful reassurance. *And such were some of you* (verse 11a). If these are the sins that rightly exclude us from God's heaven, then which of us could ever hope to enter? But the glory of the gospel is that the church is composed of redeemed sinners, people whose values at one time were exactly the opposite of those of the Lord Jesus, yet who have since experienced a change that is almost too wonderful to imagine.

Three times in the original of verse 11, Paul uses the word 'but'. It precedes the three great things that God has done for us through the person of his Son and applied to our lives by his own Spirit. We are *washed*, *sanctified*, and *justified*. The stain of sin in our lives has been eradicated by the death of the Lord Jesus. The blood of God's Passover Lamb has washed us clean. We have been set apart by God so as to belong to him and he claims us as his very own. And through the work of Christ on the cross we have been made right with God. 'Justified' is the opposite of 'unrighteous' in verse 9. It means that we are declared righteous, freed from guilt and acquitted of all charges. Such an amazing transformation is possible only through the person and work of the Lord Jesus Christ, in giving himself up for us on the cross, and by the activity of God the Holy Spirit, making these things real in our personal experience, granting us the gift of faith and shaping our characters more and more into the likeness of Christ. The contrast in these verses is very striking. Verse 11 is a description of what the gospel of God's free grace achieves in a sinner's life when he, or she, repents. But, if we remain complacent about our sin and content in our quarrels, how can we claim to be real believers in such a Saviour? The challenge to us all is that we make sure that we are not deceived. The privilege of entry into God's kingdom has been purchased for us at Calvary through the grace of Christ, but the corollary is, 'Let everyone who names the name of the Lord depart from iniquity' (*2 Tim.* 2:19).

17

Members of Christ

12"All things are lawful for me," but not all things are helpful.
"All things are lawful for me," but I will not be enslaved by
anything. 13"Food is meant for the stomach and the stomach for
food" – and God will destroy both one and the other. The body
is not meant for sexual immorality, but for the Lord, and the
Lord for the body. 14And God raised the Lord and will also raise
us up by his power. 15Do you not know that your bodies are
members of Christ? Shall I then take the members of Christ and
make them members of a prostitute? Never! 16Or do you not know
that he who is joined to a prostitute becomes one body with her?
For, as it is written, "The two will become one flesh." 17But he
who is joined to the Lord becomes one spirit with him. 18Flee from
sexual immorality. Every other sin a person commits is outside
the body, but the sexually immoral person sins against his own
body. 19Or do you not know that your body is a temple of the Holy
Spirit within you, whom you have from God? You are not your
own, 20for you were bought with a price. So glorify God in your
body (1 Cor. 6:12–20).

If the radical change of verse 11 has actually taken place in the
lives of Paul's readers, then it will be manifested in a radically
different lifestyle. However, it seems that this was lacking in certain
quarters of the congregation, and the basic problem that Paul is
addressing in this section is their misunderstanding of the significance of their physical bodies in their lives as Christian believers.
How does the Christian gospel affect our understanding of sexual
morality? It is a common fallacy today to argue that one religion is

very much like another and that there is really nothing to choose between them. Because the concept of absolute truth is so widely denied, it is imagined that a pick-and-mix approach to religion is perfectly acceptable. However, when you study Christianity, you find that it is totally different. The common denominator of all the religions of the world, with the exception of the Christian faith, is that they describe ladders by which their devotees may attempt to bring themselves into the presence of the divine, or to the ultimate good which is envisaged. Based as they are on human effort, these religions are inevitably governed by works. The unique factor of the Christian revelation is the grace of God, which brings God down the ladder to man, to rescue us when we have no means of saving ourselves. Legalism (law-keeping as a way to righteousness) is at the heart of all man-made religions, but God's revelation is one of true liberty. The Corinthian Christians seem to have grasped that well enough, but Paul is concerned about the implications they have drawn from it. He therefore picks up their slogan *'All things are lawful for me'* and begins to argue that this does not mean that they can behave in whatever way they choose. In this section, therefore, Paul is getting to the root of the question, 'What is true Christian freedom?'

UNDERSTANDING THE PRINCIPLES (verses 12–17)

There are three affirmations that Paul makes in the course of these verses, upon which his teaching is clearly based. It is significant that he does not deny the slogan that he twice quotes in verse 12, but he modifies and focuses it in a way that seems to have been absent from the Corinthians' thinking. In claiming that their spirituality set them free to do anything, they were in fact redefining morality. So, Paul's first principle is that Christian liberty is not licence. It is certainly true that in Christ we are set free to be our true selves. The gospel is not a strait jacket. But it makes nonsense of that freedom if it is used to claim that sin does not exist any more and that everything has become permissible. A man who uses his imagined freedom like that will inevitably destroy both himself and others; for the freedom that comes through the gospel is a freedom that exists only under Christ's lordship. Our human nature remains fallen and sinful, and sin always destroys. The only wage it pays is death, and the only way out of that cul-de-sac is the gift of God that brings eternal life.

Paul now exhorts his readers to ask two questions which are designed both to define and control their use of freedom. The first is, 'Is it beneficial?' By this Paul means that when we are considering something we may think is permissible, we should also ask the question whether it helps us to develop a Christian life that is more evidently like the Lord Jesus. It is fascinating to see how fundamentally different from the non-Christian's viewpoint this question is. Before we became Christians, it is likely that the only controlling question we might ask is, 'What's wrong with it?' Now, we are to ask, 'What's right with it?' Does this 'lawful', or permissible, attitude or behaviour actually have any value in developing my discipleship?

The second question is, 'Does it tend to master, or enslave, me?' Here, Paul's point seems to be that freedom involves the choice to refuse as well as to accept. Something may be lawful but if it dominates my life so that Christ is being squeezed out of the central position, then I am no longer free. There is some other controlling principle at work and my life is being taken over by a 'bottom line' that is contrary to my creed that Jesus Christ is Lord. The subtlety involved is that this controlling principle may be something that is eminently permissible. Business activities, professional commitment, hobbies, family life, even Christian ministry, can so take us over that we begin to serve the activity rather than the Lord. As chapter 4 reminded us, we are only truly free when we are Christ's bond slaves. These two questions are therefore set to challenge the use of our freedom in a truly godly way. It is all too possible to enslave ourselves in the name of freedom; to be dominated by practices that do not help us, trapped in our own desires, rather than living as God's free people. Licence, we need to remember, is less than liberty, not more.

The second principle (verses 13–14) is that what a Christian does in the body has eternal significance, because it is not simply confined to this world. Since it is true that in every age the church tends to be conditioned by the society of which it is a part, it is hardly surprising that Greek philosophy infected the Corinthian thinking. The fundamental dualism between the spirit and the material showed itself in a variety of ways. For some, this led to extreme asceticism, where the body was despised and so rigorously treated that it came to be regarded as the enemy of true spirituality. Everything to do with the body was insignificant for the life of the spirit or the fate of the soul. At the other end of the spectrum, such thinking could lead to libertarian lifestyles. If only the spirit can inherit God's kingdom, then what one does with the body is of eternal *in*significance. Ultimately, this led to a denial of the resurrection of Christians, and Paul has to deal with this point later in the letter (chapter 15).

The argument is spelt out in verse 13a. *Food is meant for the stomach and the stomach for food.* In its relevance to sexual behaviour, the argument is this: It may be claimed that just as you satisfy your appetite for food by eating, which is simply a natural physical process, so one may satisfy the sexual appetite by casual sex. But by taking his readers back to the fundamental principle, Paul shows that the comparison between food and sex is invalid. The body is more than animal tissue, more than matter informed by the soul or spirit. The stomach may be an organ of the body which is used during our earthly life, but the body is the whole person, created by God to glorify God and serve him. He sanctifies and dwells within the Christian's body and he will raise it up at the last day, just as Christ was raised in glory from the grave. Thus, the body is *for the Lord, and the Lord for the body* (verse 13). On this analogy, therefore, sexual intercourse is not equivalent to eating a meal. It is an act of the whole person, a self-giving at every level of the personality, and it belongs to that which is destined for eternity, the real person raised in the likeness of Christ. If God regards our physical bodies with such importance, then they must be dedicated to him and life lived in them must reflect his character and priorities.

This leads Paul to his third principle, which is that you cannot live a divided life (verses 15–17). Rather than being destined for destruction, our bodies are destined for resurrection, a pattern that is proved by Christ's own resurrection. Since a Christian is united to Christ by faith, his body, by definition, belongs to the Lord. If, then, the Christian's body belongs to Christ and one day he is going to raise it up in glory, how can that body be united with a prostitute? (verse 15b). Such behaviour would be both inappropriate and contradictory. Central to Paul's argument is his quotation from Genesis 2:24 in verse 16, '*The two will become one flesh.*' On that basis, sexual union is clearly meant exclusively for marriage. It represents the union of two persons who are transformed into a new unit in society. Sex is not like a limb of the body. It represents an activity in which the whole person is involved, and in many ways determines character, outlook and lifestyle. That is why there is no such thing as free love. Love demands loyalty. If it is free, then it is not love, but if it is love then the couple should publicly commit themselves to one another. To use what God has designed as a life-changing union in order to gratify lust, or to gain temporary pleasure, is to invite deep personal disintegration. It is certainly clear that multiple liaisons lead to an inability to make a deep and lasting relationship. Christians, who are in such a relationship with the living God, cannot possibly live in that way. You cannot be truly united to Christ and leave your sex life outside his authority. For *he who is joined to the Lord becomes one spirit with him* (verse 17). Our love must reflect Christ's devotion in loyalty to his bride, the church. Indeed, the proof of union with Christ is that we surrender to him all that we have, including every aspect of our physical bodies.

WORKING OUT THE PRACTICE (verses 18–20)

How then are we to live Christ's way in a pressingly pagan world? We can thank God for the clarity of Paul's opening statement in verse 18. *Flee from sexual immorality*. This is not just human advice but the divine command through the apostle. The verb is a strong one; it means not just 'avoid', but 'run away from'. This reminds us that Christian sexual standards are not preserved by cowardice but by courage. Yet, running away from sexual sin is often not given the credit that it deserves. After all, it is neither clever nor courageous to put one's head into the lion's mouth, and then pray fervently that it will not be bitten off! Paul is always a realist in these matters. Because sexual sins affect us so deeply, within our personality, and because the sex drive is so powerful, Christians must take determined and strong action. In practice that means putting a distance between ourselves and temptation. We need to be disciplined in what we read and what we watch. The physical side of friendships or relationships that may lead to marriage needs to be kept under control, so as not to dominate or dictate. It is not a godly thing to put oneself in a situation where temptation may prove too strong. The right thing to do is to run away.

As the section concludes, Paul gives three very good reasons why we need to be so drastic. Firstly, because sexual immorality is a sin against oneself (verse 18b). All sin harms the sinner, but this sin may do deeper harm and leave deeper scars than we tend to imagine. We must avoid thinking of sexual sins as the worst of all sins, and of course like all sins they can be forgiven, through repentance and the forgiveness that flows to us from the cross. But, as with all other sins, we may have to live with the consequences of our rebellion, and Christians are to be realists about the damage which immoral relationships can cause in so many ways. The devil never tells us about the small print.

Secondly, Paul reminds us that sexual immorality is a sin against God (verse 19). The Christian's *body is a temple of the Holy Spirit* and therefore *You are not your own.* It is a sin also against the other person involved, of course, but here the focus is on God. Paul again seems to be particularly concerned to attack the false Greek view of the body. Rather than regarding it as a despised prison for the pure spirit, from which it needs to be released, Paul describes the body as the temple of the Holy Spirit, the dwelling place of God himself. For that reason it must be pure and holy, kept for his exclusive use. As redeemed sinners we belong to the one who bought us with his own blood, the corollary of which is that we have no right to do what we like with our bodies. We belong to the Lord, our bodies are to be used for the Lord and to glorify the Lord in everything we do.

Lastly, Paul teaches that sexual immorality is a sin against our redemption (verse 20). It is all too easy for us to forget the slavery in which we lived when we were sons of Adam and daughters of Eve. Sin and death held authority over us and tyrannized our lives. Nor should we forget the immense cost which God was prepared to pay in order to bring us to freedom. The lifeblood of his own Son was the only means by which we have been redeemed, and when we consider the costliness of that price it is not difficult for us to see its application in the last sentence of the chapter. *Therefore honour God with your body.* Just as the slaves in Corinth, many of whom were doubtless members of the church, were bought by their masters and belonged to them, so Christ has sovereign rights over all of his people. He makes us his children, welcomes us into his family, but he expects us to honour him with all that we are and have. If we use our bodies for immorality we deny his cross and frustrate his redeeming grace.

18

Marital Duty

¹Now concerning the matters about which you wrote: "It is good for a man not to have sexual relations with a woman." ²But because of the temptation to sexual immorality, each man should have his own wife and each woman her own husband. ³The husband should give to his wife her conjugal rights, and likewise the wife to her husband. ⁴For the wife does not have authority over her own body, but the husband does. Likewise the husband does not have authority over his own body, but the wife does. ⁵Do not deprive one another, except perhaps by agreement for a limited time, that you may devote yourselves to prayer; but then come together again, so that Satan may not tempt you because of your lack of self-control.

⁶Now as a concession, not a command, I say this. ⁷I wish that all were as I myself am. But each has his own gift from God, one of one kind and one of another (1 Cor. 7:1–7).

Chapter 7 forms the last main unit of the section that began at 5:1, in which Paul corrects the wrong thinking of the Corinthians in the area of morality, especially sexual morality. In a pagan city like Corinth, many of the converts to Christianity would have brought with them a background of sexual behaviour profoundly at variance with the Creator's instructions. Clearly, it was a matter of much debate and potential disagreement within the congregation, as to how the gospel ethic was to be worked out in this challenging context.

NO EXCUSES? (verses 1–4)

Verse 1 indicates that Paul is answering a principle advanced by at least some of the believers in Corinth in their letter to him. *It is good for a man not to have sexual relations* or, more literally, 'not to touch a woman'. Their reasons for adopting this view are not hard to understand. Since Corinth was a by-word for sexual immorality in the Græco-Roman world, it would be natural for keen Christians to swing towards the opposite end of the spectrum and to elevate complete abstinence from sexual relations as a mark of true spirituality and godliness. Such self-discipline would prove that a superior divine power really was at work in them and might be a further sign that 'already . . . you have become kings' (4:8). Further support could be given to this view by the concept of the dualism of body and spirit that was foundational to Greek thinking. If the body is inferior to the pure spirit, simply a prison house of the real person, as was widely believed, then to ignore and so nullify its sexual demands would clearly be a sign of superior spirituality. Abstinence from marriage would then clearly be 'good'.

But Paul will have none of it. Supremely the realist, he begins his rebuttal of this view with the potent consideration *because of the temptation to sexual immorality*. He knew that you do not correct the excessive swing of the pendulum in one direction by an equal, but opposite, swing in the other. The question that has rather to be asked is: 'Where does the Bible, God's revelation, draw the perpendicular? What is the biblical norm?' This is what Paul now begins to expound. Marriage is not a second-best spiritual option. *Each man should have his own wife and each woman her own husband* (verse 2). The exclusivity of one man to one woman within Christian marriage is built into this statement, echoing the Genesis 2:24 principle of leaving father and mother and cleaving (being united to) to one's wife, as 'one flesh'. The apostle is not saying that marriage is a remedy against immorality for those who are single and are tempted not to be chaste. At this point, he is dealing with Christians who are already married, either to another believer or perhaps to an unbeliever, if the Christian has been converted since their marriage. Both these groups will be in view again later, in verses 10–11 and 12–16. His point is that withdrawing from marriage or abstaining from sexual relations within marriage is not 'good', since faithful monogamous marriage is God's good gift for humankind.

Verses 3 and 4 develop the argument, exactly balancing the equivalent privileges and responsibilities of husband and wife to each other in the marriage union. In speaking of mutual *conjugal rights,* husband and wife to each other (verse 3), Paul uses a word that literally means 'debt', implying obligation to meet one another's sexual needs. This is expanded further in verse 4 where the point is that at the heart of the marriage relationship there is a giving of oneself away. The essence of love is self-giving, and that is expressed in the physical union of the married couple, confirming and deepening their oneness at every other level of life and personality. It is likely, however, that a view was developing in Corinth that said, 'You cannot be fully devoted to Christ and be married.' Or, if you remained married, then real spirituality would be evidenced by the 'Platonic' nature of the marriage, the abstaining from sexual intercourse. Paul's response is to deny not only the division between spiritual and physical but also the view that there can be any personal rights of abstinence in marriage, just because marriage involves the giving of the whole self. The wedding service expresses the biblical principle very succinctly: 'All that I am I give to you and all that I have I share with you, within the love of God.'

Because we are whole people, it is no part of Christian piety to imagine that some higher 'spirituality' can be attained by physical abstinence. In fact, it is more likely to lead to an increasing self-centredness, since one's own spiritual ambitions may be pursued at the expense of the one person to whom one has the greatest obligation of love. It is a common experience that recently married couples are soon brought to realize just how selfish they have been as individuals; so much so that marriage must be one of God's most powerful ways of dealing with our deep-rooted selfishness.

NO EXCEPTIONS? (verses 5–7)

Verse 5 shows that there is one set of circumstances that can be regarded as an exception to this 'rule'. Those circumstances are: *that you may devote yourselves to prayer.* But even here, the exception is carefully qualified by two restrictive requirements. It must be *by mutual consent* and *for a time.* Neither party is to feel aggrieved or deprived because the other has imposed his or her will unilaterally, nor is this to be without a definite terminus in view. Again, Paul is supremely realistic about it all. He has no time for a humbug, other-worldly, false spirituality. It may sound very 'spiritual' for a Christian married couple to tell their friends that they now abstain from sex, to devote themselves to 'higher things' and exhort other couples to follow their example. But Paul knows that unless the limitations of the first half of verse 5 are clearly operating, the temptations of the second half of verse 5 are likely to overwhelm them, *because of your lack of self-control.* Throughout the letter Paul continues to remind them that *Satan* is a powerful enemy and that refusing one another proper sexual relations within marriage is playing into his hands. Temptations to sexual immorality will inevitably increase in such a situation, since the sexual drive in human beings is a gift – part of God's good creation. Like every other aspect of our humanity, sex is profoundly affected by the Fall, but that does not make it evil or inferior, of itself. It is our manner of dealing with it that indicates whether or not we are godly. And Paul's point is that it is not godly to pretend that you are above sexual temptation, or to try to ignore that aspect of our continuing warfare against the world, the flesh and the devil.

Now as a concession, not a command, I say this (verse 6) is Paul's final caveat in this paragraph. He is not making a strait-jacket for every married couple, by instituting an apostolic instruction that they *must* periodically refrain from sexual relations, in order to pray. Rather they *may*, if they so choose. Verse 7 sums up his general outlook and attitude, though it is not easy to be completely sure of what he means by *I wish that all were as I myself am.* Does he mean that he wishes everyone was single, as he was presumably, whether as never married, or perhaps as a widower? Can this be construed as a call for celibacy, as a more excellent way than marriage? Certainly the verse has been pressed into service for that cause. Or does he mean, as some commentators suggest, that he wishes everyone were free from the unhelpful dualism and its resulting asceticism, which he is correcting in this passage? He wants the Corinthians to come round to his point of view.

The fact of the matter is that all are not as he is (single) *but each has his own gift from God.* In recognizing marriage as God's good gift, Paul denies implicitly that he would want to take it away from those to whom God has given it. Therefore, as he will develop in the following verses, those who are already married are not to seek to extricate themselves from this God-given state, but neither should those who are unmarried regard it as mandatory that they should end their single state. Though it remains true that 'it is not good that the man should be alone' (*Gen.* 2:18), yet some may be given the state of singleness as an equal gift of God, at least for a time. After all, neither state is automatically permanent. The important perspective is to recognize God's providence in our current situation, to receive it and use it faithfully as his 'gift', according to the Maker's instruction, recognizing that it may change with time, and that all this is under God's sovereign wisdom. The danger is always that we look at the unfavourable ingredients of our circumstances and argue with ourselves that, if only our circumstances were different, we would be much more effective, holy Christians. This is very rarely the case. It is much better for us to live in the enjoyment of God's current providential provisions and sovereign overruling of our circumstances and to prove his faithfulness *within* the circumstances rather than concentrating all our energies on changing them. After all, the state God has currently given us is his '*charisma*', that is, a gift of his grace – an expression of his undeserved favour and mercy. To see *that* in the word Paul uses must surely change our perspective.

19

God Has Called You to Peace

⁸To the unmarried and the widows I say that it is good for them to remain single as I am. ⁹But if they cannot exercise self-control, they should marry. For it is better to marry than to be aflame with passion.

¹⁰To the married I give this charge (not I, but the Lord): the wife should not separate from her husband ¹¹(but if she does, she should remain unmarried or else be reconciled to her husband), and the husband should not divorce his wife.

¹²To the rest I say (I, not the Lord) that if any brother has a wife who is an unbeliever, and she consents to live with him, he should not divorce her. ¹³If any woman has a husband who is an unbeliever, and he consents to live with her, she should not divorce him. ¹⁴For the unbelieving husband is made holy because of his wife, and the unbelieving wife is made holy because of her husband. Otherwise your children would be unclean, but as it is, they are holy. ¹⁵But if the unbelieving partner separates, let it be so. In such cases the brother or sister is not enslaved. God has called you to peace. ¹⁶Wife, how do you know whether you will save your husband? Husband, how do you know whether you will save your wife? (1 Cor. 7:8–16).

In this next section, Paul addresses three different groups within the Corinthian congregation, defined not by their preferences (as in chapter 1) but by their situation in life. He begins with the singles (verses 8–9), moves on to those married to fellow-Christians (verses 10–11) and concludes with those married to unbelievers (verses 12–16).

SINGLE? (verses 8–9)

In this first short section, Paul is addressing those who *are* like him (cf. verse 7) in that they are currently unmarried, *as I myself am.* The term translated *'unmarried'* is a little more specific than it appears. *'Agamoi'* is masculine and balances *widows*, which is clearly feminine. So, rather than speaking about those who have never been married and those who have been widowed (men or women), Paul is probably addressing only the widowed of both sexes. This is supported by the observation that *'agamos'* is used again in verses 11 and 34, where it seems in both contexts to refer to those who have been married previously but are no longer. Following up his comment in verse 7 about God's good gifting, Paul is concerned to remove from the single members of the church any pressure to change their unmarried status. *It is good for them to remain single as I am* (verse 8). They were not to be made to feel that their state is somehow inferior, or less fulfilled, than those who were married, since it is far better to be unmarried than to be unhappily married or unequally matched.

However, Paul again enters a caveat. It is the inner attitude that concerns him – *but if they cannot exercise self-control.* Every normal human being struggles with sexual temptation and those who are single, or who are no longer married, face particular types of temptation. They are not necessarily stronger than those faced by married people, but the fulfilment of a happy marriage, which is a defence against this temptation, is not available to them. It is normal, therefore, for unmarried people to struggle with issues of self-control, but those in view here are failing noticeably in that struggle. If they have been taught only that 'it is good for them to remain single', then that solution is barred to them and so they have no legitimate outlet for their sexual drive. The result is likely to be that they will *be aflame.* Paul does not say 'with passion'; that is an addition of the translators. Others have suggested he could mean 'with shame', because of their lack of self-control. But clearly the image is a destructive one, and so the apostle's teaching is *they should marry. For it is better to marry than to be aflame.* Repression is not the right solution. Marriage, which is the good gift of God in creation, is. Paul therefore wants to rehabilitate marriage in Corinthian thinking, not as a remedy for lust, but as the divinely provided channel for wholly positive human sexuality.

In passing, it is worth reflecting on the fact that single people often *do* feel less accepted and valued than they should be in contemporary congregational life. They are not helped to see their current singleness as God's gift and to use its opportunities accordingly. Paul will return to this theme in verses 32–35. So many churches are marriage and family dominated, to the extent that the unmarried and childless are almost 'frozen out'. Of course we want to build strong Christian marriages and families, but to emphasize that to the exclusion of valuing, supporting, and using the many unmarried members of our congregations is an imbalance, that can become sinful. Why are so many widows no longer invited out to homes in the church family after their husbands have died? Why are so many singles seen simply as potential babysitters? Why when singles *are* invited out to meals in a church family are they so often invited as a group, or, even worse, as a pair (a man and a woman)? We need to be much more self-critical about our attitudes and unspoken assumptions about the role and state of singles within the family of God.

MARRIED TO A CHRISTIAN? (verse 10–11)

Paul is still defending the importance and value of Christian marriage, answering the objection of verse 1, and he moves on now to deal with the married Christians in Corinth, who wished to extricate themselves from their marriages. At verse 12, he will start to address the particular issues facing believers married to unbelievers, but first he addresses all Christians who are married. What he says is a *command* (not an option as in verse 6), and it is a command with full dominical authority – *not I, but the Lord*. Its substance is very clear. Marriage is a lifelong commitment that neither partner is to break. Again we must not read too much into the modern translations of 'separate' (verse 10) and 'divorce' (verse 11). In current legal practice, separation may be a halfway house on the road to a full divorce. But Paul is not legitimising such a view, and we must not read our social conditions back into the biblical text. Both verses signify the end of the marriage relationship and that is off limits for a Christian.

Yet, almost immediately, as we are often seeing in this chapter, Paul looks at an exception, *but if she does* (verse 11a). Although the Bible is uniformly clear that God hates divorce and it is never his way (*Mal.* 2:16), yet in the reality of a fallen world and human sinfulness, that same God regularizes the process by which divorce may happen, if that is the least of the evils available (*Deut.* 24:1–4). Just as God made provision in the Old Testament for the breaking of his commands, so here Paul follows suit. As with all of God's commands, Christians do sometimes break them. This grieves the Lord and harms his people, but the addition here, in verse 11, is designed to restrict the growth of evil. *She should remain unmarried or else be reconciled to her husband.* The one relates to the other. It is because of the hope of reconciliation and of the rebuilding of the marriage, that re-marriage is forbidden.

We must not require these two verses to present us with a comprehensive biblical view of marriage and divorce. They have an important role to play, but must stand alongside the teaching of the Lord Jesus in Matthew 5:32, Mark 10:2–12, Luke 16:18 and, especially, Matthew 19:3–9, with its important exception clause. Recognizing that divorce was permitted in the law of Moses, 'because of your hardness of heart', Jesus decrees that the only circumstances in which it is acceptable are those of 'sexual immorality', because this sin destroys the 'one flesh' unity on which marriage is based. Even in such a case, divorce is permitted, rather than required, in order to regularize the situation publicly, which is that the marriage has been destroyed. Just as marriage is contracted in a public leaving and cleaving, so, sadly, divorce is the equivalent public declaration of its end. And since divorce carries with it the possibility (at least) of remarriage, Paul's statement in verse 11 is specifically geared to that situation. Any divorce, outside of Christ's exception, is not in accordance with God's will for his people, so that any remarriage based on such an unacceptable divorce would only multiply the offence. The issue of remarriage for the 'innocent' party is not dealt with directly here.

MARRIED TO A NON-CHRISTIAN? (verses 12–16)

To the rest (verse 12) indicates those who have not been covered by the two previous paragraphs, whom we are therefore justified in defining as believers married to unbelievers. In a Gentile community like Corinth, much as in our own culture, this situation would often arise. It is certainly correct to teach, from Paul's second letter, that a Christian believer should not enter into the 'unequal yoke' of marriage with an unbeliever (*2 Cor.* 6:14–15). How can a strong marriage be built on the different foundations of different ultimate reference points – God or self? But marriage is a gift of God to *all* humanity, and we should rejoice when unbelievers commit themselves to one another, according to God's structures. What happens, however, when one of the partners is converted? That is Paul's focus here. And again, he was particularly addressing immediately relevant issues for the Corinthian church. In their climate, where marriage was being spiritually downgraded, the new converts were probably being encouraged to come out of their pagan marriages in order to be more spiritual Christians. They would otherwise be contaminated by a sexual relationship with an unbeliever, hindered in their spiritual development. But again, Paul will have none of that.

Carefully balancing the situations of both sexes equally, in their responsibilities for making their marriages work, the apostle's clear teaching is that the Christian must not divorce the unbelieving partner, if it is the case that he or she *consents to live with* them. Some have argued that this is just Paul's opinion and does not have binding authority because of the introductory clause *I say (I, not the Lord)*, in contrast to the claim of the Lord's authority in verse 10. But Paul is not saying these few verses are less divinely inspired than all of the rest of his writings, or that they lack divine authority. He is simply affirming that unlike the previous case (verses 10–11) we have no direct teaching from the Lord Jesus about this. That, in itself, is hardly surprising, since the ministry of the Lord Jesus on earth was almost exclusively to the 'lost sheep of the house of Israel', within the boundaries of Israel and Jewish communities, built on and instructed by the 'Torah', the Old Testament law. That law forbade cross-religious marriages, but this new set of circumstances, with the spread of the gospel in the Gentile world, now required new definitive instruction, which the apostle gives.

His reasons are highly instructive. The Christian is to do everything possible to hold the marriage to an unbeliever together, to make it work, because the unbeliever *is made holy*, through the believing partner (verse 14). What does Paul mean? Clearly, he is not referring to salvation, since repentance and faith are everywhere taught in the New Testament as a personal, individual response. For an answer we need to go back to the Old Testament idea of ritual purity and contamination. The idea of being made holy, or sanctified, is that of being set apart, to a special purpose or ownership. 'Saints' are 'set apart' people, within the sphere of God's grace. This refers to their standing rather than character and certainly does not indicate perfection. But a man could become ritually unclean in a variety of ways and this would exclude him from entering the presence of God in the Temple. This, for example, was what concerned the priest and the Levite in the parable of the Good Samaritan (*Luke* 10:31–32). They 'passed by on the other side' because if the man were dead they would have become ritually unclean by their proximity to his dead body and therefore unable to officiate at the Temple.

However, the emphasis of the gospel is not that of contaminating uncleanness, but of contagious holiness. The unbelieving partner and the children produced by the marriage come within the sphere of God's grace. Because of the believer's influence for holiness within the home, the gospel is there lived out and explained. Far from seeking to get out of the marriage, the Christian partner has a new calling to pray, love and serve the unbeliever, in the expectation and hope that God will graciously move in upon the whole family and eventually unite them together in faith in the Lord Jesus Christ. The Christian does not withdraw, give up or move out. Quite the opposite! Confident of God's infinite mercy and grace, he or she becomes the channel of Christ-like reality in the family – an expectant instrument for gospel contagion.

But sometimes such faithful love and commitment meets only with resistance and rebellion. What if the unbeliever decides to end the marriage and walks out on the believing partner (verse 15)? The marriage will undoubtedly have changed, as the Christian partner will no longer be living according to their old pagan norms. In such a situation Paul indicates that nothing is gained by trying at all costs to prevent the unbeliever from leaving. *In such cases the brother or sister is not enslaved.* This then becomes the only other ground envisaged in Scripture on which divorce can be an acceptable option for the believer. The reason is important too. *God has called you to peace*. Where conflict predominates in the marriage and the home, because the believer is trying at all costs to keep the unbeliever in a marriage, for which there is no longer any enthusiasm or desire on the unbeliever's part, it is better to allow them to leave.

This is the connection then to verse 16. Is its tone optimistic or resigned? Clearly the great desire of the believing partner is for the unbeliever to be saved, but they are now removing themselves from the sphere of God's grace and holiness. So, it would not be unreasonable for the Christian to reason that leaving the family home puts them outside the circle of gospel influence and much less likely to be saved. This could lead them to apply undue pressure on the unbeliever not to leave. But Paul's point seems to be not to argue in such limited and humanly-centred ways. You don't know whether staying in the marriage or leaving the family home is more likely to influence the unbeliever towards saving faith. Distance may be an asset, whereas insistence on remaining may impose an intolerable strain which is actually spiritually counter-productive, particularly if the Christian's 'witness' is insensitive or coercive. The certain stress is not justified by the uncertain outcome. The Christian must have sufficient faith in God's sovereign grace and constant mercy to let the unbelieving partner go, if that is what they really want to do. The outcome is always in wiser, stronger hands than ours.

20

The Place in Life the Lord Has Assigned

¹⁷Only let each person lead the life that the Lord has assigned to him, and to which God has called him. This is my rule in all the churches. ¹⁸Was anyone at the time of his call already circumcised? Let him not seek to remove the marks of circumcision. Was anyone at the time of his call uncircumcised? Let him not seek circumcision. ¹⁹For neither circumcision counts for anything nor uncircumcision, but keeping the commandments of God. ²⁰Each one should remain in the condition in which he was called. ²¹Were you a slave when called? Do not be concerned about it. But if you can gain your freedom, avail yourself of the opportunity. ²²For he who was called in the Lord as a slave is a freedman of the Lord. Likewise he who was free when called is a slave of Christ. ²³You were bought with a price; do not become slaves of men. ²⁴So, brothers, in whatever condition each was called, there let him remain with God (1 Cor. 7:17–24).

This relatively uncomplicated section is, in fact, the heart and centre of this whole chapter. It is instructive to see how the apostle has put it together, since it leads us clearly to his major concern. It begins in verse 17, *let each person lead the life that the Lord has assigned to him* and concludes with exactly the same instruction, at the end of verse 24, *each man . . . should remain in the situation God called him to.* In addition, and so that we stand not the slightest chance of missing or forgetting the point, it is reiterated at the mid-point of the paragraph, in verse 20. *Each one should remain in the condition in which he was called.* Either side of this central assertion, Paul develops an example. The first is from the religious sphere, concerning circumcision, and the second is social, concerning slavery. Neither of these seems to have been a particularly live or contentious issue in Corinth; indeed, that is probably the very reason why Paul chose them as his examples. As they do not in themselves raise any hackles, he is able to use them illustratively to drive home his main point, so that his readers will hear it and understand it more clearly.

STAY AS YOU ARE!

We need to ask why Paul stresses this so much and what it reveals about the Corinthian challenges and problems. Generally, in the first-century world, as the radical nature of the Christian gospel became clearer and more extensively spread across the Roman Empire, the levels of hatred and fear increased, and with them grew opposition and persecution. It was understandable that at first Christianity was seen as simply a variant form of Judaism, an ethnic religion that was afforded full rights of practice under Roman rule. Under the umbrella of Judaism Christians might find themselves attacked by Jewish religious authorities, but they were relatively safe from political persecution. However, as the Jews increasingly exposed and denounced the 'heretical' belief in Jesus as Messiah and pointed out the rivalry of his kingly claims to those of Caesar, the Roman authorities gradually perceived the radical nature of this new threat.

When Paul wrote this letter such developments had hardly begun, but he undoubtedly saw the danger to the gospel which unnecessary social upheaval could cause. If Christians insisted that their freedom in Christ had to be exercised in a confrontational way, even against those norms of ordinary everyday culture, which did not involve any gospel or ethical compromises, then there might well be negative consequences to the spread of the good news. What if slaves were to form a liberation movement to free themselves from their earthly master as an expression of their liberty in Christ? Would that commend the gospel? What if marriages within the Christian church began to be annulled and the numbers of unsupported wives and children multiplied? What would that say about a gospel of restoration, forgiveness and love? For these, and other similar, reasons Paul repeats his central statement three times.

It is a statement based on the conviction that God's sovereignty extends over all the detailed circumstances of every individual life. God assigns everybody a place in life and calls each one to his particular function. The fact that a new believer is in a particular position, at the time of his conversion, is not therefore an accident. God's sovereignty does not come into play when an individual's spiritual life begins; it has governed everything from the beginning of creation. *This is my rule in all the churches* (verse 17b) is an indication of the total historical and geographical relevance of this principle. It is always true for everybody, everywhere, and so the principles derived from it are equally comprehensive in scope and relevance. The circumstances of our personal lives are not accidental – they are laid down by God. Each one finds his or her own special tasks and duties, in keeping God's commands, within the sphere in which he has placed us, in his infinite wisdom and love.

TWO EXAMPLES

The first example he takes (verses 18–19) relates to the issue of circumcision, which we know was considered in the Graeco-Roman world as one of the defining characteristics of Jewishness and which, for the Jews, was the supreme evidence of being a son of Abraham. We also know that from the earliest days of the Gentile mission there were Judaizers who wanted to insist that non-Jewish believers in Jesus should first become Jews before they could become true Christians. Paul consistently opposed such irrelevant religious imperialism and these verses show his typical response. Christian Jews should not try to change their status with regard to circumcision, any more than Gentiles needed to. *For neither circumcision counts for anything nor uncircumcision.* It just does not matter any more. What does matter is *keeping the commandments of God* (verse 19). With the advent of Christ and the gospel, the external sign had given way to the internal reality, which is not now a physical rite, but a heart-obedience. After all, that is what the external sign was originally intended to indicate. Circumcision was the mark in the flesh of covenant obedience to the Law (*Gen.* 17:9–14), and so when the inner reality of the law written on the heart becomes a reality through the gospel of Christ, the outer sign is redundant. How foolish then for a Christian to devote his energies to worrying about his physical state and seeking to change it, rather than devoting his life to obeying the Lord and so changing his whole character!

Verses 21–22 take us to the second example, namely, that of slavery. The Christian slave will not be troubled to the point of distraction over his social circumstances, for they are no longer what matters most to him. Of course, freedom is not a bad thing, and if he is offered the opportunity to gain it, he is perfectly right to do so. He does not have to be a slave to being a slave, as though God could never change his social condition. But *he who was called in the Lord as a slave is a freedman in the Lord. Likewise he who was free when called is a slave of Christ* (verse 22). This is the priority by which all Christians, slave or free, must live their lives – their relationship to Jesus Christ as Lord. The distinctions of status in this temporal world are irrelevant in comparison with this eternal relationship. The Christian agenda is not to abolish social differences, but to put them into their proper eternal perspective by transcending them through the gospel, so that they gradually fade away into irrelevance. Those who seek to preserve them simply demonstrate their spiritual immaturity. Of course, it is better for all men to be free rather than slaves, but that is only a relative good compared with the absolute of being Christ's bond-slave, 'whose service is perfect freedom'.

This leads on to Paul's concluding application in verse 23. *You were bought with a price; do not become slaves of men.* This is an echo of his earlier words in 6:20, at the end of his argument against sexual immorality. There he reminded his readers that as it cost the precious blood of God's Son to redeem them from sin and grant the gift of the Holy Spirit to indwell them, they could not contemplate uniting themselves to a prostitute. Here, what they must not contemplate is drifting back from their freedom into a bondage to man-made rules and regulations, whether religious or social. Christians are responsible to God first of all (verse 24) and all that really counts is the reality of our relationship to him, as Lord, seen in our obedience to his Word. Once we allow other people to put their rules in the place of God's commands, we have lost our Christian freedom.

If the Corinthian Christians yielded to the pressures from purely human sources to change their circumstances and situation in life, they would become 'slaves of men'. It is as though Paul is replaying the tapes of the conversations that they had been having and which could so easily produce this new slavery. 'Give up marriage . . . leave that pagan husband . . . you really should be circumcised . . . aren't you going to buy your freedom?' and so on. Instead he wants them to stay where they are and keep on obeying God's commands, so that they might enjoy the only true freedom any human being can have, in recognizing and submitting to Jesus Christ as Lord. The circumstances of life are not the most important things in life. The great priority is that, irrespective of our circumstances, we have been set free, in Christ, to be our true, redeemed selves.

21

Free from Anxieties

²⁵*Now concerning the betrothed, I have no command from the Lord, but I give my judgment as one who by the Lord's mercy is trustworthy.* ²⁶*I think that in view of the present distress it is good for a person to remain as he is.* ²⁷*Are you bound to a wife? Do not seek to be free. Are you free from a wife? Do not seek a wife.* ²⁸*But if you do marry, you have not sinned, and if a betrothed woman marries, she has not sinned. Yet those who marry will have worldly troubles, and I would spare you that.* ²⁹*This is what I mean, brothers: the appointed time has grown very short. From now on, let those who have wives live as though they had none,* ³⁰*and those who mourn as though they were not mourning, and those who rejoice as though they were not rejoicing, and those who buy as though they had no goods,* ³¹*and those who deal with the world as though they had no dealings with it. For the present form of this world is passing away.*

³²*I want you to be free from anxieties. The unmarried man is anxious about the things of the Lord, how to please the Lord.* ³³*But the married man is anxious about worldly things, how to please his wife,* ³⁴*and his interests are divided. And the unmarried or betrothed woman is anxious about the things of the Lord, how to be holy in body and spirit. But the married woman is anxious about worldly things, how to please her husband.* ³⁵*I say this for your own benefit, not to lay any restraint upon you, but to promote good order and to secure your undivided devotion to the Lord.*

³⁶*If anyone thinks that he is not behaving properly toward his betrothed, if his passions are strong, and it has to be, let him do as he wishes: let them marry – it is no sin.* ³⁷*But whoever is*

firmly established in his heart, being under no necessity but having his desire under control, and has determined this in his heart, to keep her as his betrothed, he will do well. ³⁸So then he who marries his betrothed does well, and he who refrains from marriage will do even better.

³⁹A wife is bound to her husband as long as he lives. But if her husband dies, she is free to be married to whom she wishes, only in the Lord. ⁴⁰Yet in my judgment she is happier if she remains as she is. And I think that I too have the Spirit of God (1 Cor. 7:25–40).

Once again, Paul's concern shifts to different groups within the Corinthian congregation, but he never moves far from the central, guiding principle of verses 17–24, 'Stay as you are!' In this concluding section, the focus begins with single people who have never been married, signalled by the opening heading: *Now concerning the betrothed.*

FREEDOM TO LIVE (verse 25–31)

Throughout the letter, the phrase '*Now concerning ...* ' is used to indicate a change of subject matter, but probably also to introduce and deal with various issues the Corinthians have raised with the apostle. Paul is again keen to present his teaching as a '*trustworthy*' judgement, rather than a divine command (verse 25), but this does not imply any diminution of apostolic authority or reliability. Verse 40, the concluding note of this section, makes that clear. The particular issue of *the betrothed* or 'virgins' probably reflected the situation found in the culture of the first century, where the decision of a single woman's parent or guardian, on whom she would be dependent for support, determined whether or not she was allowed to marry. The men (fathers, and perhaps fiancés too – see verse 36) seem to have asked Paul's advice on whether they should plan marriages for their children, whether engaged couples were committed to one another, and whether Christian widows were at liberty to marry again.

His basic answer is verse 26. *In view of the present distress it is good for a person to remain as he is.* The use of 'good' here matches the

Corinthians' use of the same word in verse 1. It does not carry an absolute moral sense of good as opposed to evil but rather the sense of a wise or expedient course of action. This view is supported by verse 25: *no command from the Lord*, and verse 28: *if you do marry, you have not sinned*. The point of contention in the verse, however, is what is meant by *the present distress*. Many suggestions have been offered, including the occurrence of sexual immorality in the Corinthian church; the imminence of persecution; or the fact that the church is to view itself as living in the last days, suspended between the two comings of Christ. This latter view is supported by the comments of verse 29, that *the appointed time has grown very short*, and of verse 31, that *the present form of this world is passing away*. In this sense, Paul's words would be relevant to every generation of believers in history. But there have been specific times and specific places in the world where the intensity was particularly strong, even to this day, and first-century Corinth was a very evident example of this.

Since Paul's desire is for the unmarried to be *free from anxieties* (verse 32a), this perspective of living in the last days seems to make the best sense. It frees us from the anxieties that can arise from being bound up in this world. In order to keep our lives focused on what matters most, the sorts of decisions that have to be made about marriage need to be reached within the perspective of the eternal kingdom. We must follow Paul's argument through the verses. 'Are you bound to a wife [by marriage]? Do not seek to be free. Are you free from a wife [by death or divorce]? Do not seek a wife.' This is the principle of staying where you are because a time of emergency and crisis is no easy context in which to start a new life-style. Of course, marriage is not a sin (verse 28), but Paul wants his readers to be realistic about it. A married man's troubles will be greatly multiplied in a time of hostility and persecution by the important and proper consideration he must give to his wife and family. It does not even need external pressure to produce that effect. Not surprisingly then, some of the greatest advances for the gospel in history have been accomplished by single men and women – men and women who have devoted themselves to the Lord's work without the distraction of other human loyalties and responsibilities.

It is this gospel perspective, as we might call it, which seems to drive the next section, verses 29–31. *The appointed time has grown very short* is always true, whether it is used to mean that the Lord Jesus may return suddenly and soon, or to mean that for each of us our life in this world is comparatively brief. Our problem is that we are tempted to live as though this world is the ultimate reality and is going to last for ever. In fact that is the essence of worldliness. In contrast, Christians know that this world and everything in it is fragile and temporary. As citizens of another, better country, a heavenly one (*Phil.* 3:20, *Heb.* 11:13–16), we must beware of settling down too comfortably, or holding on too tightly to anything we have gained, or been given, in this world. None of these things is lasting. *From now on, let those who have wives live as though they had none* (verse 29b). How this verse has been greatly abused over the years by men that have been unwilling to shoulder their proper responsibilities in marriage! Such behaviour cannot be what Paul means, as the opening verses of the chapter should be sufficient to show us. What, then, is he saying? Simply that those who are married recognize that it cannot be for ever; they do not build their whole lives on their marriage, because death will end it, and marriage is not part of the new creation, as Jesus taught in *Matt.* 22:29–30. It is a wonderful gift of God for *this* world, but therefore, by definition, transient.

In verses 30–31, the examples become more general, but all make the same point, expressed at the end of verse 31: that *the present form of this world is passing away*. Neither tears nor laughter are a permanent state; they are transient emotions in a transient world. We all love to be happy, but to build one's life solely on that basis is total self-centredness and would ultimately disqualify oneself from ever attaining such a goal. Things we own and use, trade and commerce, professional and social relationships, are all part of the world as created and given to us by God in his goodness, but they are not ours to keep and we are not to be engrossed by them. If we are, we shall end up worshipping and serving created things rather than the Creator, and to do so is to exchange the truth of God for a lie (*Rom.* 1:25). Christians are not to be absorbed by this world, because they know it has no permanence and can provide no lasting satisfaction. Applying this to the main theme of the chapter, we can say that the single Christian is not to become fretful, anxious or frustrated, because he or she is not yet married. We have been set free from the idolatry of sex and marriage, in order to use God's greatest gifts in the gospel to his glory. We can be free from concern because we are confident in the grace and goodness of God, which allows us not to be irresponsible towards others but to sit loose to this world and its values.

FREEDOM TO SERVE (verses 32–35)

Paul now pursues his rationale for the single person to stay single by showing how the gospel can be well served through such a lifestyle. *The unmarried man is anxious about the things of the Lord.* That is the freedom he has in his single state. His interests are not divided between how to please the Lord and how to please his wife (verse 34a). These two concerns are not automatically opposed to one another, of course, but the married man will sometimes have to prioritise his use of time, in one direction or the other, and the same is true for the married woman (verse 34). Unmarried Christians can devote their energies and time to the service of God without distractions. But is that how unmarried believers view things today? Is that how the state of singleness is used?

Because we live in a sexually idolatrous society, it is all too easy for young people especially, but single people of any age, to buy into the devil's lie that unless you are 'in a relationship', you cannot be a fully-rounded, fulfilled person. As a consequence, the pressure is on for young Christians to pair off into an exclusive relationship as early as they can, often with long-term disastrous results. Christians need to hear that they are not 'on the shelf' at 18, 21, 30 or any other age! There is no shelf to be on, if you are a Christian, only the will of a loving heavenly Father to be in. We need to encourage younger Christians to see the potential of giving some of the most energetic years of their life to the service of God, instead of drifting through a series of 'relationships' with the aim of getting married as soon as possible. Some will get married early, as God's '*charisma*' (gift) to them, but if that gift does not come, the alternative gift of singleness has great potential for gospel work. churches everywhere need the dedicated service of undistracted singles, who are not divided by other pressures and considerations.

Paul wants singles to use their gift, however long or short it may last, to *please the Lord* (verse 32) and *to be holy in body and spirit* (verse 34). That is why verse 35 emphasizes that Paul's considered judgement is not a strait-jacket to restrict freedom, but an open door *to promote good order and to secure your undivided devotion to the Lord.* In a context where the Corinthian opinion was being restrictive or prescriptive, Paul is not denigrating marriage to a second best, any more than he writes off singleness. He wants his readers to see the benefits of both states – each a gracious gift from God – and to use their passing opportunities for eternal profit.

FREEDOM TO DECIDE (VERSE 36–40)

This concluding paragraph poses some challenges for the translators. In a nutshell, the issue is whether the 'anyone' of verse 36 is a father (guardian) or a fiancé. If the betrothed strongly desires to marry, then, in such a case, it is no sin to marry! *He who marries his betrothed does right,* verse 38 affirms, *and he who refrains from marriage will do even better.* This preference is entirely at one with the views Paul has already expressed, namely that singleness gives greater opportunities for undistracted gospel service and that individuals should remain in the state in which they were called. But Paul adds that individuals have freedom to choose in these areas, and that either choice may be right. This is not a black and white, sin and obedience, choice. Individual responsibility and freedom mean that none of us has the right to 'lay down the law' for others in such matters. This is also the principle that governs the apostle's judgement about widows remarrying. A Christian widow is entirely at liberty to remarry, provided she marries a believer (verse 39). However, Paul's view again is that *she is happier if she remains as she is* (verse 40) for the reasons already explained. We can recognize how such a woman's rich experience of family life, combined with a single-minded devotion to the Lord, can equip her to be a wonderfully effective pastoral carer in her community. We have freedom in Christ and our choices, naturally, will vary. So, Christians are not to sit in judgement on one another, but to respect one another's liberty, within the sovereign will of God as revealed in Scripture. *You were bought at a price; do not become slaves of men* (verse 23). In other words, Paul is saying that we should enjoy our liberty to be Christ's slave, and in doing that, whether single or married, we shall find our true fulfilment.

22

Love Builds Up

¹Now concerning food offered to idols: we know that "all of us possess knowledge." This "knowledge" puffs up, but love builds up. ²If anyone imagines that he knows something, he does not yet know as he ought to know. ³But if anyone loves God, he is known by God.

⁴Therefore, as to the eating of food offered to idols, we know that "an idol has no real existence," and that "there is no God but one." ⁵For although there may be so-called gods in heaven or on earth – as indeed there are many "gods" and many "lords" – ⁶yet for us there is one God, the Father, from whom are all things and for whom we exist, and one Lord, Jesus Christ, through whom are all things and through whom we exist (1 Cor. 8:1–6).

The first issue dealt with in this new chapter and section may seem remote for many Christians today, at least for those in the west, but in many parts of the world it is as urgent now as it was in first-century Corinth. *Now concerning food offered to idols* (verse 1) indicates that Paul is answering another question already raised by his readers. Although his focus has changed from marriage and singleness to idolatrous sacrifices, these are both matters in which the proper exercise of Christian freedom is vital. This is why Paul, once he has noted his new heading, appears to digress from answering the question immediately and does not return to it until verse 4. But far from verses 2 and 3 being merely a digression, they state the most basic principle on which Paul's argument over the next few chapters will be based. They are therefore extremely important verses for our understanding and application of this whole section, where Paul continues his discussion of aspects of true Christian freedom.

KNOWLEDGE OR LOVE? (verses 1–3)

We know that all of us possess knowledge is Paul's opening reaction, presumably echoing the Corinthians' assertions that the way to deal with the issue was on the basis of what everybody 'knows'. In verse 4 we see the immediate point – *we know that an idol has no real existence*. Paul does not deny that. He has already described his readers as those who 'in every way ... w ere enriched ... in all kno wl- edge' (1:5). So the point is not to dispute what the Corinthians know about idols, but to make them aware of how they are using that 'knowledge'. For the real issue is that *"knowledge" puffs up, but love builds up*. And by introducing the idea of love into the discussion, Paul dramatically shifts the focus.

When we reflect on it, the point of verse 1 is clear, both in theory and experience. It is a commonplace to say that knowledge is power, but this is a worldly, not a spiritual, truism. Knowledge alone simply inflates its possessor, because it separates him out from those who do not know, and provides perceived advantages over others that he will be tempted to make use of to advance himself and to put others down. No Christian community is immune from this basic sinful stratagem. Indeed, Christians are sometimes dominated and side-tracked by a quest for ever more obscure and esoteric knowledge. They devour books dealing with the farther reaches of speculative theology, or accentuating the more unusual, even bizarre, sorts of spiritual experience, and then from their lofty citadels look down on 'the ignorant'. Everybody else is pigeon-holed according to their own 'test questions' and is usually accounted a miserable failure, by comparison, in the knowledge stakes. The knowledgeable person therefore becomes increasingly puffed up, remote, and superior; and, ultimately, increasingly dry, barren and loveless. Real Christ-likeness is seen in love – the full heart not the full head – for only love builds up.

We immediately have to introduce the caveat (as we did in 1:18–21) that Paul is not being anti-intellectual. We do require knowledge because God has revealed himself and the mysteries of his sovereign will in his Word. Ignorance is not a Christian virtue. But even our greatest knowledge is partial, as Paul will argue in 13:9, and it is therefore inadequate as the sole basis for determining Christian behaviour. Verses 2 and 3 help to make this clear. In any sphere of life, the really knowledgeable person knows how little he or she knows, and how much therefore he or she has yet to learn and discover. How much more must this be the case when the subject matter involved is the knowledge of God! *But if anyone loves God, he is known by God* (verse 3).

The problem with this verse is not its teaching, which is confirmed elsewhere in the New Testament. It is the teaching that we only come to love God because he takes the initiative in knowing us and in bringing us into a saving relationship with himself. The issue involved is the question as to why Paul suddenly seems to deflect off to this point and how it helps his present argument. In what sense is the man who loves 'known'? Perhaps it is that knowledge of God is relational and reciprocal; it exists not in the dimension of factual correctness, so much as that of loving inter-action. We only truly know God to the extent that we love him, and where that love exists, it itself is the evidence that we are known, or recognized, by God. To be known by God is to live in his love. The deeper point that Paul is making is that love is actually the only true way to know God, since love is the ultimate and eternal reality in God's universe. 'God is love' (*1 John* 4:8).

By way of application, we need to remind ourselves that the model of New Testament church life is not the university lecture room. Teaching is not an end in itself. Its purpose is to lead us to a deeper knowledge of God and so to a deeper love relationship with him. The divine being is not a collection of data to be examined or processed, but an infinite person to be loved and adored. Yet we so readily reduce the Bible to the level of a textbook, and maturity to mere learning of doctrine. However if a head full of knowledge is not governed by a heart full of love, all you have is a swollen head!

KNOWLEDGE AND TRUTH (verses 4–6)

In verse 4, Paul returns to the 'knowledge' on which the Corinthians were basing their behaviour, by making a foundational theological statement that *there is no God but one*. Everyone who knows the true and living God knows that idols have no real existence. All sorts of human creations, pseudo-deities, are dignified with the title of 'god' or 'lord' (verse 5), but they are merely the products of rebellious, sinful human imagination. They have no objective reality. *There is one God, the Father, from whom are all things and for whom we exist* (verse 6). This wonderful statement of healthy Christian realism underlines the self-revelatory knowledge that lies at the heart of Christian assurance. The Father is the only 'god' and Jesus is the only 'lord', in contrast to all the confusion of man-made religions. There is but *one Lord, Jesus Christ, through whom are all things and through whom we exist* (verse 6b). It is of supreme importance that the Lord Jesus is here bracketed with God, the Father, in the closest unity, making this one of the strongest assertions of his deity in the whole of Paul's writings. The Father is the originator of all creation and his Son is its agent and sustainer (see also *Col.* 1:15–17).

But also, we must not miss the application as to how we are to live. Christians live *for* the Father, *through* the Son. To do the Father's will is the ultimate purpose of all his creatures, as was supremely demonstrated in the earthly life and ministry of the Lord Jesus. See, for example, John 5:19–20, 6:38–40 and Hebrews 10:5–10. It was his perfect will of fulfilled obedience that was substituted for our rebellious wills in Christ's atoning death on the cross. That is why it is only possible for us to live for God *through* Christ, and the glory of the gospel is that the life of Christ is brought into our experience through the gracious ministry of the Holy Spirit, indwelling every believer.

All this means that the way in which the Corinthians were to deal with the problem of idolatrous sacrifices was for their lives to be patterned on the love of Christ. To deduce the fact that *an idol has no real existence*, from their knowledge that there is only one God, was correct, but to take the further step and claim that going to pagan temples to eat food offered to idols in sacrifice is harmless, because it is meaningless, is dangerous. For Christians to assert that their freedom, based on knowledge, must be exercised at all costs, irrespective of its effect on others, is to exalt knowledge above love. That is not the way of love and so cannot be the way of Christ. It is to such practical concerns that Paul's argument now turns.

23

The Exercise of Your Freedom

> *⁷However, not all possess this knowledge. But some, through former association with idols, eat food as really offered to an idol, and their conscience, being weak, is defiled. ⁸Food will not commend us to God. We are no worse off if we do not eat, and no better off if we do. ⁹But take care that this right of yours does not somehow become a stumbling block to the weak. ¹⁰For if anyone sees you who have knowledge eating in an idol's temple, will he not be encouraged, if his conscience is weak, to eat food offered to idols? ¹¹And so by your knowledge this weak person is destroyed, the brother for whom Christ died. ¹²Thus, sinning against your brothers and wounding their conscience when it is weak, you sin against Christ. ¹³Therefore, if food makes my brother stumble, I will never eat meat, lest I make my brother stumble* (1 Cor. 8:7–13).

In the second part of this chapter, Paul presents the case of a fellow-Christian whose *conscience is weak*, as the focus for his argument that love, rather than mere knowledge, is the criterion by which Christian behaviour should be determined. To err in this area may have the devastating consequences of destroying a brother for whom Christ died, and so sinning against Christ and his body.

THE WEAK BROTHER (verse 7–10)

However, not all possess this knowledge (verse 7a) is the turning point of the chapter. Clearly Paul is referring back to the facts outlined in verses 4–6 that there is only one God and that idols are the creation of the human imagination. One might imagine that this would be basic knowledge for every Christian, but there are degrees of knowing and for the young convert, as yet untaught and insecure, the example of older and more stable, experienced Christians often proves crucial. Verse 7 puts his readers into the shoes of such a person. He might have been recently delivered from paganism. Up to his conversion his whole life revolved around the pagan temples with their trade guilds, markets and social friendship groups. He would have been brought up never to question the reality of all this superstition. So it would hardly be surprising that *through former association with idols* (verse 7), the old ways of thinking often re-imposed themselves on his new mind-set and that long-held prejudices took time to eradicate. The same pattern is observable in new converts today.

Such believers were unable to separate the food from the idols to which it was offered. However much they 'knew', and had it reinforced by older Christians, that idols were nothing, just the lumps of stone or wood shaped by men, and that the food was only ordinary food, they could not shake off the pagan, demonic associations of the temples so easily. Paul recognizes that this is due to the state of *their conscience, being weak* (verse 7b). He does not dispute the fact, but neither does he condemn them for it. The weakness is explained by the next phrase – it *is defiled*. The meaning is that if such persons are coerced, or encouraged, into eating meat offered in pagan sacrifices, their consciences will convict them that they have drifted back into pagan ways of worship, and so denied the uniqueness of the Lord Jesus Christ and their submission to him. Paul's point is that no Christian should dare to compromise another Christian's conscience, by imposing their 'knowledge' on one whom they consider ignorant, or their 'strength' on one who is weak. The particular issue about food is comparatively trivial (verse 8) but the state of a Christian's conscience is not. The Corinthians need to recognize, therefore, that far from building up their weaker brothers and sisters in love, by urging them to neglect their scruples and eat the food offered to idols, they may in fact be destroying them. They are encouraging them to neglect, or silence, the witness of conscience.

This sobering possibility is more clearly spelled out in verse 9, where we are told that the exercise of God's good gift of freedom may be carried through in such a way as to *become a stumbling block to the weak*. They will not be made strong by insisting on the irrelevance of food (verse 8) or the non-existence of idols (verse 4). Paul agrees with both views, of course, 'knowing' that they are true, but he is determined to operate on the even more important basis of love. His primary concern is with his brother's spiritual well-being, not his own freedom. Verse 10 supposes a situation where someone whose *conscience is weak* sees *you who have knowledge eating in an idol's temple.* What will his reaction be, if he respects the more mature Christian as an example? Clearly, he will *be encouraged* to follow suit, but at the cost of his conscience. The subsequent process is one in which he learns to act against conscience, to follow flawed human models and effectively to harden his heart. It is a road to potential spiritual ruin.

Some of Paul's readers might have replied that all this was the weaker Christian's problem, not theirs, but Paul puts the ball firmly back in their court (verses 11–13). Such an attitude is the essence of worldliness. In the world, individuals continually fight for their freedom, at whatever cost, even if it damages others. Many of the armed conflicts of history have broken out for precisely this reason: Whose 'freedom' is to prevail? It is all about the imposition of power for personal advantage. But a Christian wants to use the God-given liberty of the new life in Christ to set others free to be their best for God. As we will discover in the powerful argument of chapter 12, we belong to one another because we belong to Christ. Membership of his body carries the inevitable consequence that we are members one of another. Indeed, the fellowship of love within the family of God is the greatest distinguishing mark of gospel reality and a quality that the pagan culture can never even begin to counterfeit. In this context, the key question has to do with how I use my freedom. Is it to build up my brother? These last three verses explain how corporate responsibility may well restrict private liberty.

THE DISASTER SCENARIO (verses 11–13)

It is important again here to realize that Paul is not denying, nor attacking, the two realities of knowledge and freedom that flow from the gospel. The problem is the self-centred use made of them by the Corinthians. Paul shows them the end of the road on which they are travelling in order to stop them in their tracks. The awful possibility is that *by your knowledge this weak person is destroyed, the brother for whom Christ died* (verse 11). The reference to the death of the cross immediately heightens the issue, and in two ways. Firstly, it reminds us that the church only exists because the Lord Jesus denied himself the freedom rights to which he was fully entitled, and chose instead to lay down his life, in loving self-sacrifice, in order to purchase the freedom of his people. To adopt the opposite pattern in our behaviour is to deny Christ and devalue his cross. But it also reminds us that a weaker brother is as equally precious to God as the strongest saint, since he too is saved at the same infinite cost – the death of God's one and only Son. To despise someone who is that valuable to God is to oppose Christ's values and purposes, and constitutes, therefore, not only *sinning against your brothers*, but even more alarmingly, Paul says, *you sin against Christ* (verse 12b). Whenever we sin against another member of Christ's body, the church, we sin against the head himself.

In the final verse, Paul applies these over-riding principles to the matter in hand, personalizing it to himself, in the first person singular, and thereby both bringing himself under the same authority, and also setting his readers an example, which the following chapter will expound. Since love, not knowledge, is Paul's governing principle, he is prepared to surrender his freedom, rather than to exercise it in such a way as to harm his brother (verse 13). If necessary, *I will never eat meat, lest I make my brother to stumble.* They are very strong words and imply a readiness to sacrifice freedom of choice that is rare even among mature believers. Perhaps we have not learned as deeply as Paul that sacrifice is always the characteristic by which love is recognized. That may explain why we choose 'knowledge' as the easier option. We don't have to deny ourselves; it is more likely to inflate our egos. But the way of love meant the way of the cross for our Lord, and it was the only path by which we could be set free. 'It is the way the Master went. Should not the servant tread it still?'

As the chapter ends, we come back to the great paradox of the Christian faith: that in God's Kingdom, the way up is down, and the route to self-fulfilment is by giving oneself away. We still find it hard to believe that in the weakness of Christ crucified the power of God is uniquely and savingly revealed. We accept it readily enough as a doctrinal proposition and it becomes part of our 'knowledge', but to live the crucified lifestyle is a much more deeply challenging option. It will mean that our choices are governed by the good of others and that our decisions are made on the basis of their spiritual well-being. Whether it is in the big things of life – marriage or single-ness, career, where to live – or in the smaller, almost unnoticed, choices of every day, Christ calls us to the radical discipleship which denies itself and picks up the cross to follow him, not out of duty but out of love. biblical spirituality is motivated entirely by love, because it is cross-shaped.

24

Am I Not Free?

¹Am I not free? Am I not an apostle? Have I not seen Jesus our Lord? Are not you my workmanship in the Lord? ²If to others I am not an apostle, at least I am to you, for you are the seal of my apostleship in the Lord.

³This is my defence to those who would examine me. ⁴Do we not have the right to eat and drink? ⁵Do we not have the right to take along a believing wife, as do the other apostles and the brothers of the Lord and Cephas? ⁶Or is it only Barnabas and I who have no right to refrain from working for a living? ⁷Who serves as a soldier at his own expense? Who plants a vineyard without eating any of its fruit? Or who tends a flock without getting some of the milk?

⁸Do I say these things on human authority? Does not the Law say the same? ⁹For it is written in the Law of Moses, "You shall not muzzle an ox when it treads out the grain." Is it for oxen that God is concerned? ¹⁰Does he not speak entirely for our sake? It was written for our sake, because the ploughman should plough in hope and the thresher thresh in hope of sharing in the crop. ¹¹If we have sown spiritual things among you, is it too much if we reap material things from you? ¹²If others share this rightful claim on you, do not we even more?

Nevertheless, we have not made use of this right, but we endure anything rather than put an obstacle in the way of the gospel of Christ. ¹³Do you not know that those who are employed in the temple service get their food from the temple, and those who serve at the altar share in the sacrificial offerings? ¹⁴In the same way, the Lord commanded that those who proclaim the gospel should get their living by the gospel (1 Cor. 9:1–14).

One of the most important principles of biblical interpretation is the setting of the text under consideration in its immediate context, within the argument of the whole book. There are some great chapters of Scripture – chapter 9 is one and chapter 13 another – that are often detached from their context and seem to float free, as self-contained entities. They are used in this way to extract important spiritual principles for a more general application, but are not always interpreted properly in the original context according to the author's original purpose. But 'a text out of its context can become a pretext'. We must therefore be always asking, 'Why does the writer say these particular things here, at this particular stage in his argument?' if we are to benefit fully from the Holy Spirit's intention.

The opening argument of chapter 9 is a case in point. It begins, *Am I not free?*, and continues, verse after verse, with a veritable avalanche of rhetorical questions, in which the apostle is exploring the nature of his Christian freedom within the context of his ministry. It is obviously valid to see this section as a discussion about the apostle and his rights; a discussion that has profound implications for the financial support of gospel work, on a much broader front. But we must not lose sight of the Corinthian argument, or switch off from the book's melodic line, which we have been trying to discern. Paul is certainly discussing the nature of Christian freedom, but not in the abstract. Having warned his readers to 'take care that this right of yours does not somehow become a stumbling block to the weak' (8:9), he now illustrates how this principle of loving, self-sacrificing service has governed all the decisions that he himself has made as to the circumstances of his own ministry – financial and otherwise. He is following in the spiritual footsteps of 'Jesus Christ and him crucified' (2:2), so that his freedom is always cross-shaped. Moreover, as the passage proceeds, we see that this is precisely what his Corinthian detractors are criticizing him for.

DEFINING THE ISSUE (verses 1–6)

There are no less than sixteen question marks in the first twelve verses of the ESV translation of this section. They do not express an uncertainty in Paul's teaching, so much as a building up, stone upon stone, of a towering argument in which he deals with the criticism of his ministry-style by some of the Corinthians. Earlier, in 4:3, he had asserted, 'With me it is a very small thing that I should be judged by you or by any human court', but clearly he was being judged by the supporters of other parties or leaders within the congregation, and now is the time to deal with the issue in more detail. The immediate trigger is 8:13 where Paul affirms his willingness to forego the freedom to eat meat at all, if the exercise of such freedom causes a brother to fall. This readiness to give up his personal rights for the gospel benefits of others has, we now learn, directed and animated his whole apostolic ministry.

As he begins his argument, it is precisely on his status as a true apostle of Christ that he focuses. Some in Corinth, presumably, were denying Paul this authoritative role and seeking therefore to undermine his influence. The *others* of verse 2 is perhaps a reference to them. If they were objecting to the radical, counter-cultural context of Paul's message and ministry, then the best way to oppose it would be to undermine his authority. This would cut off his authority to teach and invalidate his teaching at root. After all, they argued, he was not one of the original apostolic group, and he had been a monstrous persecutor of Christians. He had come very late on the scene, as an apostle of Christ, and perhaps had simply arrogated this authority to himself, so that his gospel extremism could be ignored and his apostolic claims rejected. Paul replies by referring to the two great marks of apostolic authenticity seen in himself.

Have I not seen Jesus our Lord? (verse 1) draws attention to the fact that the apostles (literally 'sent ones') received their personal commission directly from the risen Lord himself. They were the witnesses of his resurrection and had been commissioned to preach 'repentance and forgiveness of sins . . . in his name to all nations' (*Luke* 24:46–48). Paul's own life-changing conversion and commission on the Damascus road was a parallel experience to the apostles' encounter with the risen Lord (*Acts* 9:1–6). It was an equivalent visible meeting with Jesus our Lord in all his risen power and glory, and made Paul not one whit inferior to Peter, or John, or any other member of the original band, though he would gladly describe himself later as 'one untimely born . . . the least of the apostles' (15:8–9).

The other distinguishing mark of apostolic authenticity is highlighted in the next rhetorical question. *Are you not my workmanship in the Lord?* This is undeniable evidence of his apostleship. The apostolic commission was to preach the gospel to all the nations, and the very existence of the church in Corinth was proof positive of a divine enabling in Paul's ministry and a divine vindication accompanying it. This point has already been well made in 1:21 and 2:4–5. So, the Corinthians of all people cannot possibly deny Paul's apostolic authority. They would not exist without it, *for you are the seal of my apostleship in the Lord* (verse 2). Having established his apostleship by these two distinctive authentications, Paul now proceeds to cross-examine his critics, who, he sees, are only too keen to *examine me* (verse 3). He has successfully refuted their denial of his apostleship. He now begins to attack their criticisms of his life-style and behaviour.

To begin with, Paul establishes his rights as an apostle of Christ; rights that the Corinthians seemed quite ready to allow to all the other travelling messengers of the Lord Jesus. These focus on material support – *the right to eat and drink* (verse 4) and on the right to be accompanied by *a believing wife*, who would also be supported. This does not mean that Paul was married; it only means that such a right was generally recognized. What he questions is the situation in which he and Barnabas were being treated differently and had to *work for a living* (verse 6, NIV). Clearly there were no adequate grounds for such discrimination and Paul establishes that there is no reason why he should be denied these rights of support. He is an apostle and should be treated as such.

PRESENTING THE ARGUMENTS (verses 7–12a)

In this section, Paul confirms his legitimate rights even more cogently by the use of two supporting examples. The first comes from what he calls *human authority* (verse 8). It is the common experience of all human societies that work is rewarded by payment, whether in cash or in kind. The exertion of labour and the commitment of time, it is universally agreed, should be recognized and rewarded (verse 7). But the stronger argument comes in verse 8b. *Does not the Law say the same?* This matter is not a mere human arrangement and therefore, arguably, dispensable; it is, in fact, an unchanging principle of God's decree in the 'Torah'. Paul quotes Deuteronomy 25:4, *You shall not muzzle an ox when it treads out the grain.* The principle is clear. The ox, that is expending its labour to enable the farmer to thresh his crop, should be rewarded by being able to eat some of the product that its energy has produced.

But since this is part of the law of God, it is reflective of his unchanging character and concerns and so, verse 10 asserts, *Does he not speak entirely for our sake?* God *is* concerned about oxen, but not merely about oxen. The principle, when applied to a farmer and his harvest, is that the farmer's labour must be rewarded by a share in the end-product (verse 10b). But then Paul takes another step, from the material harvest to the spiritual harvest (verse 11), indicating that he has every right to share in that spiritual harvest; and to share, not simply in spiritual things, but in the material as well. *If we have sown spiritual things among you, is it too much if we reap material things from you?* Once again he has clearly established his right to full financial support. In fact, because he was the one who brought the gospel to the Corinthians, he ought to be their main priority and responsibility with respect to material help (verse 12). He has exactly the same divinely given authority as all the other apostles and exactly the same right as to material support. We are, therefore, set up and ready for the conclusion to be drawn. They should stop criticizing their apostle and support him gladly and generously as far as his material well-being is concerned.

But then, suddenly, by Paul's next words, his readers are totally wrong-footed!

DRAWING THE CONCLUSIONS (verses 12b–14)

The hammer blow falls in the middle of the verse, with the most unexpected of statements. *Nevertheless, we have not made use of this right.* In other words, Paul has neither asked for, nor been willing to accept, any financial support from the Corinthian congregation. Clearly this was a major cause of contention between them. We have already noted how conditioned the Corinthian believers were by their powerful, surrounding culture. As in our days, pagan culture valued everything in terms of money. The public speaker, or rhetorician, was the equivalent of today's media performer, where the highest monetary rewards flow to the most successful and most popular, though not necessarily the most talented, individuals. Paul insisted on not being paid and therefore had to work with his own hands at his trade of tent-making, which he learned as a young rabbi as part of his training. This meant that he was not wealthy and had none of the trappings of the successful public orator. In the world's eyes, therefore, he would not be worth listening to and his message would be as despised as his methodology.

Undoubtedly, this caused real offence to some of the Christians in Corinth, who wanted a much more culturally acceptable approach and a far less radical message than the gospel of the cross. This therefore is why Paul is being criticized. They see his approach as working against the gospel, in that no one who counted in Corinth was going to bother with a down-at-heel, renegade, Jewish, tent-making rabbi with his talk of a 'god' crucified in shame and utter weakness. What nonsense! And surely we can recognize the force of that sort of thinking. I recall a pastor in London who was turned out of the congregation that he had established by his faithful gospel preaching, when this sort of thinking came cascading into the church. If he was really a 'man of God', it was argued, he would be wearing a better suit, driving a better car, be more influential, popular, and wealthy. He was not prosperous, so they would no longer have him as their pastor. As measured by their acquisitive ambitions, he did not come up to the standard of a messenger from God. It is all very contemporary and very Corinthian.

However, the last sentence of verse 12 provides Paul's concluding and decisive thrust. *We endure anything rather than put an obstacle in the way of the gospel of Christ.* This explains why he would not yield an inch to the Corinthians' demands. There is something far more important than his perfectly legitimate rights, or the Corinthians' foolish and illegitimate compromise, and that is the gospel itself. This is a central gospel issue for Paul, because the primacy of the clear proclamation of the gospel and of its unhindered spread is the driving force of his whole life and ministry. Verses 13 and 14 not only reaffirm that the rights they want him to take up are not in themselves wrong, but also recognize that he is bucking the trend and swimming totally against the prevailing cultural and religious tide. Yet he remains adamant and unabashed. Whether it is the temple in Jerusalem, or the pagan temple of Corinth, the same principle is universally observed that *those who are employed in the temple service get their food from the temple.* The general principle is reinforced by the equivalent *command* from the Lord himself, applying it to *those who proclaim the gospel* (verse 14). But still Paul will not budge. He doesn't criticize others who do use their rights. There is no taking the moral high ground, or adopting a position of spiritual superiority. He just will not risk hindering the gospel in any way, and in the next section he will reveal his reasons, both principled and pragmatic.

25

All for the Sake of the Gospel

¹⁵But I have made no use of any of these rights, nor am I writing these things to secure any such provision. For I would rather die than have anyone deprive me of my ground for boasting. ¹⁶For if I preach the gospel, that gives me no ground for boasting. For necessity is laid upon me. Woe to me if I do not preach the gospel! ¹⁷For if I do this of my own will, I have a reward, but not of my own will, I am still entrusted with a stewardship. ¹⁸What then is my reward? That in my preaching I may present the gospel free of charge, so as not to make full use of my right in the gospel.

¹⁹For though I am free from all, I have made myself a servant to all, that I might win more of them. ²⁰To the Jews I became as a Jew, in order to win Jews. To those under the law I became as one under the law (though not being myself under the law) that I might win those under the law. ²¹To those outside the law I became as one outside the law (not being outside the law of God but under the law of Christ) that I might win those outside the law. ²²To the weak I became weak, that I might win the weak. I have become all things to all people, that by all means I might save some. ²³I do it all for the sake of the gospel, that I may share with them in its blessings (1 Cor. 9:15–23).

Chapter 9 began with that powerful and searching question: 'Am I not free?' Thus far, in answering that question, Paul has affirmed that the essence of his freedom lies in his ability to use it to deny himself, for the sake of the gospel. While he is perfectly free to use his 'right' to financial support as a gospel minister, he has elected to make use of his freedom by denying himself all this, because he fears that to use it could lead to a gross misunderstanding, which might actually undermine the progress of the gospel and so defeat his central purpose. There is more than mere pragmatism, however, to Paul's decision, as this present section now reveals.

The argument revolves around the apostle's two key personal convictions, strongly expressed and convincingly argued. *I have made no use of any of these rights* (verse 15) and *I have made myself a servant to all* (verse 19). Each of these reflects the cross-centred spirituality that has come to dominate all his decision-making and subsequent behaviour. There is an important point here, which we must not miss. Our tendency is to regard the gospel of Christ crucified simply as the way in to the Christian life, rather than recognizing that it is the way on in the Christian life, for it is the very essence of God's self-revelation. The cross is not just the key that opens the door to heaven, it is also the road by which we must travel through that door, and to the eternal realities. To grasp this will prevent us from simply reducing the gospel to a set of propositional truths that are to be believed, thereby producing a dry, cerebral faith. We should, rather, embrace its essentials as principles for our everyday living. Not only is the cross the glorious expression of God's grace by which our sin is covered and our redemption accomplished, it is also the shape of the application of that saving work in life and character. The apostle Peter draws the two aspects together and shows them to be theologically inseparable in 1 Peter 2:21–25. 'He himself bore our sins in his body on the tree, that we might die to sin and live for righteousness' (verse 24). But also, 'Christ also suffered for you, leaving you an example, so that you might follow in his steps' (verse 21).

GOSPEL SACRIFICE (verse 15–18)

In this paragraph, Paul explains the reasons that lay behind what the Corinthians probably saw as his wilful and stubborn refusal to exercise his right to their material support. The climax of his line of thought is expressed in verse 18, *that in my preaching I may present the gospel free of charge.* That, says the apostle, is his *reward*, rather than any financial or material benefits. We need to unpack his reasoning.

After insisting that all this is not some underhand subtlety by which he is actually hoping to squeeze money out of the Corinthians in spite of all his protestations, he identifies his free preaching of the gospel as his *boast*, which he would rather die than give up (verse 15). The next verse insists that it is not his preaching about which he boasts, *that gives me no ground for boasting. For necessity is laid upon me* (verse 16). Perhaps Paul is attempting to forestall criticism that might have accused him of some sort of inverted snobbery in that he separated himself from other gospel preachers by not being supported. He is not boasting about how 'spiritual' he has shown himself to be by deciding to be an unrewarded gospel preacher. On the contrary, he did not choose this life-style at all. He is under a divine compulsion to devote his life to the work of the gospel, and there can be no escape for him into any imaginable, let alone comfortable, alternative. *Woe to me if I do not preach the gospel!* In this he mirrors the compulsion of the Christ who *is* the gospel. Christ resolutely set his face, as a flint, to go to the cross in Jerusalem, and taught his disciples not only that the 'Son of man must suffer ... be killed, and after three days rise again' (*Mark* 8:31; 9:31; 10:33–34), but also that, 'if anyone would come after me, let him deny himself and take up his cross and follow me' (*Mark* 8:34–38). Paul has grasped that a life of gospel preaching is inseparable from a life of gospel sacrifice. How can an evangelist of the crucified Saviour do anything other than shoulder his own cross and follow him? The apostle therefore sees his self-denying sacrifice as expressing and demonstrating the very essence of the message of Christ crucified, and he will therefore allow no one to deprive him of that opportunity.

However, divine compulsion is not the whole story. There is also a voluntary ingredient in the apostle's response to the Master's commission. Choosing not to be disobedient, he both discharges his trust and also offers his labour, which, according to the principle of verses 7–12, should rightly generate its own reward. For Paul, freedom means not the right to command a salary, but the right to choose his own satisfaction, which for him is not in terms of positive material benefits, but in a much more gratifying reward. As he preaches the free gospel of the sacrificial love of Christ, he can offer it without cost, *so as not to make full use of my right in the gospel* (verse 18b). That is his greatest reward, because that is how he most closely follows in his Master's footsteps. And that explains why he would rather die than be deprived of his *boast*. Before we look at the implications for ourselves, we must turn to the second of Paul's great affirmations.

GOSPEL SERVANTHOOD (verses 19–23)

Once again the apostle returns to the fact of his freedom as a believer in Christ, which he nowhere down-values or underplays. He does so in order to take up the powerful imagery of slavery, which was so central an experience in the life of the Graeco-Roman first-century world. *Though I am free from all, I have made myself a servant* [or, a slave] *to all* (verse 19a). The stress is clearly on the voluntary nature of his sacrificial service, something that would occur only very rarely, if at all, in a slave's experience. Most slaves would be only too anxious to gain their freedom, if that were at all possible (7:21), but the paradox is that the gospel freedman is only too ready to commit himself as a slave *to all*. This would mean that there would be a limit-less potential demand for his services. It will be a totally consuming life-style, in that no slave has control over his own time and energy. Of course, Paul is using the phrase metaphorically; this is why he underlines the fact that actually he does not *belong* to anybody. It would be foolish, because impossible, to assume that a gospel worker is to be 100% at the beck and call of everybody twenty-four hours a day. No human being could live like that, particularly not Paul, who very clearly prioritised his time and strategised his ministry. But he does want his readers to feel the force of the metaphor and to see its implications by understanding its purpose – *that I might win more of them* (verse 19b).

In the next three verses, Paul spells out three specific examples of how his becoming the slave of others results in fruitful gospel work. The three examples identify different categories of people (within the composite *everyone* of verse 19) to whom he is committed. He begins with the Jews, whom he describes as *under the law* (verse 20). The apostle's slavery here consists of laying aside his freedoms and his rights so that the gospel might not be hindered by any unnecessary cultural differences. In this way he hopes to *win those under the law*. We have important examples, elsewhere in the New

Testament, of how this worked out in practice. When Paul wanted to take the young convert, Timothy, with himself and Silas, on a missionary journey, he 'circumcised him because of the Jews who were in those places, for they all knew that his father was a Greek' (*Acts* 16:3). Was that compromise? After all, this is the same Paul who could write that 'in Christ Jesus neither circumcision nor uncircumcision counts for anything' (*Gal.* 5:6) and again that 'neither circumcision counts for anything, nor uncircumcision, but a new creation' (*Gal.* 6:15). The answer must be negative, because the reason why Paul had Timothy circumcised was nothing whatsoever to do with the gospel *per se*, and everything to do with not causing needless offence to legalistic Jews, who otherwise might never have begun to listen to his message about their Messiah. Similarly, in Acts 21:26, we find him carefully observing the rules of Jewish purification at the Jerusalem temple, along with his companions, precisely to avoid needless offence, even though he knew that he did not need the temple and its rules to bring him to God. When preaching in the Jews' synagogues, Paul habitually used Old Testament arguments, examples and quotations, in order to prove the identity of the Lord Jesus as the Christ, to those who were in bondage to the law. Of course, he refused to return to that slavery and would never compromise the free grace of the gospel, but he was prepared to become their slave in all the areas of Jewish culture that were neutral with regard to the gospel, so as to win the Jews.

When dealing with Gentiles, *those outside the law* (verse 21), he followed the same principle. In all the neutral areas, he was prepared to accommodate himself to Gentile cultural thought and practice so as not to raise unnecessary barriers to the gospel. The book of Acts furnishes examples of this at the historic Council of Jerusalem (*Acts* 15:13–21) where it was agreed, 'that we should not trouble those of the Gentiles who turn to God' (verse 19). It was not necessary to follow Jewish rites and ceremonies, in order to be Christian. Similarly, when addressing the Areopagus in Athens, it was the cultural setting and thought-forms of the Gentiles that dictated Paul's presentation and applications of the good news. Since the Gentiles did not have the law, he did not use it with them, although this does not mean that he had become antinomian (lawless, or against the concept of law). The parenthesis of verse 21, here in

1 Corinthians 9, clearly explains that while the apostle no longer saw the law as a means of righteousness, he submitted to the authority of his Lord, Jesus Christ, and sought to live in obedience to his commands. Christians must always recognise the 'rubbish' of any supposed 'legalistic righteousness' (see *Phil.* 3:4–9), which is merely 'confidence in the flesh' and must be replaced by 'the righteousness from God that depends on faith'. But the needed balance to that is to remember the words of the Lord Jesus when he said, 'If you love me, you will keep my commandments' (*John* 14:15). Having made this distinction clear and ensuring that the word of Christ was in no way compromised, Paul was always prepared to adapt to Gentile culture, *that I might win those outside the law.*

But the third example seems a little unexpected. *To the weak, I became weak, that I might win the weak* (verse 22). Why should Paul introduce such an apparently insignificant category, after having been dealing with the two great people-groups of Jews and Gentiles? Is this not an anticlimax? In fact it is the opposite, because it returns us, at this point, to the main focus of the letter's argument. Suddenly, the weak brother of chapter 8, whose conscience could so easily be compromised by an unloving use of personal freedom, is back in the frame. Rather than asserting his freedom, the gospel slave is prepared to sacrifice his rights so as to win the over-scrupulous and not cause him to stumble. The principle of cross-shaped spirituality is therefore at the heart of all real ministry. *I have become all things to all people, that by all means I might save some* (verse 22b). That is the sign that the gospel proclaimed has truly gripped the heart of the messenger. The salvation of as many as possible becomes the dominating concern of both life and lip. As a result, all the personal, daily life-decisions are arrived at on a new basis: How will this affect the progress of the gospel? Will it make it easier or harder for others to hear, to believe and so to be saved? Verse 23 makes it very clear that the salvation of others is *the* supreme gospel blessing, both now and in eternity, which motivates that type of slavery seen so consistently in Paul's ministry, and that ultimately produces the harvest, in God's good time and will. The challenge for Paul's original readers was whether they were prepared to be sacrificial servants, following Christ's model and that of their apostle, or whether they would insist on the arrogance of knowledge and the power of freedom to live as they wanted, irrespective of the effect on others. The future of the gospel and of the authentic church in Corinth hung in that balance.

But what about us? The Corinthian context, with which we can so readily identify, only serves to heighten the contemporary nature of these challenging paragraphs. So often we also are tempted to write off such a testimony as apostolic extremism; necessary, perhaps, for Paul and the Early Church, but not appropriate for Christians today. To arrive at my life-decisions on the basis of how they will help or hinder the progress of the gospel may seem unnecessarily narrow and daunting. What if it would mean rearranging my career plans, reassessing my use of time, or revolutionizing my attitude to money? Supposing I might have to give up some things that I really want to do, or to buy, in order to give myself to a specific work of service? Supposing I chose whether or not to move home; where to live; whether or not to work full or part-time in paid employment; all on the basis of whether or not these decisions forwarded the cause of the gospel? How would I view that? With relief that it was Paul who was called to be an apostle and not myself?

Yet, is it not true that real Christianity not only declares but also lives out the lordship of Christ? The half-hearted, lukewarm variety is repulsive to God (*Rev.* 3:16), for reasons that are not hard to see. He did not send his only Son to die that agonizing death on the cross and to rescue us from sin and hell, in order to give us the luxury of being spare-time, amateur Christians. We are set free to choose. A young man may therefore decide, much as Paul did, not to pursue a well-paid career because Christ's love is compelling him to preach the gospel, at home or abroad. He is free to give up his rights (which are not wrongs!) to make that sacrifice for his crucified Lord. He will want to sit loose to his material blessings, to travel light, ready to receive and use God's good gifts, out of gratitude to the Giver, without being bound by them. A wife may sacrifice the time that she would otherwise spend with her husband in order to set him free to do God's work, or to pursue her own God-given ministry. She may sacrifice her own career to give her children a stable, loving secure family life and to bring them up to trust and serve her Lord as their own. She has the freedom to deny her rights for the sake of the gospel, 'to share in its blessings'.

The great principle of biblical evangelism is the building of bridges to people where they are, not the expectation for them to build bridges to us within our citadel churches. As congregations, we need to see how we can make proper concessions and not stand on our rights, so as to enable others to hear and believe. If we insist on their jumping through our (sometimes outdated) cultural hoops, a church may die within a generation. And while the Lord Jesus is committed to building *his* church, he does not promise its presence in any specific geographical location in any generation. That depends on how far his people are willing to become 'slaves to everyone', to win as many as possible. To bring it right down to earth, we need to ask, 'Whose slave am I, for the sake of the gospel?' God does not call us to be 'oddballs', as though the work of evangelism was like an alien invasion from another planet! He calls us to be adaptable to others and available to serve, to put ourselves out for those who do not yet know Christ, so that they may experience his love through us. This may involve us in not always doing things quite the way we would have chosen. But then the cross was not like that, was it? Perhaps the challenge to us today is to realize that we do not sufficiently share in the blessings of the gospel because we are not sufficiently committed to the sacrificial servanthood, which is the spiritual lifestyle of the cross.

26

A Crown That Will Last

²⁴Do you not know that in a race all the runners compete, but only one receives the prize? So run that you may obtain it. ²⁵Every athlete exercises self-control in all things. They do it to receive a perishable wreath, but we an imperishable. ²⁶So I do not run aimlessly; I do not box as one beating the air. ²⁷But I discipline my body and keep it under control, lest after preaching to others I myself should be disqualified.

¹I want you to know, brothers, that our fathers were all under the cloud, and all passed through the sea, ²and all were baptized into Moses in the cloud and in the sea, ³and all ate the same spiritual food, ⁴and all drank the same spiritual drink. For they drank from the spiritual Rock that followed them, and the Rock was Christ. ⁵Nevertheless, with most of them God was not pleased, for they were overthrown in the wilderness (1 Cor. 9:24–10:5).

As though to underline the point he had made in verse 21, about becoming as a Gentile to win the Gentiles, Paul now adopts another strongly Corinthian metaphor, that of the Greek games, and applies it to the gospel life-style he has been outlining. The victor's garland was not won without training, discipline and hard work. By contrast, Paul looks back to the generation of the children of Israel who experienced God's miraculous deliverance from Egypt in the exodus, but who failed to reach the land of promise, in spite of all God's blessings. The purpose of this section and of the next is to move from exhortation and motivation to warning, as Paul begins to apply his cross-centred principles to the church at Corinth, not as optional extras but as the very essence of godly living.

THE NECESSITY OF DISCIPLINE (verses 24–27)

It is always impressive to see the dedication of top-class athletes to their chosen discipline and event. Take, for example, the hundred metres sprinters. Can you imagine what it must be like to work through years of training, with all the self-denial and discipline involved, to come through all the trials and selection procedures, and eventually to be selected to represent your country at the Olympic Games? What if you were then to come last in the first heat and be eliminated, perhaps only a second slower than the eventual winner? It is all over so quickly! Up to four years' work, but all decided in 10 seconds. What makes them do it? *They do it*, says Paul, *to receive a perishable wreath that will not last* (verse 25). There may be many conflicting motives, but ask any athlete why they are at the games and they will tell you, 'I want to win the gold medal'. That is what explains the endless training schedules, the disciplined diet, the early nights and mornings. The end is clearly in view. It is undoubtedly a great moment when the athlete mounts the victor's podium, when their national anthem is played and the gold medal is hung around their neck, but after a year, or a decade or two, they will just be a name in a record book; the garland fades and the fame with it – it will not, cannot, last. It may be the greatest moment in that in-dividual's life, but nothing can preserve it forever. And if that is true for the winner, how much more for the losers? Remember that there is only one gold; for *only one receives the prize.*

Nevertheless, the discipline and determination of the athlete frequently puts to shame the half-hearted, casual nature of much Christian discipleship. *So run that you may obtain it*, Paul exhorts his readers. One traditional attitude to sporting competitions is that 'it matters not who won or lost, but how you played the game', but in the twenty-first century world where professional sport is very big business, it does matter, and so it should! It mattered also in first-century Greece. The exercise of *self-control* of verse 25 probably refers to the necessity for an athlete to train for ten months before being allowed to compete. The rules had to be kept and the course had to be run, if the crown was to be won. Anything that militated against the athlete being at peak fitness had to be rigorously excluded. The whole of life was geared to this single achievement. It is still true today that if you want to win gold, there is a price to pay. And it is this same attitude of dedication and determination at the heart of the Christian's spiritual life that Paul insists upon. He would not be satisfied by anything less.

But we do it to receive *an imperishable* wreath (verse 25b). Once again Paul surprises us by the contrast that he draws. We might expect him to motivate us to replicate the athlete's dedication, but it is the contrast in the rewards gained that provides his major thrust. The prize awaiting the dedicated Christian runner is so much greater, because it is eternal. With such an amazing potential reward in view, it would be the height of folly not to bother, to *run aimlessly* or to *box as one beating the air* (verse 26). That certainly would not win you a gold medal in the games, and therefore how could it be assumed that it would be sufficient for winning an eternal crown? However, the reward is not the only incentive. The glory of the heavenly reward is that it is available not just to one winner but to all the faithful servants of Christ, who make the prize their goal. The final motivation, in verse 27, is the example of Paul himself and the self-discipline exercised in his own apostolic ministry. He is painfully aware of the possibility of personal disqualification, even though he may have preached *to others*. The whole course has to be run and the issue is not decided until the finishing tape. There can be no let-up in self-discipline, or in keeping the rules, if the athlete is to complete the race successfully. *I discipline my body and keep it under control* is Paul's remedy for the danger of missing out on his reward by not finishing his course faithfully (verse 27). The prize he has in mind cannot be his salvation, for that is already his by God's gracious gift. He is thinking, rather, of the heavenly reward for faithful service, of which he has spoken already in 3:12–15 and 4:5.

These are stirring and profoundly challenging words, the more so when we consider how easy it is for individual believers and whole congregations to run aimlessly or shadow-box. Many churches are aimless. They drift on from one week to another, maintaining their programmes, 'keeping the doors open', but with very little gospel urgency and even less focus on eternity. They become dedicated to the preservation of the status quo, they settle into a comfortable rut and remain unchallenged and unchallengeable, as many a keen young pastor has found. We shall all inevitably drift into comfortable half-heartedness, unless we are actively running the race, putting the gospel first and bringing our lazy, self-indulgent bodies and our proud, selfish spirits under the daily challenge of Christ's radical authority. The only remedy for drift into ineffectiveness is forward movement for the sake of the gospel. We need often to be reminded that time is the only one of God's good gifts that is constantly decreasing. Every day the finishing line is nearer; what then are we doing with our lives? Paul's disciplined dedication in this chapter challenges us deeply. 'I have made no use of any of these rights' (verse 15). 'I have made myself a servant to all' (verse 19). 'That by all means I might save some' (verse 22). 'I do all for the sake of the gospel' (verse 23). 'They do it to receive a perishable wreath, but we an imperishable' (verse 25). Life is not a game; it's the real thing and has eternal implications:

> Only one life, it will soon be past.
> Only what's done for Jesus will last.

What better epitaph could any of us hope for than Paul's great motto, 'All for the sake of the gospel'? The wonderful thing is that everything *can* be 'for Jesus' if we are prepared to make Christ and his gospel the controlling factor of our lives. Whatever age or stage of life we may be at, there is not a Christian living that does not need to be running today in such a way as to obtain the prize. As Jim Elliot famously wrote, 'He is no fool who gives what he cannot keep, to gain what he cannot lose.'

THE PERILS OF PRESUMPTION (10:1–5)

As Paul moves his focus away from the athletic track to the history of Israel, and specifically to the exodus generation, he begins to tackle one of the biggest threats to perseverance that any Christian will face, namely, presumption. It is that mentality that imagines that we shall all muddle through in the end, because we always have done so throughout life. Our culture is full of it, whenever people are challenged to think about eternity. All roads must eventually lead to heaven, it is thought; that is, if heaven really exists. 'I like to think of grandpa in that great golf club in the sky', was a comment once put to me. 'Death is nothing at all; it's just like passing into another room next door.' But it is especially sad when Christians are infected by this virus of presumption and begin fondly to imagine that everything must be all right, no matter how they live, or whatever happens.

Chapter 10 shows us that the Christian life cannot be lived at half pace. The Victorian hymn asks whether we shall 'float to heaven on flowery beds of ease', and, to the credit of the hymn-writer, affirms that we shall not! But many Christians seem secretly to imagine that they can. Paul, however, always the realist and never succumbing to weak-eyed sentimentalism, asserts that if we are going to be people who persevere, it will only be because we are people who are not presumptuous. Such a danger is not only clearly Corinthian but pressingly contemporary.

The message of verses 1–5, therefore, is that merely external identification with God's work and purposes will never be enough. Paul refers to the people of Israel in the old covenant, and shows how their deficiencies should act as a warning to his readers about the perils of presumption. It is important to remind ourselves that in the context of the letter, the apostle is still dealing with the issue of food offered to idols. He accepts that strong Christians know that idols are really nothing, but that the real danger is that they may be led into an over-easy attitude to the whole thing. It seems that the Corinthians were saying, 'We don't need to worry about pagan festivals; we are safe because we're Christians. We know that idolatry is empty and meaningless and because we've been baptized and are regularly eating at the Lord's Supper, nothing can injure us. We can go to pagan temples and eat whatever we like – it won't have any effect upon us.' They have their twenty-first- century descendants who hold exactly the same view. There are people who rely on their baptism, or who think that their involvement in Christian activity, in Christian meetings, in listening to the Word of God preached, or in being at the Lord's Table, must guarantee that they will be acceptable to God in the end. They believe that these activities act as an 'immunization' against God's judgement. What Paul is demonstrating is that this is not the case. The sacraments of baptism and the Lord's Supper are signposts to Christ, but they are never vehicles to take us to the journey's end, and Paul is emphasizing this point. He does so, firstly, from the Old Testament, by comparing the experience of Israel in the Old Testament with that of the New Testament church.

In verses 1–2 he is concerned with baptism, and in verses 3–4 his reference is to feeding on Christ, which is what is symbolized by the communion service. When the Jews came out of Egypt they shared a common experience of salvation. Led by God in the pillar of cloud, they came to the Red Sea and by God's miraculous deliverance, they passed through on dry land. They were *all under the cloud and all passed through the sea, and all were baptized into Moses in the cloud and in the sea.* The analogy of baptism here is not primarily about getting wet. It is about taking on a new identity, sharing the destiny of the common leader. When they were baptized into Moses, they became people led by Moses, as God's agent. They were God's redeemed people, but Moses was God's man given to them to lead them. Through that experience of crossing the sea, they were initiated into their new life as God's covenant people. Similarly, baptism in the Christian's life experience stands, at the beginning of spiritual life, as an initiation. We only experience it once. It does not make anybody a Christian. It is not a vehicle to heaven, but it is a signpost, a symbol of having left the kingdom of darkness and entered the kingdom of light.

Following this great deliverance, God's people were miraculously sustained by him throughout their journey. Verses 3–4 speak of the *spiritual food* and *spiritual drink* that came in the form of the daily provision of manna and water from the rock. This provision for their physical life has its parallel in the Lord's Supper, which reminds us of the broken body and poured out blood of the Lord Jesus and which encourages us to feed on Christ in our hearts, by faith, with thanksgiving. What we experience physically as we take bread and wine into our physical bodies is a symbol or sign of what God is doing for us spiritually as he sustains us by the life that is in Jesus Christ alone. As the Old Testament Israelites drank the water from the rock and ate the manna day by day, God was feeding and refreshing them, so that they were learning that God himself was the only resource for all their needs, physical and spiritual, and that he was committed by covenant promises to them as his people. Nevertheless, *with most of them God was not pleased* (verse 5). Their great privileges did not guarantee security. That is what Paul wants his readers to understand. We can go through all the rites and privileges of God's grace and yet in the end still be under God's displeasure. We can be greatly favoured by his grace, but then become so presumptuous about it, so easy or careless in the way we respond to him that God is not pleased with us and has to stretch out his chastening hand upon us. *They were overthrown in the desert.* That generation did not actually reach the land of promise because of their unbelief, seen in their carelessness. Although they received huge privileges, they succumbed to the perils of presumption.

For us, as for them, the warning is very clear. It is a great thing to start to run the Christian race, to be brought out of Egypt by the blood of our Passover Lamb (5:7–8). But membership of God's covenant people carries obligations along with its massive privileges. To start well is good, but to finish well is even more important. Paul therefore wants the Corinthians to be under no illusions. In the gospel of Christ they have experienced even greater blessings than the Israelites, since they now know the reality of fellowship with Christ, of which the manna and the rock were only symbols, or foreshadowing types. For Christians to drift away from this reality of fellowship, through careless presumption, would be an even greater tragedy than Israel's. That is why the discipline of consistent daily running, with the prize in view, is so essential to every believer's well-being.

27

Examples and Warnings for Us

⁶Now these things took place as examples for us, that we might not desire evil as they did. ⁷Do not be idolaters as some of them were; as it is written, "The people sat down to eat and drink and rose up to play." ⁸We must not indulge in sexual immorality as some of them did, and twenty-three thousand fell in a single day. ⁹We must not put Christ to the test, as some of them did and were destroyed by serpents, ¹⁰nor grumble, as some of them did and were destroyed by the Destroyer. ¹¹Now these things happened to them as an example, but they were written down for our instruction, on whom the end of the ages has come.

¹²Therefore let anyone who thinks that he stands take heed lest he fall. ¹³No temptation has overtaken you that is not common to man. God is faithful, and he will not let you be tempted beyond your ability, but with the temptation he will also provide the way of escape, that you may be able to endure it (1 Cor. 10:6–13).

Complacency is a serious danger in any sphere of life. This is particularly the case when a set of actions is performed so often and with such regularity that the attention is easily disengaged. One thinks of the busy hospital nurse rushed off her feet with a multitude of demands, or the baggage X-ray machine controller at an international airport, where lives may depend on the fight against complacency. This is clearly Paul's view of the Corinthians' spiritual situation. Their super-spiritual tendencies seem to be lulling them into a false sense of security. They believed that they were standing firm; that as they exercised their gifts and developed their knowledge, they were not in the slightest danger (see verse 12). They might have appreciated the danger of Israel's situation in the Old Testament, but presumed that this was because Israel did not have all the blessings of the outpouring of the Spirit that were now enjoyed at Corinth. Paul's urgent message is that the danger is the same; that the symptoms of spiritual decline were all too visible in the congregation at Corinth; and that complacency was the root of the problem. We should not be at all surprised to find that his message is also a word in season to our own generation and to our own hearts (verse 6).

The divided heart is a well-documented biblical phenomenon and one with which we can be all too familiar in personal experience. The repentance with which we first respond to God's grace in the gospel is a change of mind, or heart, about God, about ourselves and about our broken relationship with him. We are accustomed, quite rightly, to emphasizing that the Greek word for repentance, *metanoia*, indicates a change of mind – not just an emotional response, which might prove to be nothing more than remorse. But there is an equivalent danger of over-intellectualising our response to the gospel, so that a re-adjustment of thinking is considered sufficient, without any radical change of character and behaviour. The Bible sees the issue as concerning the heart, which is the control-centre, not of the emotions merely (as in current western thinking) but of the whole life. The heart is where decisions are made, where priorities are established, and where the course of life is determined. The truth of God as it illuminates the mind, focuses the direction of life, stimulates the affections, and governs the behaviour. Psalm 86:11 expresses this memorably: 'Teach me your way, O Lord, and I will walk in your truth; give me an undivided heart, that I may fear your name.' The daily battle with the world, the flesh and the devil is largely centred on the reunification of the believer's heart to do God's will, rather than on its fragmentation by the many competing agendas for which our fallen, sinful nature still craves. The examples of the exodus generation of Israelites are therefore quoted by Paul *that we might not desire evil as they did* (verse 6).

Four different incidents now occupy the apostle's attention and are passed on to his readers as examples. *Do not be idolaters, as some of them were* (verse 7). This is where God's instructions to his redeemed people began and it is where we must start too. The first

[162]

of the ten great 'words', or commandments, is utterly uncom-promising. 'You shall have no other gods before me' (*Exod.* 20:3). The second follows immediately from it, as an inevitable conse-quence. 'You shall not make for yourself a carved image, or any likeness of anything that is in heaven above, or that is in the earth beneath, or that is in the water under the earth. You shall not bow down to them or serve them' (*Exod.* 20:4–5). However, we must always recall the foundation biblical truth that the law is given to redeemed people, not as a means by which to acquire grace (which is the fallacy of a works religion), but as a proper response to grace given. God's first words from the mountain are not commands but the statement, 'I am the LORD your God, who brought you out of the land of Egypt, out of the house of slavery' (*Exod.* 20:2). It is on the basis of his redemptive grace, experienced through the Passover deliverance, that the nation of Israel was constituted as God's people, his 'firstborn son' (*Exod.* 4:22), and brought to the mountain to learn how covenant people are to live in order to please their covenant Lord, and so enter into all the blessings of his covenant grace. Such free mercy, expressed in electing grace, marks out the people of God, whether under the old or the new covenant, as his distinctive possession, his priestly kingdom, his holy nation (see *Exod.* 19:4–5, *1 Pet.* 2:9–10, *Rev.* 1:5–6).

Single-hearted devotion to worship the covenant Lord must, therefore, be the only appropriate response to such covenant grace. But even while Moses was on the mountain receiving the written tablets of the spoken law, *the people sat down to eat and drink and rose up to play* (verse 7, quoting *Exod.* 32:6). The incident of the golden calf stands in biblical history as one of the most horrifying warnings of the fickle, unstable, treacherous nature of the sinful human heart. So soon after the deliverance through the sea, and so quickly after hearing the very voice of God declaring his law to them, the calf is constructed and the pagan orgies, learned in Egypt, betray the desires of their hearts. The example was well chosen also because of the issues of idol worship with which the Corinthian church is grappling. We have seen Paul declare that 'an idol has no real existence, and that there is no God but one,' (8:4), so that with regard to food offered to idols, 'we are no worse if we do not eat, and no better off if we do' (8:8b). What he is concerned about are those occasions when a weaker brother's conscience is offended by a stronger Christian's insensitive and unloving use of his knowledge and freedom (8:9–13). But he never condones participation in idolatrous worship (see 10:20), since it identifies them with all that is opposed to God's sovereign rule and rescuing grace. The nature of those objects upon which our hearts are focused is his great concern.

It has become almost a cliché to describe the gods and shrines that dominate our increasingly pagan western culture, in terms of materialistic values and desires. This is such a familiar truth that we often lose the sense of betrayal and treachery that should strike our consciences whenever we desert the living God for our own tawdry trinkets. Complacency is indeed the great danger. And it remains the stubborn and persistent truth that 'no one can serve two masters, for either he will hate the one and love the other, or he will be devoted to the one and despise the other. You cannot serve God and … ' (*Matt.* 6:24). The continuation of the text reads: 'money', or 'mammon', but there is a sense in which anything else which presumes to share the control-centre of our lives, alongside God, could be equally included there. We speak of our alternative priorities as indicative of our divided hearts, but the chilling diagnosis of the Lord Jesus is that the attempt to serve God and anything or anyone else actually reveals that we do not serve God at all. In reality, Jesus says, we hate and despise him. Pluralism is never a possibility in relationship with the living God of the Bible. We dare not fall into the complacency of the Israelites. This is not just a matter of avoiding the grosser manifestations of our godless culture in what we see or read, in the places we go, or in the leisure activities we embrace. It *is* that, but more than that. This verse demands that we look deeper at what is really driving our lives, our choices and our values. Where do we look to find fulfilment in life? What is the bottom line that we would never be willing to give up? What could we not live without? If there is any serious rival to God and the gospel then we may already have fallen into secret idolatry.

Sexual immorality – the second great snare – always seems to follow on the heels of idolatry in Scripture. *We must not indulge in sexual immorality, as some of them did* (verse 8) is Paul's serious warning, with reference to the twenty-three thousand who died, as recorded in the book of Numbers . The text there establishes the link with idolatry very specifically. The men of Israel indulged in sexual immorality with Moabite women, who 'invited the people to the sacrifices of their gods' (*Num.* 25:1–2). The logic is that if we will not worship God as our creator, we shall in the end worship ourselves, the creatures. Paul uses the same argument in Romans 1:18–32, where the same sequence of God-rejecting idolatry leading to immorality is exposed. Self-worship is the root of all immoral sexual behaviour, since its basic motivation is self-gratification and sexual pleasure. But God's opposition to such behaviour and his designation of it as 'evil' is grounded in his own character of unchanging faithfulness, revealed in his covenant commitment to Israel. You cannot worship the God of covenant faithfulness and be untrue to your marriage partner, or try, before marriage or outside of marriage, to snatch the sexual fulfilment that God has designed for the marriage covenant relationship alone. Such sins of the body reveal the disease of the heart. It is not set on God's will and God's way, but on the evil of self-centred rebellion. The appalling judgement suffered by thousands in the resulting plague, brought about by the Lord's anger (*Num.* 25:11), indicates how seriously God views such complacent indulgence.

Paul continues, *we must not put Christ to the test, as some of them did and were destroyed by serpents* (verse 9). Again we are taken back to the book of Numbers and to the incident of provocation recorded in chapter 21. Fired by impatience at the length of the wilderness journeyings and their boredom with the manna, graciously provided on a daily basis by the Lord to sustain them, 'the people spoke against God and against Moses, "Why have you brought us up out of Egypt to die in the wilderness? For there is no food and water, and we loathe this worthless food!" '(*Num.* 21:5). Even now, so many centuries later, we are shocked by the effrontery of their ingratitude, until we look at our own hearts. Their controversy with God caused them to reject and despise his great rescue plan, of which they were the daily beneficiaries. Often they revealed that their hearts were still set on Egypt and their recognition of God's preserving grace and generous provision became almost non-existent. Basically, they were rebelling against the circumstances and conditions God had decreed for them. As a consequence, they had to learn how far they could go in challenging God's goodness, and the plague of snakes was the resulting judgement. This is why the only remedy for them involved an act of faith and dependence on the part of each individual towards God. Such an act counteracted their previous faithless provocation and testing of the covenant Lord. When Moses was commanded to make a bronze snake and put it up on a pole, so that anyone who looked to it would live, this means of salvation was clearly designed to teach God's people the lesson of their total dependence on him for life itself. Complacency often leads us to imagine that we could do a better job in governing our lives than in submitting them to the Lord's all-wise providence, and so we provoke him, requiring him to prove his beneficence in ways that *we* choose and at the times that *we* want, with disastrous results.

We return again to the book of Numbers for the apostle's fourth example. This time we are in chapter 16, with the rebellion led by Korah, the Levite. *Nor grumble, as some of them did and were destroyed by the Destroyer* (verse 10). The discontent which led to Korah's presumptuous verbal attack on Moses and Aaron, in company with '250 chiefs of the congregation', found its roots in their own wilful pride and its resulting envy and resentment. It represented a very serious challenge to the authority of God's leaders, and beyond that to God himself who had chosen and appointed them. It even had a specious theological reason behind it. 'All in the congregation are holy, every one of them, and the LORD is among them. Why then do you exalt yourselves above the assembly of the LORD?' (*Num.* 16:3). But this only reveals the same heart disease, set on human pride. Grumbling is always a species of idolatry. It reveals a heart in rebellion against the way in which the sovereign God has ordered our circumstances, contradicting his providence and affirming, 'I know best.' In fact, the grumbler's heart is set on his own will, not on God's. Moses' rebuke of Korah and his company indicates that their ambition for the priesthood lay beneath their grumbling, but that 'it is against the LORD that you and all your company have gathered together' (verses 10–11). Although the ringleaders were destroyed by earthquake and fire, the people still continued to grumble, accusing Moses and Aaron of killing the LORD's people (*Num.* 16: 41) and thereby drawing upon themselves God's wrath, in the destroying angel and the resultant plague in which 14,700 died, before Aaron 'made atonement for the people. And he stood between the dead and the living' (verses 47–48).

These are truly terrifying examples of how God's chastening judgements must fall in wrath on those whose complacency leads them to rebel against his covenant mercy. Clearly, Paul is afraid that the carelessly triumphalist 'spirituality' of the Corinthian church may lead them to the same desperate experiences of covenant discipline. Nor can we distance ourselves one inch from these example-warnings. For what are the sins that continually beset the contemporary church? Idolatry; immorality; testing the Lord; and grumbling. They are right up there at the top of the list in all our congregations, because they are endemic in the fallen human heart. The greatest danger of all is the complacency that is happy to rely on an outward conformity to Christian norms, while the heart is, in reality, in a far country. 'This people draw near with their mouth and honour me with their lips, while their hearts are far from me' (*Isa.* 29:13).

These things happened to them as an example, but they were written down for our instruction (verse 11a). They were not written down for them, nor written merely as an interesting historical record. Biblical narrative was always written with a spiritual purpose, so that Paul is not at all embarrassed to affirm that God is speaking to *us* through the Old Testament text. Indeed, the whole revelation before the coming of Christ was designed to prepare for, and point to, God's final Word in his Son, and to instruct the international community of the New Covenant resulting from Christ's death and resurrection as to how we should now live *on whom the end of the ages has come* (verse 11b). Like the Corinthians, we too live in the 'last days', following Christ's ascension and preceding his return, and in which God's self-revelation is seen in all its fullness in Christ. Ours is therefore both the greater privilege and the greater responsibility. We all therefore need a dose of healthy, heavenly realism if we are to learn how to live for God in our generation.

Verse 12 is a warning that we can very easily be deluded. *Therefore let anyone who thinks that he stands take heed lest he fall.* Just as the leading athlete in a race must not relax or stumble if the prize is to be his, so we can never afford to relax our spiritual attention and grip in this world. That was Israel's great mistake, as we have seen. Having the blessings of God's covenanted grace in the promises and in the 'Torah' (law) they became complacent. God would never judge them as he judged the nations, they thought. The temple, the city of the great king, their relationship to God as his chosen people, all these came to be regarded as inviolable, right up until the moment when they were led away in exile. They made the fatal error of imagining that they could live as they pleased and still be secure in God's blessing, forgetting that his covenant involved curses as well as blessings (see, for example, *Deut.* 28).

New Testament Christians are equally prone to such errors. We too come to imagine somehow that the privileges of grace carry with them an immunity from God's chastening discipline. In Corinth, it showed in a dependence on externals, on excitement and culturally approved manifestations of power and wisdom, which in the end were carnal and worldly and not really spiritual at all. It is self-delusion to rely on anything that puts the focus upon us, rather than upon the Lord. The true Christian lives, moment by moment, in dependence upon, and by faith in, God alone. We are never off the spiritual life-support machine! Verse 12 indicates that those who imagine, because of previous experience or because of their long record of Christian service, that they are strong, independently of God, are particularly vulnerable.

However, verse 13 teaches us that while we can easily be deluded, we can also be delivered. This has become a famous verse, incorporated into many systems of Scripture memory verses, and obviously for very good reasons. But taken out of context it is often presented, without the warning ingredient, as an almost facile optimism. *No temptation has overtaken you that is not common to man* has sometimes been taken to mean that we should be encouraged by the fact that we are all 'in the same boat' and that the experience of testing is the lot of every Christian, so we do not need to be particularly bothered about it. But there is much more to it, in context, than that. We are being warned not to think that we are any different, in our human nature, or superior in ourselves to the Israelites whose bodies fell in the desert. The temptations that they faced, we face, and always will do in this world. We would be foolish to think otherwise, though complacency might encourage us to do so. Once again we are being warned to be active and watchful.

Yet there *is* great comfort in the verse, if we turn to God in our temptations and do not allow them to drive us from him. *God is faithful, and he will not let you be tempted beyond your ability.* The word 'faithful' is placed with emphasis at the beginning of the clause, and God's faithfulness can be our common experience just as much as temptation. While it is true that tests and trials are the means God uses to refine our faith, so that Oswald Sanders can even describe them as God's 'votes of confidence' in his people, it is also the case that he knows exactly how much his people can bear and will not allow us to be taken beyond breaking point. The hand that governs all our circumstances is that of a God who is totally faithful, so that while we have no ability to stand, or any security of foothold in and of ourselves, we can be completely confident in him. When the temptation is fierce, the help is increased. Moreover, at exactly the right moment, perhaps even at the point of greatest crisis, *he will also provide the way of escape, that you may be able to endure it* (verse 13b). The 'way of escape' is more than an exit sign. It is a word used of finding one's way through a mountain range, by sticking to the one pass and not deviating from that route. In similar vein, it speaks of disembarking from a boat after a perilous journey – a safe harbour and a deliverance from danger. We shall never be wrecked if our trust is in the God who is faithful. Whether therefore we have to go on bearing the heavy load of continuing bombardment, or whether the escape route suddenly opens up, the battle with temptations of every sort can be won, if our dependence is on God alone. There is always more grace and it is particularly available in time of need, matching the colours across the spectrum of our human dependence. That is the purpose of these exemplar warnings and that is the way to stand firm.

28

Flee from Idolatry

[14]Therefore, my beloved, flee from idolatry. [15]I speak as to sensible people; judge for yourselves what I say. [16]The cup of blessing that we bless, is it not a participation in the blood of Christ? The bread that we break, is it not a participation in the body of Christ? [17]Because there is one bread, we who are many are one body, for we all partake of the one bread.

[18]Consider the people of Israel: are not those who eat the sacrifices participants in the altar? [19]What do I imply then? That food offered to idols is anything, or that an idol is anything? [20]No, I imply that what pagans sacrifice they offer to demons and not to God. I do not want you to be participants with demons. [21]You cannot drink the cup of the Lord and the cup of demons. You cannot partake of the table of the Lord and the table of demons. [22]Shall we provoke the Lord to jealousy? Are we stronger than he? (1 Cor. 10:14–22).

For several years now, it has been popular for young Christians to wear a bracelet inscribed with the letters WWJD. They stand for the question, 'What would Jesus do?' and are designed, by their visibility, to encourage Christ's disciple to stop and think before they speak or act, so that they follow more conscientiously and faithfully in their Master's footsteps. This seems to me to be an excellent idea, provided we are honest enough to recognize that we need to be guided not by our own subjective assessment of Jesus' will (which will always be partial and biased) but by the authoritative revelation of his mind in Scripture. Many a sinner has imagined that Christ would condone his sin, pleading mitigating circumstances, when

Scripture would clearly deny it. But with that proviso, the question is a good one and we should all be asking it much more than we normally do.

The section that begins with *Therefore* in verse 14 really runs through to 11:1 and constitutes the climax of Paul's argument which began back at the start of chapter 8, 'Now concerning food offered to idols . . .'. When we reach the end of this section, which we shall study in two parts, we will have learnt what Jesus would do. His example is summed up in the two distinctives of Christian living in a non-Christian society: 'Do all to the glory of God' (verse 31), which is the equivalent of the first great commandment to love God with heart, soul, mind and strength. And, 'give no offence' (verse 32), matches the second great commandment to love our neighbours as ourselves. This is the example of Christ, and of Paul his apostle, that we also must follow if we are to live as authentic disciples in an alien culture.

In its immediate context, however, the command of verse 14, *Therefore, my beloved, flee from idolatry*, is the practical conclusion of the preceding warnings about the power and subtlety of temptation. God can be trusted to provide the way out, but can Paul's readers be trusted to take it? His appeal to them is personal and affectionate and this only increases rather than diminishes its strength. To 'flee' implies speed and a determination to put as much distance between you and what is after you as is possible. Idolatry is such an all-devouring monster that there can be no compromise solutions. Christian believers must have nothing to do with it. Doubtless the Corinthians would have agreed in principle, but they were blind, apparently, to the implications of their own actions. So Paul appeals to them not only as friends but also as *sensible people*, to *judge for yourselves what I say* (verse 15). He does not summon up his authority as an apostle to bludgeon their wills into submission. He knew that he had to win their minds to the truth otherwise their wills would not be sufficiently stirred up so as to change their behaviour. He therefore appeals to their wisdom to assess, approve, and agree with, his argument – an argument that hinged upon the view that to participate in a religious event is to identify with the object worshipped in the event.

[171]

PARTICIPATION IN GOD'S PROVISION (verses 14:18)

The two rhetorical questions of verse 16 make the point with great clarity. Paul begins where they are, in the Christian celebration of the Lord's Supper. Bread is broken as a sign of the body of Christ broken for his people. Wine is drunk in thanksgiving for the blood of Christ poured out for the forgiveness of sins. Paul's point is that this constitutes not just a remembrance but *a participation in the body of Christ*. The word used is *koinonia*, commonly translated 'fellowship' and referring to the sharing of the same values and concerns among partners in any enterprise. The experience of the one affects that of all the others. To eat the bread and drink the cup of blessing at the Lord's Table is not a meaningless act, but an expression of that faith in his atoning sacrifice that joins us to him, in saving grace. It expresses and deepens our dependence upon him for our salvation and encourages us to 'feed on him in our hearts, by faith, with thanksgiving'. The bread and wine remain unchanged, simply bread and wine, but the partakers, in eating and drinking, identify their interest and involvement in the death of Christ on their behalf, and so express, by faith, the saving union with Christ into which grace has brought them.

The fellowship does not end there, however, *Because there is one bread, we who are many are one body, for we all partake of the one bread* (verse 17). When we come to the Lord's Table we do so as his people, not as individuals in isolation. We join with all our fellow believers everywhere who make up the body of Christ. There is therefore a mutual participation. We are sharing a love-feast, a fellowship meal. Just as the one loaf broken into many parts is consumed piece by piece by the various participants, so we, coming as individuals, are reminded of our unity, and rather like the pieces of the loaf being re-assembled, we express our oneness in Christ's body through our personal union with him as our Head. We belong to one another because we each belong to him. That is the fellowship (*koinonia*) principle and explains why the Lord's Table can only be open to those who believe, who participate by faith in the benefits of his death.

This was not something revolutionary or new, appearing at the dawn of the gospel era. Verse 18 shows us that exactly the same principle applied in Old Testament Israel and was expressed in the fellowship of the sacrificial system. *Are not those who eat the sacrifices participants in the altar?* The animals offered according to the law of God were the means by which sinners could draw near to a holy God, in fellowship and acceptance. In some of the offerings, parts of the sacrifice were designated for the priests, other parts could be eaten by the worshippers. But in its significance this was no ordinary food like that which might be cooked at home. The participants knew that they were entering into fellowship with God, that their friendship with the covenant Lord was being sealed, just as many other expressions of trust and promise were confirmed in that culture, by eating a meal together. They also knew that they were affirming all that the altar and its sacrifices stood for as regards the character of God – his holiness, justice and grace.

PARTICIPATION IN PAGAN SACRIFICES (verses 19–21)

With the principle of participation now clearly established, Paul applies it to the vexed question of sacrifices offered to idols and meals in pagan temples. *What do I imply then? That food offered to idols is anything, or that an idol is anything?* (verse 19). Is he going back on his previous declarations in chapter 8 which made it abundantly clear that idols were nothing more than blocks of wood or stone, human artefacts? Of course not. The idol is nothing and means nothing in itself, but behind it there lurks something much more sinister – the devil and his demonic agents waiting to snare and destroy the unwary. For *what pagans sacrifice they offer to demons and not to God* (verse 20). Since idolatry is the prime expression of sinful man's refusal to worship and serve his Creator, the powers of evil are as inseparable from the pagan feasts as the grace of God is inseparable from the Lord's Supper. The participation principle applies, so that attending a pagan temple banquet and being involved in worship at an idol shrine, are not neutral activities. In fact they constitute fellowship with demons, which can never be acceptable for a believer (verse 20b). *You cannot drink the cup of the Lord and the cup of demons* (verse 21a). The two are diametrically opposite. This, then, is the force of the participation argument. For believers in Corinth to claim that their superior knowledge that an idol is nothing gives them freedom to visit pagan temples and take part in their feasts, and then equally to be at the Lord's Table participating in the benefits of Christ's death, is a logical impossibility. *You cannot partake of the table of the Lord and the table of demons* (verse 21b). How can we possibly live to the glory of God if we allow the slightest foothold to the devil, in any part of our lives?

Not only is this logically inconsistent and therefore intellectually foolish, but it will provoke God, as the Israelites did, and call out his wrath against such presumption. We have already been reminded of examples of his awesomely destructive power against which no human defences stand any chance at all. *Shall we provoke the Lord to jealousy? Are we stronger than he?* (verse 22). These are powerfully searching questions to ponder.

To apply this principle to our lives, in our very different cultural context, is not so difficult. At its most basic level it is a call to all who name Christ's name to have nothing to do with any of the manifestations of demonic activity with which our culture sadly abounds. Ouija boards, tarot cards, all forms of astrology, occult practices, fortune telling, séances, black magic, witchcraft and the multitudes of books, films and videos they spawn, all are to be fled from by those who share in the body of Christ. But although these are among the overtly demonic influences in our culture, which can be more easily identified and rejected, we need to be on our guard against the more subtle inroads of Satan's power in the other false gods of our time – the greed of gambling and materialism; the addictive power of sex, pornography, drink and drugs; the ruthless quest for power and status; all of which ruin millions of lives. If we cultivate any of these idol shrines, in the secret chambers of our hearts, how can we pretend to live to the glory of God? We have already recognized the danger of complacency, but here the equally serious and subtle challenge is the little-by-little drift of compromise.

29

Seeking the Good of Many

^{23}*"All things are lawful," but not all things are helpful. "All things are lawful," but not all things build up. ^{24}Let no one seek his own good, but the good of his neighbour. ^{25}Eat whatever is sold in the meat market without raising any question on the ground of conscience. ^{26}For "the earth is the Lord's, and the fullness thereof."*

^{27}*If one of the unbelievers invites you to dinner and you are disposed to go, eat whatever is set before you without raising any question on the ground of conscience. ^{28}But if someone says to you, "This has been offered in sacrifice," then do not eat it, for the sake of the one who informed you, and for the sake of conscience — ^{29}I do not mean your conscience, but his. For why should my liberty be determined by someone else's conscience? ^{30}If I partake with thankfulness, why am I denounced because of that for which I give thanks?*

^{31}*So, whether you eat or drink, or whatever you do, do all to the glory of God. ^{32}Give no offence to Jews or to Greeks or to the church of God, ^{33}just as I try to please everyone in everything I do, not seeking my own advantage, but that of many, that they may be saved. ^{1}Be imitators of me, as I am of Christ* (1 Cor. 10:23–11:1).

The concluding paragraphs of this section apply the second great principle of Christian distinctiveness in a pagan world, namely, that of love for our neighbour, expressed here as working for his good. At this point we return to the ongoing debate that Paul has been conducting with his readers about the responsible uses of the freedom they have in Christ and the gospel. He returns to what was probably one of the catchphrases of the freedom party in Corinth, *'All things are lawful for me'*. We have already seen Paul's reaction to this blanket justification in 6:12, namely that, whilst not challenging its assertion head-on, he has qualified its application with two other controlling criteria: Is it beneficial? Does it master me? This changes the debate from a focus on what can or cannot be done, to a discussion of the values and benefits of the choices freedom can legitimately make. In chapter 6, the argument was particularly related to sexual conduct, but here the focus is on careless idolatry, even perhaps deliberately open and provocative behaviour. Once again, Paul sees that freedom has become a virtue in itself so that to exercise it was all that seemed to matter, irrespective of the negative effects this was having on the consciences of others. This is to elevate a wrong priority, self-satisfaction, above God's dominant concern – that I should love my brother.

A MOST IMPORTANT PRINCIPLE (verses 23–30)

Paul picks up the Corinthians' motto, in order to repeat his original sanction and to add to it another that is especially relevant to the issue under review. *'All things are lawful'*, but not all things are helpful (verse 23a). He reminds his readers that it is much more important to ask the question, 'What's right with it?' than the more familiar, 'What's wrong with it?' To this he adds another, more social, consideration – *but not all things build up* (verse 23b). Does it build up? Clearly, the apostle has not only the individual believer's own edification in view, but also that of his fellow Christians within the local congregation at Corinth. The next verse stresses the point. *Let no one seek his own good, but the good of his neighbour* (verse 24). This is the distinctive use of his freedom that marks the Christian's life-style as different from that of the world around him. Each of our lives impacts many other lives around us, for good or ill. Conventional human wisdom instructs us to put our own good first. 'Look after number one,' we tell ourselves, 'because nobody else will.' From such an attitude springs all the stresses and breakdowns of human relationships, at work, in the home, and even in the church. If we seek our own good we shall treat other people as means to that end, pawns, cogs in the machine, backs on which to climb. To seek the good of others is totally revolutionary. It requires me to love them more than I love myself and it is thoroughly and essentially Christ-like. To imagine that I can cultivate a personal relationship with Christ, quite apart from my fellow-Christians, enjoying my freedom, pursuing my own godliness in an hermetically-sealed environment, detached from others in the body with all their pressing needs, is total fantasy. Therefore, whenever that sort of thinking creeps into our own attitudes, we need to be ruthless in its exposure and rejection.

But how does this most important principle work in the area of food sacrificed to idols? Paul now comes to summarize and sum up his argument. In verses 25–27, he emphasizes one aspect of the principle. A practical instruction is given. *Eat whatever is sold in the meat market without raising any question on the ground of conscience.* This indicates that a Christian is not to be involved in detailed research over such matters, to try to uncover any suspicion of evil. In a fallen world it will always be there, usually in large measure, but such an attitude will tend to make the investigator increasingly negative in attitude to both the people and the things of the world around him. Biblical theology takes up a different and much more positive standpoint, as the quotation from Psalm 24:1 makes clear. *For 'the earth is the Lord's, and the fullness thereof'* (verse 26). This reminds us of the important strand of world-affirming thankfulness in Paul's world-view, rather than the world-negating criticism into which so many Christians seem to fall. We also need this corrective. As we delight in God, we delight also in the wonder, beauty and variety of the world that is his handiwork, expressive of its Creator's nature and character. It is entirely appropriate for Christians to be alive to all that is good in God's world and to be able to be at home in any part of it. We rejoice in the myriad diversity of human achievement, in which the Creator's power and ingenuity are revealed in spite of the taint of human pride and rebellion.

Such Christians are neither afraid to mix freely in the company of unbelievers, nor to share with them the good things of God's creation that he has provided for the whole human race. They are not always pulling out of social contacts because of their own scruples, nor are they fastidious to the point of seeking to unearth everything that is contrary to God's best purposes in the unbeliever's life-style. *If one of the unbelievers invites you to dinner and you are disposed to go, eat whatever is set before you without raising any question on the ground of conscience* (verse 27). This is the necessary apostolic justification for Christians to be socially involved in normal human ways within our society; playing our part, seeking to be salt and light, and bearing our witness to Christ. One of the reasons why the gospel is not penetrating our culture, as we would wish, is that Christians are not sufficiently involved in it. We have somehow opted for the preservation of our own fragile holiness in isolation from the world, so that many of us have comparatively few non-Christian friends, and even lack the confidence to go out and make them. It is hardly surprising that such negativism and detachment have led many of the older generation to think of Christianity primarily as a list of prohibitions. I, for one, rejoice that many Christians of the younger generation are much more at ease with the company of their unbelieving contemporaries and are therefore more able than their parents were, or are, to take the gospel out into the world and meet unbelievers on their own ground.

But there is another side too, as verse 28 makes clear. When the Corinthian Christian visits the home of his unbelieving friend or colleague for a meal and is specifically informed, *'This has been offered in sacrifice'*, then the whole scenario is changed. Even though he himself is fully convinced that 'an idol is nothing', he must not eat the food, since his participation would be at best ambiguous, and would actually contradict and compromise his witness to the one true God and the uniqueness of Jesus Christ as Lord. Politely, but firmly, he must refuse the food, so as to show that he does not knowingly and willingly have any participation in, or fellowship with, idols. As Paul makes clear, this is *for the sake of conscience – I do not mean your conscience, but his* (verse 29). The point is clear. Such a refusal is, in fact, an act of love towards his pagan host. It makes clear to him how distinctively different the Christian gospel is, with its exclusive devotion to Christ, in comparison to all expressions of man-made religious substitutes. By taking this clear stand, once the reality is explained to the unbelieving friend, the Christian will be true to his own convictions. He will be challenging his friend with the exclusive claims of Christ, and, if he is being observed, he will not be risking harm to a weaker brother's conscience.

It is the unbeliever's response that governs the two concluding questions that Paul poses in verses 29 and 30. What is the advantage of using my freedom (to eat food offered to idols, provided it is not in a pagan temple) in such a way that another person's conscience judges and condemns my action? The unbeliever might well conclude, from what he sees as the Christian's inconsistency, that Christianity is no different from any other religious system; that it can be used when convenient and disposed of in adverse circumstances. Even if the meal is enjoyed with thanksgiving to the true God, rather than any recognition of the idol, there is still the very present danger that the unbeliever will denounce the Christian for his compromise and double standards. That can only serve to hinder the progress of the gospel and Paul has already taught the foundation principle that he would rather 'put up with anything', including the denial of his freedom and rights than for the gospel to be impeded (see 9:12–23). So, it is better not to partake at all in the meal than for an act of freedom and thanksgiving to be denounced as hypocrisy (verse 30). The force of the argument still pertains to our own witness today, the clarity of which can so easily be obscured by compromise, even if that compromise, as is so often the case, is due to a fear of causing offence.

A MOST SIGNIFICANT APPLICATION (10:31–11:1)

The '*So*', or 'Therefore', at the beginning of verse 31 alerts us to the fact that the argument is about to be summarized, and Paul does this with immense clarity and challenge. The first principle, which governs everything else: eating, drinking, abstaining – or indeed any other area of our behaviour – is stated as a command. *Do all for the glory of God* (verse 31). That is our first allegiance and responsibility in that the chief end of man is to glorify God, and from this obligation and privilege no area of life is to be excluded. Such love for God must issue also in love for our neighbour, therefore Paul commands, *Give no offence* (verse 32a). The addition of the three categories, *to Jews or to Greeks or to the church of God*, is designed to show how all-inclusive the instruction is. No category of person among whom Paul ministered was excluded. We are revisiting the explanation in 9:20–22 of how he made himself 'a servant to all, that I might win more of them'. This includes not only the pagan Corinthians but also religious Jews and weaker Christian brothers. All are to be treated with the same love and respect.

At first sight, the opening comment of verse 33 might seem strangely at odds with the uncompromising convictions we normally associate with the apostle. *Just as I try to please everyone in everything*, might sound a bit weak, even vacillating. We all know people who are so keen to please that they seem to be blown around by every breeze. In being attentive to everybody else's whims they seem as a consequence to lack any kind of backbone. One could hardly accuse Paul of modelling, or advocating, that sort of indecision. So what does he mean? The clue, again, has been given us already, in 9:22. 'I have become all things to all men so that by all possible means I might save some.' It is exactly the same principle here. *Not seeking my own advantage, but that of many, that they may be saved* (verse 33b). Because the salvation of many others is Paul's driving motivation, his own good will always be subordinate to theirs. He will use his freedom to deny himself the rights which are freely his if that means that others will come to be saved, through faith in Christ crucified. Because his own good, in terms of comfort, status, or any other personal goal, is not on the agenda, his own behaviour is set free to serve others, to please them in any way that does not compromise the gospel so as to win them to Christ. That is the life-style of love, kindled by the gospel, which, in turn, communicates the reality of the gospel. It is the reality-test of whether we do in fact love our neighbour and whether therefore we truly love God. By nature we say, 'Why should I not do what I want?' But by grace we say, 'How can I serve so that you may be saved?'

Where did Paul discover such an extraordinary reversal of his pre-Christian attitude? How could he live in such a radically different way? The answer began on the road to Damascus, but in its simplest terms is summarized for us here. *Be imitators of me, as I am of Christ* (11:1). Paul is a great model of both gospel ministry and committed Christian discipleship, but only because he himself is following so closely in the footsteps of the Lord Jesus.

At this point all that we have previously learnt from this letter as regards true spirituality being governed by the cross, comes powerfully to the fore. The example of Christ is one of self-sacrifice through suffering, even to the death of the cross. That was the only way by which his amazing grace and love could work for the eternal good of a lost world, so that we might be saved. This is the explanation, as we have seen, of why Paul could write, 'I decided to know nothing among you except Jesus Christ and him crucified' (2:2). Moreover, it exposes again the loveless arrogance and puffed-up 'knowledge' of these Corinthian Christians who insisted on the priority of their own freedom and their own super-spiritual gifts and experiences, rather than the humble servant-heart that carries any cross in order to win someone else to Jesus. The gulf between the two spiritualities is very wide, but there is no doubt as to where Paul stood – he was alongside the Lord Jesus himself. The challenge to our own comfort zones and easy-going, part-time Christian discipleship is profound, is it not? It is the greatest joy and privilege in all the world to be able to say from the heart, 'Be imitators ... of Christ.'

Horatius Bonar's urgent, penetrating verses capture it so well:

> Go, labour on; spend and be spent;
>   Thy joy to do the Father's will.
> It is the way the Master went
>   Should not the servant tread it still?
>
> Go, labour on, it's not for nought;
>   Thy earthly toil is heavenly gain.
> Men love thee, heed thee, praise thee not.
>   The Master praises – what are men?

30

Everything Comes from God

²Now I commend you because you remember me in everything and maintain the traditions even as I delivered them to you. ³But I want you to understand that the head of every man is Christ, the head of a wife is her husband, and the head of Christ is God. ⁴Every man who prays or prophesies with his head covered dishonours his head, ⁵but every wife who prays or prophesies with her head uncovered dishonours her head – it is the same as if her head were shaven. ⁶For if a wife will not cover her head, then she should cut her hair short. But since it is disgraceful for a wife to cut off her hair or shave her head, let her cover her head. ⁷For a man ought not to cover his head, since he is the image and glory of God, but woman is the glory of man. ⁸For man was not made from woman, but woman from man. ⁹Neither was man created for woman, but woman for man. ¹⁰That is why a wife ought to have a symbol of authority on her head, because of the angels.

¹¹Nevertheless, in the Lord woman is not independent of man nor man of woman; ¹²for as woman was made from man, so man is now born of woman. And all things are from God. ¹³Judge for yourselves: is it proper for a wife to pray to God with her head uncovered? ¹⁴Does not nature itself teach you that if a man wears long hair it is a disgrace for him, ¹⁵but if a woman has long hair, it is her glory? For her hair is given to her for a covering. ¹⁶If anyone is inclined to be contentious, we have no such practice, nor do the churches of God (1 Cor. 11:2–16).

There are two major difficulties frequently encountered in Bible study. Some passages are hard to understand, and so engage the mind at full stretch as we try to work out their meaning. Other passages are hard to accept, and so engage the will at full stretch as we try to respond to them in obedience. But this passage comes into both categories, so that as we approach it we need to do so in humility and dependence on God, expressed in prayer, that he will be pleased to make its message clear and plain to us, and give us grace to put it into practice.

At its most superficial level the passage has been used often to exhort Christian women to wear a head covering in worship, or even in private prayer. I still remember, vividly, hearing a church elder using the passage in this way and informing the sisters that 'a piece of greaseproof paper is quite adequate'. But is that really the burden of these verses? The determination with which they have been attacked and rejected, both by the Christian feminist lobby and by liberal Bible commentators, seems to indicate that there is much more at stake here – and so there is, indeed.

Given the letter's context, Paul's opening remarks in verse 2 are, perhaps, surprisingly positive. Having exhorted his readers, in verse 1, to follow Christ's example, he does not want them to think that he is implying that they do not wish to do so, or that they are resistant to his apostolic teaching. On the contrary, he begins on a note of praise, commending them because they had remembered what he had taught them when he first established the church at Corinth. This is demonstrated by the fact that they are continuing to hold on to the instructions (or traditions) that he delivered to them. It is on that basis, therefore, that Paul now wants them to deepen and increase their understanding, or as the opening phrase of verse 3 puts it – *But I want you to understand.* There are implications of the gospel's teaching that they may not yet have grasped, and ignorance of them was resulting in malpractice in their congregation. This is what the apostle now sets out to correct. It all revolves around the concept of headship.

1. HEADSHIP EXPLAINED (verses 3–6)

Paul's exposition begins with a very clear statement of the foundation principle on which his corrective argument will be based. *The head of every man is Christ, the head of a wife is her husband, and the head of*

Christ is God (verse 3). Clearly, there is a chain of relationships being explored, in which one person is related to another by the concept of headship: God to Christ, Christ to man, and man to woman. Our understanding of these verses will depend, therefore, on what this concept means, and about this there is considerable debate. The Greek word *kephate* means firstly the physical head (as of a body); secondly, and metaphorically, a person in authority (as in the head of state, or of a school); and thirdly, and even more metaphorically, a source or origin (as in the head of a river). There is evidence for the use of all three meanings in first-century literature.

Principles of biblical interpretation teach us that words must be interpreted within their own context, both in the book of which they are a part and in the wider context of the author's other biblical writings. Wider still, their context in the whole Bible must be considered, since Scripture interprets Scripture. Thus, Bible words have Bible meanings. They must also be interpreted in a way that is consistent, theologically and practically, with the overall teaching of Scripture. Divine authorship predisposes us to look for unity, not contradiction, in the Bible. Applying these principles, we can then work out what meaning is intended in any specific context.

Here in 1 Corinthians, Paul is clearly using one of the two metaphorical meanings. If the word 'head' is understood as meaning an 'origin' or 'source', then, God would be the 'source' of Christ, when he sent the incarnate Son to be the Saviour of the world; Christ is the 'source' of man, both as Creator and Saviour; man is the 'source' of woman, in the sense of Genesis 2:22–27, where woman is said to be 'taken from the man'. There are difficulties with this interpretation, however. It seems to ignore the fact that Christ is the 'source' of woman, as well as man, since they were both created in God's image, in equality (*Gen.* 1:27). Also, it contradicts the emphasis in Genesis, supported also in the narrative of the Fall, that the order of Creation suggests a more hierarchical chain of responsibility (God-man-woman).

The much more common interpretation, throughout church history, has been to view the verse as teaching a relationship of authority/responsibility in the context of headship. This is not to be understood as a matter of inherent superiority, so much as one of differing functions. A similar situation exists within the Persons of the Holy Trinity. There is an equality of the three Persons within the Trinity but it is an equality that allows for the role of the Son in his work of salvation to be subordinate to that of the Father. Paul will in fact teach this very point later in the letter (see 15:28). This is certainly a more consistently biblical interpretation of headship than the suggestion that Christ originated from, or found his source in, the Father, in that there never was a time when the Son was not (see *John* 1:1). This interpretation is further supported by the apostle's use of the term 'head' in the famous passage on marriage in Ephesians 5. There he states that, 'the husband is the head of the wife even as Christ is the head of the church, his body, and is himself its Saviour' (*Eph.* 5:23). That authority of Christ was revealed in the self-giving love that led him to give himself up for the church, on the cross, and calls forth the submission of his people to him as Lord (*Eph.* 5:24–25). This is then declared to be the pattern for a husband's 'headship' relationship with his wife, the authority of loving responsibility, since Christ is not merely the source of the church, but also its Lord.

With this principle established, Paul, in verse 4, begins to comment upon the aberrant practices that existed in the congregation at Corinth. He starts with a general application. There is a distinction between the sexes that should be exemplified in public worship. A man should not pray or prophesy (i.e. vocalize in worship) *with his head covered*, or literally 'with the head down'. Here, the apostle is possibly making use of wordplay. Such behaviour *dishonours his head*, that is, in terms of verse 3, dishonours Christ, the head of every man, rather than dishonouring the individual's physical head. The next verse states the opposite, with regard to *every wife*. For a woman to pray or prophesy *with her head uncovered dishonours her head*, that is her husband. The theological justification for this has to wait until verse 7, but at this point Paul is concerned to affirm the normal, common practice and to alert his readers to the contentious nature of any deviations from it.

It is probably for that reason that he develops the concept of dishonour, or shame and disgrace, at the end of verse 5. *It is the same as if her head were shaven*. To have one's head shaved was clearly a shameful thing for a woman to have to suffer, as verse 6 makes clear, but the uncovered head is equivalent to the cropped or shaven head, and equally disgraceful. At this point, we need to enquire as to the nature of the 'covering', and here again there are different interpretations. Indeed, it is easier to determine its significance than its nature. Verse 10 will describe it as *a symbol of authority*, that is, the authority or headship to which the woman submits. Its cultural significance, therefore, represents the submission of a godly woman to the male leadership of the congregation, or of a godly wife to the headship of her husband. Its absence should well be interpreted as a rebellion against that situation, in contrast to the mistaken view that was probably present at Corinth, namely, that it was a further privilege of the believer's gospel freedom. The only reference to the nature of the covering is found in verse 15, where it is defined, not as a veil, or a hat, but in terms of the woman's own long hair. This explains why the NIV offers an alternative translation of verses 4 to 7 in its footnotes, with 'long hair' instead of 'covered', and 'shorn' or 'short hair' instead of 'uncovered'. There is an argument, though with apparently little conclusive evidence, that a cropped or shaved head indicated that the woman was an adulteress or a prostitute, so that Christian 'freedom' to appear in this unorthodox way would bring the gospel and its followers into disrepute. The only Old Testament reference that would help us here certainly indicates something of this sort. In Numbers 5:18, a woman suspected of adultery had to appear before the priest with her long hair loosed, and the terminology in the Greek version of the Old Testament text (the Septuagint) is exactly the same as that used here. Perhaps Paul is asking, not for a veil or hat, but for the long hair to be worn up, on the head, as a sign of living under her husband's authority, as was the custom in that culture for all respectable women.

This opening section affirms a role for women in the congregation, both in prayer and prophesying, which is neither restricted nor forbidden. The very fact that it was happening at all is a mark of the new found freedom these women now enjoyed in Christ. But these legitimate activities must not obscure the differentiation of the roles of men and women that God has built into his creation order. The structures of verse 3 must still be observed, and if gospel freedom is being used to obscure or overturn these norms, then it is being abused. There must be no usurpation of the other sex's role, either in appearance or activity.

2. HEADSHIP EXPLORED (verses 7–10)

Having made the practical application plain, the apostle now supports and bolsters his argument theologically, so as to convince the doubters and challenge the deviants. In order to do this, he argues, not primarily from the cultural norms of the first-century Græco-Roman world, but from creation itself (verse 8). Man is *the image and glory of God* (verse 7) – an allusion to the passage in Genesis 1:26–28 where both man and woman are described as being created in God's image. But the second term 'glory' is governed more by the language of Genesis 2, where we learn that man was created first and reflected God's glory in his role as the vice-regent of creation; he was God's representative and 'head' of the created order. While the woman shares that role equally and fully as a human being, nevertheless in her relationship to man there was a differentiation, which was indicated by the two facts of her being created from the man, and being created for the man as a helper suitable for him. Thus the *woman is the glory of man* (verse 7b) as the man is the glory of God. The explanation is made clear in verses 8 and 9, where the sequence of woman's creation (verse 8) and the purpose of her creation (verse 9) are spelt out. As the man 'glorifies' God by fulfilling the headship role assigned to him by the Creator, so the woman 'glorifies' man by recognizing him as her head.

With this firmly established, Paul returns to the statement he began in verse 7 – *a man ought not to cover his head* – balancing it now, in verse 10, with the equivalent application required of women. *A wife ought to have a symbol of authority on her head.* These are clearly twin obligations, in Paul's view. They could hardly have stronger justification than the argument from creation that he has adduced in verses 7–9, but he now adds a further reason – *because of the angels.* What does Paul mean? Many commentators have suggested that the 'authority' a woman ought to have on her head is to indicate her own submission, to her husband or to the male leadership of the church. This might be her long hair put up, or a covering. But the words '*a symbol of*' have been imported by the translators into the text, and the Greek word *exousia* (authority) is usually active in meaning – having, or exercising, authority. On the basis of this more normal, active sense, recent commentators see the 'covering' as symbolic of her own authority, or freedom, to be a woman rightly fulfilling her

God-given role in the congregation, in prayer or prophesying. In doing this she submits to male headship, as the man submits to Christ's headship. Thus, she 'glorifies' man just as the man 'glorifies' God, in that both fulfil their proper functions under Christ, the Head, within the church, which is his body.

This would also make sense of the reference to angels. We have already been introduced to angels (in 4:9) as those who observe what goes on in the world, and who serve God in executing his purposes among human beings. These angels would clearly be offended by, and opposed to, any challenge to the created order, as determined by God, or any deviations from its principles. They want to see Christian women enjoying both the freedom and the dignity that the gospel has brought them. But this will only come about by such women fulfilling their God-given role and not usurping that of the men. It is arguably the most tragic legacy of the Fall that since Eve took the initiative in assuming her husband's role, as leader of the partnership, and Adam apparently only too willingly acceded, mankind has connived at the same skewing of the roles, in the long history of human rebellion against God's norms, on both sides of the gender divide.

3. HEADSHIP APPLIED (verses 11–16)

The last paragraph begins with another change of tack, designed to stop the reader jumping to extreme and erroneous conclusions. '*Nevertheless*' is perhaps the best translation in verse 11, rather than the 'However' of the NIV. What is Paul so keen to guard against here? *In the Lord* (that is in the church, the body of Christ) *woman is not independent of man, nor man of woman* (verse 11). Here, then, is a qualification of his teaching about relationships between men and women in the life of the congregation. Independence is out; interdependence is in. The argument again looks back to creation itself for its theological justification. At the beginning, woman came from man, as Genesis 2:22–23 unequivocally states. But after that first act of creation, man has always been born of woman – a fact that is manifestly true, even of the incarnate Son of God himself. Behind both activities stands God, who is alone the author and giver of life, so *all things are from God* (verse 12b). The force of Paul's line of argument is that this created order, ordained by God, provides the natural way in which men and women are to live in relationship to one another and that none of the freedoms of redemption negate the priorities of creation. The larger theological point is that redemption restores the image of God in man, so that patterns of behaviour in the church (and ultimately, and perfectly, in heaven) will reflect the pre-Fall relationships in what has sometimes been called 'Eden restored'.

The apostle is now ready to conclude the section. *Judge for yourselves*, he says (verse 13), appealing to their minds to weigh his arguments and to act rationally. Two questions follow. The first hinges on the phrase, *is it proper*, or appropriate, or fitting. He reminds them again, implicitly, that the uncovered woman's head represents an unwillingness to accept her different female role from that of her husband, or from the church's male leadership. In appearing like a man she seems to be moving towards the usurpation of his role in worship, and probably in many other areas as well. Similarly, for a man to appear as a woman, with long hair, is against the very nature of things, or, 'Does not nature itself teach you?' (verse 14a). That is how things are, normally, just as it is normal for women to grow their hair long, *for her hair is given to her for a covering* (verse 15b). So what is a *disgrace* to man (verse 14b) is *her glory* to a woman (verse 15a) and Paul is not willing to countenance the upsetting of the natural order of things. Thus, in most cultures, gender differences are established and indicated by differentiation in clothing and in appearance, especially in the hair. Refusal to accept these norms is usually an indication of difficulty in accepting gender differences, or one's own gender definition.

The last argument is from the unity amongst all the churches on this issue. To those who are *contentious*, Paul warns that *we have no such practice, nor do the churches of God* (verse 16). There is no room for negotiation or for compromise on these creation-redemption principles. Several times in the letter Paul stresses the unity of the churches, relating back perhaps to his original devastating question, in 1:13, 'Is Christ divided?' If the only answer to that is 'No', then the Corinthians are not at liberty to invent their own version of the Christian faith, independent of their sister churches, merely in order to tune in to the demands of their city's culture. Paul does not change his message or his behaviour from place to place. Timothy will remind them of his 'ways in Christ, as I teach them everywhere in every church' (4:17). Corinth cannot be an exception. Similarly, in 7:17, during the discussion on marriage, we find Paul affirming, 'This is my rule in all the churches'. And here in verse 16 the section closes on the same note of uncompromising apostolic authority. Corinth has no right to claim to be an exception.

We have seen, then, that what at first sight might appear to be a peripheral social issue is actually regarded by Paul as a foundational gospel principle. Rightly understood, gospel freedoms and kingdom values fulfil creation principles and never undermine them. By wearing her hair as her covering, the Christian wife, or woman, in Corinth, indicated her submission to her head, and through that, her obedience to God. In that way, she was able to worship with reverence, fulfilling her God-given roles within the congregation, and finding in her obedience to the Creator's order all the personal fulfilment that God had intended from the very beginning. While the cultural symbols may change, the principles do not.

31

Do You Despise the Church of God?

[17]But in the following instructions I do not commend you, because when you come together it is not for the better but for the worse. [18]For, in the first place, when you come together as a church, I hear that there are divisions among you. And I believe it in part, [19]for there must be factions among you in order that those who are genuine among you may be recognized. [20]When you come together, it is not the Lord's supper that you eat. [21]For in eating, each one goes ahead with his own meal. One goes hungry, another gets drunk. [22]What! Do you not have houses to eat and drink in? Or do you despise the church of God and humiliate those who have nothing? What shall I say to you? Shall I commend you in this? No, I will not.

[23]For I received from the Lord what I also delivered to you, that the Lord Jesus on the night when he was betrayed took bread, [24]and when he had given thanks, he broke it, and said, "This is my body which is for you. Do this in remembrance of me." [25]In the same way also he took the cup, after supper, saying, "This cup is the new covenant in my blood. Do this, as often as you drink it, in remembrance of me." [26]For as often as you eat this bread and drink the cup, you proclaim the Lord's death until he comes.

[27]Whoever, therefore, eats the bread or drinks the cup of the Lord in an unworthy manner will be guilty of profaning the body and blood of the Lord. [28]Let a person examine himself, then, and so eat of the bread and drink of the cup. [29]For anyone who eats and drinks without discerning the body eats and drinks judgment on himself. [30]That is why many of you are weak and ill, and some have died. [31]But if we judged ourselves truly, we would not be

judged. [32] But when we are judged by the Lord, we are disciplined
so that we may not be condemned along with the world. [33] So then,
my brothers, when you come together to eat, wait for one another
– [34] if anyone is hungry, let him eat at home – so that when you
come together it will not be for judgment. About the other things
I will give directions when I come (1 Cor. 11:17–34).

Throughout the letter, we have been reminded often of the
centrality of Christ's sacrificial death. It was the foundation of
the gospel message that Paul brought to Corinth (2:2) and the shaper
of the life-style of those who subsequently became Christ's followers.
Biblical spirituality finds its shape and focus in the cross of the Lord
Jesus. But one of the many ironies of the situation in the Corinthian
congregation was that when they came together to remember
Christ's death for them, in the fellowship meal which he instituted,
the behaviour of some was a profound denial of the very realities they
were allegedly celebrating. Already Paul has spoken about the Lord's
Supper as an expression of that unity in him into which the gospel
has brought every believer. 'Because there is one bread, we who are
many are one body, for we all partake of the one bread' (10:17). It
takes us right back to his original stunning question: 'Is Christ
divided?' (1:13). Of course, the answer must be, 'No', but you would
not have known that if you were in attendance at the Corinthian 'love-
feast'. Its essential meaning was being denied by their practice.

1. THE PROBLEM DIAGNOSED (verses 17–22)

Many of the problems at Corinth seem to have been caused by the
failure of the new believers in Christ to realize how radical and
distinctive was the break that had to be made with their former pagan
life-styles. The Christian *agape*, or love-feast, was totally different
in its origin and significance from anything equivalent in their secular
culture, but there were some superficial similarities. Cultic meals
were a feature of the pagan temples, where feasting on food offered
to idols would be combined with free-flowing drink and much more
besides. There is evidence that these could also be charitable
occasions when the poor were invited and fed from a common table.

Superficially, the Lord's Supper might appear to have certain features in common with these fellowship meals. Paul's point, however, is that the customary behaviour at such feasts is totally inappropriate among believers.

The paragraph begins with a sharply worded rebuke: *When you come together it is not for the better but for the worse* (verse 17). That is a devastating claim to be made against any local congregation, but the accusation is sharpened by the irony of verse 18. *When you come together as a church, I here that there are divisions among you.* Their gatherings in order to meet together only revealed how divided they actually were. Clearly, Paul is acting on what he had been told – *I hear ... and I believe it in part* – and there can be little doubt that he had considerable confidence in his sources and that he saw here a major issue that had to be addressed.

In this context, verse 19 may seem to be something of a surprise. Several times Paul has made the point that the divisions in the church are a sign of immaturity and cannot be allowed to continue. Now, however, he says *there must be factions among you*. Is he softening his opposition? Not at all; rather, he is explaining how God is working out his purposes even in the failures and immaturity of the congregation, *in order that those who are genuine among you may be recognized*. At base, this is a recognition that every congregation will be made up of genuine believers and superficial adherents, true disciples who follow in Christ's footsteps, and externalists who come along merely for the ride. In the words of the Lord Jesus, 'you will recognize them by their fruits' (*Matt.* 7:20). So Paul addresses the behaviour of the Corinthian congregation. He sees that behaviour as an infallible indicator of who it is who have God's approval – those who are genuine Christians – and who it is who do not. It is the latter group that are in his sights, particularly, in verses 20–22.

What is going on invalidates any claim that they are partaking of the Lord's Supper, since Christ would never own such attitudes (verse 20). The meal that he gave to his church as a special remembrance of himself is being so desecrated that it can no longer be described as his. Rather than honouring the Lord's self-sacrificing love, these greedy Christians cannot wait to fill their own stomachs, irrespective of how this affects others in the group. The wealthy were providing food and drink in considerable quantities for this social meal, but only for themselves. The result was obvious. *One goes hungry, another gets drunk* (verse 21). Those who have insufficient are therefore being mocked and denigrated by those who have excess. This arrogant individualism, together with its conspicuous consumption, is scathingly denounced by the apostle. It would be reprehensible enough in the privacy of their own homes but to bring such behaviour to the meeting of the church of God is to *despise ... and humiliate those who have nothing*. There is no difference in such an attitude from that of the wealthy pagan who uses every social occasion to proclaim his own membership of a particular elite, and to put down his inferiors so that they keep their place. Paul's resulting indignation is directed against the misrepresentation of the gospel that results. The cross spells the end of all human pride, all distinctions of wealth, education, birth or background, all elitism. But the very meal that should be the enactment of unity in Christ and in the gospel has become the expression of division, through pride, selfishness, greed and envy. *Shall I commend you in this? No, I will not* (verse 22).

How selective therefore are we in our 'fellowship'? At the cross, all the old sinful divisions are obliterated, as every individual, whoever he or she may be, prays the same prayer: 'God, be merciful to me a sinner' (*Luke* 18:13). And yet, how many contemporary Christian congregations are still divided? Social and financial distinctions are allowed to harden into indifference and separatism. Snobbery, whether social, intellectual or even 'spiritual', denigrates gospel humility. Members of the church of God are despised and degraded. How can such a 'church' call itself by Christ's name when its life-style betrays its belief?

2. THE CORRECTIVE EXPOUNDED (verses 23–26)

The only answer is to return to the original Supper and to the Lord's own words of institution, so as to remind the readers of how far they have drifted from the Master's intentions. As we are referred to the upper room with its Passover resonances, Paul affirms that he is simply the channel of revelation, not its source (verse 23a). The upper room also was a scene of division. It was *the night when he was betrayed*. That stark verb powerfully reminds us both of the comparative ease with which betrayal can happen and of the appalling disloyalty of the action. Yet, ultimately, this is what the behaviour of the Corinthians at the supper table of the Lord was – a betrayal of him, of his values, and sacrifice. It was however at that hour of darkness that *the Lord Jesus, on the night when he was betrayed, took bread, and when he had given thanks, he broke it, and said, 'This is my body, which is for you. Do this in remembrance of me.'* (verses 23b–24).

These are profound words on which much ink has been spent. Clearly, they cannot be teaching the doctrine known as transub- stantiation, by which it is believed that the bread and wine become the body and blood of Christ. The unleavened bread on the table was evidently *not* the body of Christ. He was there, before his disciples, in his physical body. When he had taught them, 'I am the door of the sheep' (*John* 10:7), they had not imagined for one moment, that he had changed into a thing of stone or timber, and no more do we. He was then speaking of a profound spiritual reality, and the broken bread was emphasizing the same message, of a body soon to be broken on the cross. It was 'for you'. Here, the Lord Jesus clearly teaches his substitution in his death; the bearing of God's righteous wrath; the meeting of sin's punishment justly, on behalf of his people. The Passover reference is inescapable. Every first-born Israelite son, who was redeemed in Egypt, experienced the sub- stitution of the lamb for himself on Passover night. As Exodus 12:30 poignantly expresses it, there was not a home in Egypt without a death.

Could a Christian ever forget such amazing love? Yet the Lord Jesus instituted the supper as a perpetual reminder, not simply to rekindle our memories but also to prompt us to an appropriate response in newness of life. When the Bible calls upon us to remember a truth, it is always in order to provoke us to appropriate action. Participation in the Lord's Supper therefore is always a spur and a challenge for us to live a godly life, by 'feeding on him in our hearts by faith with thanksgiving', making his word our food and his person our sustenance. In moving from the bread to the wine (verse 25), the apostle emphasizes the unity of relationship with God, and therefore with all fellow-believers, in the new covenant com- munity created through the shed blood of the cross. *This cup is the new covenant in my blood.* With these words we move from Passover to Sinai, where Israel received the terms of the old covenant, declared in the law and written in the Book of the Covenant, with the affirmation, ' "All that the LORD has spoken we will do, and we will be obedient." And Moses took the blood [of the young bulls] and threw it on the people and said, "Behold the blood of the covenant that the LORD has made with you in accordance with all these words"' (*Exod.* 24:7–8). On that day, Israel declared herself to be a covenant community, bound in obedience to her sovereign Lord, set apart from all the nations to live a distinctively different life-style as his holy people, his treasured possession. Nor are the terms of the new covenant any less demanding for those who have been covered by the precious blood of Christ. His blood has created one new covenant community, and to deny that by contrary behaviour is tantamount to rejecting the very work on the cross by which the church was brought into existence.

But in verse 26, the situation is shown to be even more solemn and demanding. *For as often as you eat this bread and drink this cup, you proclaim the Lord's death until he comes.* The Lord's Supper is far more than a social meal. It is a proclamation to God and men, a declaration of good news, about our faith in Christ's death. The eating and drinking commit us to an immediate and active public response; the presentation of the elements confronts each individual with a personal challenge. Do I believe that Christ's body was broken for me and that his blood makes me a member of his new covenant community? To eat and drink at the *Lord's* Table implies not only saving faith, but a life-style lived under his active lordship. It is an act of identification with the Christ who identifies with me in all my sin, by committing myself to live in fellowship with him and with all my fellow believers. The divisive supper at Corinth could never be the Lord's Supper, while it undermined the very purpose of his death. It was more like a pagan festival.

The last three words of verse 26 put the whole issue firmly into an even more demanding eternal perspective – *until he comes.* The Lord's Supper is not simply an event in time, but an anticipation of eternity. The Christ, whose death is proclaimed, is the Christ who has risen and will come again in power and glory, as King of kings and Lord of lords. How can his death be proclaimed by those who are unwilling to die to themselves, whose attitude of despising their less privileged brothers and sisters abuses and denies the central purpose of the event they claim to be remembering?

3. THE REMEDY REQUIRED (verses 27–34)

Whoever, therefore, eats the bread or drinks the cup of the Lord in an unworthy manner will be guilty of profaning the body and blood of the Lord (verse 27). As we consider this searching verse, it is important to keep in mind the flow of the argument, signalled by the word 'therefore'. Many a believer has been hindered from coming to the Lord's Table because of the warning of this verse about an 'unworthy manner'. Of course, the verse *is* a warning and it must not be soft-pedalled. But it is not designed to send us, especially the more sensitive personalities and consciences, on an endless, but ultimately fruitless, internal quest to find some worthiness in us as we approach the communion table. Rather, to sin against Christ's body and blood must mean to deny the very purpose of his death, namely, the formation of a new community of redeemed people whose life-style demonstrates the radical, transforming power of the cross. The Supper proclaims salvation through humble dependence on Christ's substitutionary, atoning death – and that is the only 'worthiness' any of us can ever offer. We shall always, forever, be debtors to mercy alone.

What self-examination is appropriate, then, before participating in the Lord's Supper? (verse 28). The verb 'examine' (*dokimazo*) is used frequently in the New Testament, and bears the idea of testing something in order to prove it and so approve its validity, or quality. Every individual coming to the Lord's Supper is charged with the necessary duty of testing one's attitude towards all that it speaks of and conveys. Do I trust this Christ as my sin-bearing substitute? Am I living, in humble obedience to his lordship, the life-style of the cross? The Supper also challenges me regarding my attitude to my fellow believers who are with me, at the table, as God's family. Do I love and honour them? Do I recognize in them the body of the Lord (verse 29)? For my obedience to the gospel, which the Supper proclaims, includes my obedience to the Lord's command to love one another as he has loved us. While this verse therefore is a warning against carelessness in coming to the table, in its Corinthian context it is an even stronger warning against despising my fellow Christians and not *discerning* them as the body of the Lord. The one loaf proclaims the one body (10:17). The next chapter teaches that 'the body is one and has many members' (12:12). The Lord's Table is the place where that oneness, equality before God on the basis of redemption alone, is proclaimed most clearly, and brings greatest glory to the crucified King. To behave at that very event in a way that denies these central realities is to bring judgement on oneself.

Apparently, judgement was already in operation. *Many among you are weak and ill, and some have died* (verse 30). Paul is quite prepared to see sickness, and even death, as evidence of God's chastening hand on the Corinthian believers. Verse 32 refers to this as being *judged by the Lord*, or *disciplined so that we may not be condemned along with the world*. Gordon Fee suggests that this may relate to the 'present distress' of which Paul spoke in 7:26, and it is a stimulating idea. God's erring people are subject to his correcting judgements in order to deliver them from final condemnation. The church should respond, then, in repentance and amendment of life. To be honest and discerning in judging ourselves will deliver us from the Lord's judgement (verse 31).

The practical applications are clear as Paul now relates his teaching to the actual situation he has exposed (verses 33–34). Respect and acceptance of one another lie behind the word translated 'wait' (verse 33). There is to be a mutual valuing of one another as members of the church of God that should destroy all the remaining evidences of the sinful life-style of pride or envy. Those who want to insist on lavish meals will have to eat them at home, for they dare not import their divisiveness into the church's love-feast, with the very real risk that their meeting together would *be for judgement*. Proclaiming the crucified Saviour means living the crucified life-style and when that is so flagrantly denied by the professing church, God cannot be expected to sit idly by in inactivity. He will not allow his Son's name and work to be despised and maligned. We too need to be warned.

32

Varieties of Gifts

¹Now concerning spiritual gifts, brothers, I do not want you to be uninformed. ²You know that when you were pagans you were led astray to mute idols, however you were led. ³Therefore I want you to understand that no one speaking in the Spirit of God ever says "Jesus is accursed!" and no one can say "Jesus is Lord" except in the Holy Spirit.

⁴Now there are varieties of gifts, but the same Spirit; ⁵and there are varieties of service, but the same Lord; ⁶and there are varieties of activities, but it is the same God who empowers them all in everyone. ⁷To each is given the manifestation of the Spirit for the common good. ⁸To one is given through the Spirit the utterance of wisdom, and to another the utterance of knowledge according to the same Spirit, ⁹to another faith by the same Spirit, to another gifts of healing by the one Spirit, ¹⁰to another the working of miracles, to another prophecy, to another the ability to distinguish between spirits, to another various kinds of tongues, to another the interpretation of tongues. ¹¹All these are empowered by one and the same Spirit, who apportions to each one individually as he wills (1 Cor. 12:1–11).

It is the height of tragedy that spiritual gifts have become such a divisive issue amongst Christians in our generation. It is also a supreme irony, because the purpose of the gifts is to build up, unify and edify Christ's body, not to pull it apart. However, we are in good company, or at least Corinthian company, because this chapter begins the most extended passage of biblical teaching about the gifts of God's grace (the *charismata*). It is in this context of a church being torn apart by factions and jealousies that Paul focuses the clearest teaching about the identity and use of spiritual gifts. Obviously this was a major ingredient in the problems that beset the church in Corinth.

Why is it so often like that? Almost all Christians today know of churches that have suffered severe division and persistent wounding as a result of this very controversy. Let me suggest two reasons. Firstly, because of the existence of an enemy who counterfeits all of God's gracious works and gifts, the spurious will always be found alongside the genuine. In a city like Corinth, where every sort of religious experience under the sun was practised and promoted, it was not always easy to determine what was of God and what was not. Satan is an arch deceiver who loves to throw dust in the eyes of God's people so as to confuse them about what God is saying in his Word. Secondly, the sinful nature of every Christian ('the flesh') is at war with the Spirit and obstructing the work of making us holy. The Holy Spirit, who is carrying out this work in our lives, is always being opposed and frustrated by the world, the flesh, and, behind them both, the devil. Satan continually uses the world, with its temptations, and our own weaknesses in the flesh, to divert us from God's purposes. One of his most successful tactics is to puff us up with pride, and to keep us concerned about our status in the church and our imagined place in the spiritual pecking order. We then begin to think that in some way we are better, more blessed, more gifted, and more spiritual, than other believers. The Corinthian church was facing all of these issues, but blindly, not realizing that they were in a battle with an enemy.

As we consider this passage in its biblical context, we realise that it is a corrective section, addressing the Corinthians about the wrong, worldly judgements into which they had fallen. Gaston DaLuz, a French commentator, puts it this way:

> The chief mistake of the Corinthians, which falsified their judgement and made them spiritually ignorant, seems to have been this: they imagined that it was a proof of the power of the Holy Spirit working in him if a man became beside himself, and the greater his ecstasy the more sublime the state to which the Spirit had raised him. If, on the other hand, he remained in control of himself, the less was he

thought to be under divine inspiration. From this point of view, the teacher ranked below the prophet, and the prophet below the man with the gift of tongues. Greek and even Jewish ideas agreed with this. Plato said, 'We reach the highest state of good through frenzy', and again, 'No man in full possession of his senses can be touched by the divine *afflatus*'.

The Corinthian Christians seem not to have queried these false assumptions. They were being truly Greek; very Corinthian. The more you are taken over or possessed – the less you are in control – the more spiritual you must be.

These same ideas often circulate in Christian circles today, but Paul wants his readers to know that such thinking is essentially worldly. This is not what gospel spirituality is about at all. Already in the sections on food offered to idols and on the Lord's Supper (chapters 8–11) we have been taught that true Christian spirituality is cross-shaped, and that its focus is self-sacrificing love that builds up others. It is no accident that 'the most excellent way' taught in chapter 13 is the way of love, without which all the spiritual gifts, even in their most impressive manifestations, come to nothing. Chapter 14 will show us that love requires that we speak intelligibly in a Christian assembly, and have orderly meetings, so that other Christians can be built up. Indeed, the measure of greatness of any spiritual gift is not its degree of impressiveness, or its apparent miraculous nature, but its usefulness in building up the body of Christ, in love and in truth.

1. FOUNDATION TRUTH (verses 1–3)

As the chapter begins, Paul uses his characteristic formula to indicate a change of subject matter and a major new section. *Now . . . brothers, I do not want you to be uninformed.* Such ignorance or agnosticism is characteristic of the pagan mind-set, because it has not yet been illuminated by God's self-revelation in the truth of Scripture. Paul's comment, *you were led astray to mute idols, however you were led* (verse 2), is a description that typifies all forms of pagan religion that tend to subvert the mind and concentrate on the passions and emotions. But Christian faith is directly opposite to this in its intention and direction. It does not lead to speechless idols, because it is the revelation of the one God who speaks, the only true and living God. Although the Corinthian temples were strong on mystical experiences, ecstatic states, trances and visions, with plenty of noise and excitement, at the centre of it all were lifeless 'gods' who could not therefore communicate at all. Doubtless there were prophecies, ecstatic language and miracle cures, but they did not, and could not, lead to a knowledge of, and relationship with, the Creator of the universe. His Spirit is not mute. He speaks with penetrating clarity as he declares that Jesus Christ is Lord (verse 3). That is how genuine Christians come to recognize the living God, and to recognize one another.

Verse 3 makes it inescapably clear that one's attitude to Jesus is the acid test of true spirituality. *No one can say, 'Jesus is Lord,' except in the Holy Spirit*. The Spirit will always bear witness to the true nature of the true Son of God, and never anathematise him. Therefore, real Christians will have this common foundation, which is strong enough and deep enough to bridge all their divisions and heal all their differences. It is not just our confession in words, important though that is, but the devotion of our lives to Christ's lordship in practical, everyday obedience that is the proof of the Holy Spirit's presence in our lives.

2. FUNCTIONAL DIFFERENCES (verses 4–6)

Throughout the chapter we find the twin themes of unity and diversity being explored, but the appropriate diversity is always within the framework of fundamental unity. Thus, *there are varieties of gifts, but the same Spirit* (verse 4). So as to underline the unity theme (so much needed at Corinth) Paul takes us to God himself, from whom all the gifts of grace spring, and focuses on the unity of the Holy Trinity. He speaks of *the same Spirit* (verse 4), *the same Lord* (verse 5) and *the same God* (verse 6). Clearly, these are not three different deities working in three different ways, but the Persons of the Godhead in perfect unity, providing for us a perfect model of unity in functional diversity. The inescapable implication is that if we are members of his body, we must reflect the unity of God in the way we relate to one another in our different functions, gifts and ministries.

Another way of understanding the same point is to ask, 'What is

God doing through the church in his world?' The most fundamental answer must be that he is bringing men and women to acknowledge that 'Jesus is Lord'. Such is the Father's gracious purpose and the Spirit's constant work (*Phil.* 2:9–11). Yet an infinite variety of ways and means are employed by the Spirit to bring people under Christ's rule, and verses 4 to 6 categorize three distinctive groups. Before we examine them, we need to realize that the purpose of the 'gifts, services and activities' is not to draw attention to any human channel but solely to honour Christ as king.

The *varieties of gifts* (verse 4) are, literally, *charismata* – gifts of grace. These are freely and generously given by God with different provisions for different individuals. In verses 8–10, we shall discover some of these abilities, and others are added later in verse 28. Further places where gifts are listed in the New Testament include Romans 12:6–8; Ephesians 4:11–12 and 1 Peter 4:10–11. The *varieties of service* (verse 5), or *diakonia*, refer to the way in which God-given abilities are to be used. The emphasis is on serving others, whatever demands that may make on the servant. Verse 6 speaks of *varieties of activities*, or energies, (*energemata*), stressing that it is God's energy or power working through them all. We must, therefore, accept our differences as God-given and thank him that in his mercy we are not all clones of one another. It will prevent us from expecting other Christians to be just like us, or expecting them to jump through our hoops. Our common confession of the lordship of Christ will be expressed through a wonderful variety of channels and ministries.

3. PRACTICAL OUTWORKINGS (verses 7–11)

To each is given the manifestation of the Spirit for the common good. This classic statement of verse 7 encapsulates the theme tune of the whole chapter. It instructs us that every believer has a *manifestation*, or unveiling, or appearing, of the Spirit. And that is a very significant statement. Just as the Holy Spirit indwells every believer (*John* 7:39; *Acts* 2:38–39; *Rom.* 8:9) so he will reveal himself to be present; he will appear in a variety of ways (see verses 8–10). Wherever God's people are serving out of love for God and for their neighbours, with the intention of expressing their conviction that *Jesus is Lord*, there is to be found a manifestation of the Holy Spirit, whatever the form of that service might be.

But if each Christian has something to contribute, each Christian is also a beneficiary, since these gifts are given *for the common good.* If this is the reason God has given them it must also be the criterion for their exercise. But so often the fulfilment of the person using the gift is given priority over the benefit of the body as a whole. In a culture obsessed with self-fulfilment, the church is easily conditioned to express her 'spirituality' in a culturally acceptable currency. We so easily translate secular priorities into a church context. Gifts and energies are then diverted into the seeking of our own spiritual satisfaction, the acceptability and 'success' of our church, the meeting of our own inward needs of significance, value and happiness. Subtly, we become introverted, whereas the Spirit's work is always for the good of others. We are back to the error of mainstream Corinthian thinking and Paul's insistence that true spirituality is measured, not by the yardstick of the world, but by the selfless sacrifice of the Lord Jesus.

Verses 8–10 contain nine gifts, or *manifestations*, of the Spirit, for the good of all. Discussion has often focused on precise definitions, probably because we are usually more gift-centred than God-centred in our thinking. However, every gift except the last two (tongues and their interpretation) was exercised by the Lord Jesus during his earthly ministry, and if the body of Christ is to continue his work on earth, one might expect these manifestations to be present as evidence of his active lordship in his church. But what we must remember is that this is a *Corinthian* list, not an exhaustive catalogue.

The utterance of wisdom and *the utterance of knowledge* characteristically head the list (verse 8) because word ministry is always the apostle's primary concern. The same point is evidenced in the later summary of verse 28. We know that the word of wisdom is the preaching of the cross (1:24) and that the knowledge of Christ and his example (10:32–11:1) is at the heart of the apostle's concerns for them. Whilst all believers have been granted the gift of *faith* in order to become Christians (*Eph.* 2:8–9), verse 9 indicates that there is a special gift given to some, to those, perhaps, who are called to serve God in unusually demanding circumstances. One thinks of missionaries serving the Lord faithfully for decades in very resistant cultures and seeing little fruit for their labours, in that faithfulness is the product of faith. *Gifts of healing* is literally 'cures', and the plural is very important. It helps us to understand that there is not *a* gift of healing that is exercised indiscriminately by an individual. Rather, there are actual cases of healings, or cures, carried out by God through his chosen human agents, perhaps, as in James 5:14 through prayer and anointing with oil. The word '*miracles*' (verse10a) has the same root as the word translated 'empowers' in verse 6 and linked with the familiar New Testament term *dunamis*, with its basic meaning of 'ability', the successful completion of a task.

The last four gifts all relate more specifically to the congregational meetings at Corinth and are dealt with in greater detail in chapter 14. Perhaps the *ability to distinguish between spirits* (verse 10) was a particularly contentious issue in Corinth. The emphasis Paul has laid on it in verse 3 of this chapter would indicate that some ecstatic utterances were not glorifying Christ as Lord, and so spiritual wisdom was needed in order to distinguish the false from the true. In a congregation inclined to value highly any ecstatic speech, this would be a much-needed gift from God. The same misuse can occur in the context of tongues, of course, a phenomenon often evidenced in non-Christian contexts – hence the need of the gift of interpretation.

Paul's dominant concern throughout this section is the unity of God's people, which he secures by his constant emphasis on the one Spirit, working for the good of the whole body. Verse 11 closes the paragraph by reiterating with even greater clarity the principles emphasized in verse 7. *All these are empowered by one and the same Spirit, who apportions to each one individually as he wills.* So there should be no cause for complaint. If we are unhappy about the gifts we have, or do not have, or that others have, or do not have, Paul wants us to know that our argument is with God. He chooses the gifts he will give and those to whom he will give them. If such matters generate rivalry and division, this is a mark of childish immaturity. Their true purpose is to unite, build up, and promote harmony and acceptance amongst Christians gathering together for the common good under the lordship of Jesus Christ. To splinter and fragment over the gifts of God's grace is a tragedy and a scandal. It indicates that the life-style of the world, with its concerns for status and prominence, prestige and fulfilment, has won out over the life-style of the cross. A church where such divisions are prominent might well be in terminal decline.

33

Many Members But One Body

¹²*For just as the body is one and has many members, and all the members of the body, though many, are one body, so it is with Christ.* ¹³*For in one Spirit we were all baptized into one body – Jews or Greeks, slaves or free – and all were made to drink of one Spirit.*

¹⁴*For the body does not consist of one member but of many.* ¹⁵*If the foot should say, "Because I am not a hand, I do not belong to the body," that would not make it any less a part of the body.* ¹⁶*And if the ear should say, "Because I am not an eye, I do not belong to the body," that would not make it any less a part of the body.* ¹⁷*If the whole body were an eye, where would be the sense of hearing? If the whole body were an ear, where would be the sense of smell?* ¹⁸*But as it is, God arranged the members in the body, each one of them, as he chose.* ¹⁹*If all were a single member, where would the body be?* ²⁰*As it is, there are many parts, yet one body.*

²¹*The eye cannot say to the hand, "I have no need of you," nor again the head to the feet, "I have no need of you."* ²²*On the contrary, the parts of the body that seem to be weaker are indispensable,* ²³*and on those parts of the body that we think less honourable we bestow the greater honour, and our unpresentable parts are treated with greater modesty,* ²⁴*which our more presentable parts do not require. But God has so composed the body, giving greater honour to the part that lacked it,* ²⁵*that there may be no division in the body, but that the members may have the same care for one another.* ²⁶*If one member suffers, all suffer together; if one member is honoured, all rejoice together.*

²⁷*Now you are the body of Christ and individually members of it.* ²⁸*And God has appointed in the church first apostles, second*

prophets, third teachers, then miracles, then gifts of healing, helping, administrating, and various kinds of tongues. ²⁹*Are all apostles? Are all prophets? Are all teachers? Do all work miracles?* ³⁰*Do all possess gifts of healing? Do all speak with tongues? Do all interpret?* ³¹*But earnestly desire the higher gifts* (1 Cor. 12:12–31).

In this extended section on the church as the body of Christ, we see the apostle Paul, as an expert pastor-teacher, instructing his immature converts. Their own deficiencies and misunderstandings are lovingly, but relentlessly, exposed, as he explores the body metaphor and its implications for life in the Corinthian congregation.

1. UNITY IS GOD'S GIFT (verses 12–13)

Before he addresses the problems of Corinth, Paul affirms the undergirding principle that unites every congregation of God's people. *The body is one and has many members* (verse 12). It is a powerful image because we do not think of our physical bodies as made up of many different parts that have come together into some form of constructed unity. The body is one – that is a 'given' – and all the parts serve the whole. Paul wants his readers to think of the church in that way. *And all the members of the body, though many, are one body.* They can have no independent life or existence. *So it is with Christ.* Every Christian, who is, by definition, united to Christ by faith, also belongs to every other Christian in the one body of Christ, which is the universal church, expressed in its innumerable local congregations. Think of the simple process of eating and digesting food. How many parts of the body are involved! The physical body is a single unit, or organism, which can only live and grow through a great variety of functions, in which different parts of the whole are involved, each performing their particular functions in harmony, for the well-being of the whole. That is how Christ's spiritual body, the church, must also function.

Verse 13 provides the theological reasoning. *For in one Spirit we were all baptized into one body.* The 'given' unity exists because every member of the body belongs on exactly the same terms. There is an experience common to all believers, described in this verse as baptism and as all being *made to drink of one Spirit*. This is one of only seven references in the New Testament to baptism 'in' or 'with' or 'by' the Holy Spirit. The Greek preposition *en* is used in every reference and can take any of these meanings. We speak about being baptized 'in water', the element or agent used, but equally of being baptized 'in the name' of the Trinity, signifying the purpose of the action. Here the one Spirit seems to be the agent, or element used, while incorporation into the one body is the purpose. This matches with Paul's teaching elsewhere, which makes it clear that immersion into the life of the Spirit, with its consequent membership of the body of Christ, is the experience of the new birth, or conversion. For example, Romans 8:9 affirms that the Spirit of God lives within every Christian. That is what defines the believer as belonging to Christ. Water baptism is therefore an outward sign of an individual's initiation into the eternal life of God, through faith in Christ. Neither here nor elsewhere does Paul teach that Spirit-baptism is a second separate experience subsequent to the new birth. It *is* the new birth; common to all who believe in Christ and are saved.

That is why Paul can use it as the foundation principle of unity for all members of the congregation at Corinth, whether *Jews or Greeks, slaves or free*. Such distinctions are irrelevant in the church, from God's viewpoint, and so they must not be re-imported into the congregation. Just as the Israelites in the desert were all sustained by drinking from the water that God provided from the rock (see 10:4), so also all believers drink the sustaining life of the Spirit and all are equally dependent upon God to satisfy and sustain us, every day of our pilgrimage. This is what unites Christ's church, and what God has put together no human being dare tear apart. Whatever diversities of gifts and operations God may choose to give to different members of the body, they are never to be used to fragment the given unity. We are all saved by the same gospel, indwelt by the same Spirit and members of the same body. But diversity is the problem at Corinth, and to this Paul now turns.

2. DIVERSITY IS OUR CHALLENGE (verses 14–26)

This section divides into two, verses 14–20 and 21–26, where Paul deals with two equal, but opposite, errors. First, he reiterates the foundation principle that the body is made up of many parts (verse 14). Then he proceeds to the first error, which is for one of the parts to say, *I do not belong to the body.* Imagining that the foot, or the ear, should take up such an attitude, Paul's point is that even if such a ridiculous claim were to be made, *that would not make it any less a part of the body* (verses 15, 16). Every part of the body has its own function and its own unique contribution to the body. No one part can be the whole body or there would be no body (verse 19). And every part is needed, so no individual member should suffer from an inferiority complex because they are not the whole body, or not similar to other parts of the body. For *God arranged the members in the body, each one of them, as he chose* (verse 18).

With there being such an emphasis on gifts, especially of the more spectacular kind, it is likely that some Corinthian believers who did not have those gifts were inclined (and perhaps encouraged!) to feel very inferior. This in turn could lead to envy, discontent and division. The foot and the ear are not able to perform the complicated functions of the hand or the eye, but where would the body be without them? No member of the body can perform another part's task. If the ear cannot see, neither can the eye hear! Similarly, in the church all the different functions are needed; they all matter. *There are many parts, yet one body* (verse 20). Yet how many Christians are there who feel their gifts to be inferior to others? They imagine that they have little or nothing to contribute; that others are more gifted and therefore more spiritual – a conclusion that Paul will not allow. From there, it is only a short step to thinking: 'I don't belong', and then to drift away from the fellowship; this only produces division and deprivation for the whole body.

But if one danger of the diversity of gifts is that some feel inferior and imagine that they have nothing to contribute to the body, a second is that others may develop a superiority complex, which in effect says to other members, *I have no need of you* (verse 21). This is equally disastrous. The mistake once again is that of comparing oneself with other Christians. In one situation it leads to discouragement and envy, and in the other to pride and complacency. Both injure the body, and both are wrong. Doubtless the more 'gifted' Christians at Corinth were assumed to be those with the more spectacular gifts, which put them in the public limelight. They became the spiritual 'personalities' within the congregation and began to regard other members as unnecessary. Against this, the apostle argues on two grounds, still using the body metaphor. *The parts of the body that seem to be weaker are indispensable* (verse 22). The body needs them all and so their apparent strength is no indicator of their significance. Secondly, *on those parts of the body that we think less honourable we bestow the greater honour* (verse 23a). Human dignity requires us to clothe the least presentable parts of the body with covering, both for decency and protection. They are not dismissed or ignored. So, in Christ's body, the church, *God has so composed the body, giving greater honour to the part that lacked it* (verse 24b), and the way this is to be achieved is that all the parts *may have the same care for one another* (verse 25b). This is the only way in which the body can function healthily as an entity. We all know that when one part of our body is suffering pain, the whole cannot be at peace. Similarly, in Christ's body, we all share one another's sufferings and all rejoice at one another's honours (verse 26).

Whenever inferiority or superiority prevails, the church is less than God intends it to be. He has organized the church in unity, and appointed its different members to different tasks. That is why the implications of how Christians treat one another *within* the church have such a profound effect on those *outside* it. The authenticity of the gospel is at stake.

3. HARMONY IS THE PRIORITY (verses 27–31)

Once more Paul hammers his point home, with the emphasis on 'you', as he applies his teaching to the situation at Corinth. This is not a theoretical flight of fancy but an urgent, practical matter. *Now you are the body of Christ, and individually members of it.* To the extent that the harmony and well-being of our physical bodies is central to our continuing existence, to the same degree these priorities apply to the spiritual body of Christ. Every believer really does belong. Each one counts and needs to contribute. But what we contribute depends entirely on God's appointment (verse 28a). The verse lists a wide range of gifts with those at the beginning of the list suggesting to the idea of a hierarchy of importance. *God has appointed in the church first apostles, second prophets, third teachers,* followed by five other giftings. It is, of course, ludicrous to interpret these words in such a way that we end up with the apostle denying what he has just taught, namely that the different contributions of all members are important. But verse 31 does make the point – *earnestly desire the higher gifts*. That is, the truth that all contributions are important does not deny the fact that some gifts are greater than others in their immediate and longer-term benefits to the church. Obviously, Paul's own apostolic gifting was a greater gift to the Corinthian church than the tongues-speaking of one of its members (see 14:19) in terms of its beneficial effect. We are here, today, still studying Paul's apostolic teaching but the words of the Corinthian tongues-speakers have long since been buried in the dust of history. One is undeniably greater than the other. But that does not make Paul superior. The 'ranking' has nothing to do with the individual that God has chosen to be the channel of his grace, but everything to do with the gift's effectiveness in building up the body of Christ (14:1–3).

The apostles were of first importance since they were the foundation gift of God to his church, the channels of divine revelation to the people before the Scriptures were written, and the means by which that truth was recorded. This argument is further developed in Ephesians 2:19–3:6. The prophets and teachers carried on that ministry, passing on sound doctrine and relating it to their hearers' lives, exhorting, encouraging and rebuking. These word gifts always were, and still are, essential for the health and growth of the churches. There are also other gifts needed, and Paul lists some more of them. It is interesting, however, that in the case of the word gifts at the beginning of the list Paul's emphasis is on the people rather than the gifts, thus supporting his comments about the different parts of the body. That is also, probably, the reason why, sandwiched between the more spectacular public gifts of healing and tongues, he includes the more mundane but vitally important gifts of helps and administration. His aim is not to produce a comprehensive catalogue, but to underline his point that each member has a distinctive contribution to offer and each part counts towards the harmony of the whole body.

The rhetorical questions of verses 29–30, all expecting the answer 'No', come like a series of hammer-blows to nail beyond all dispute the principles the chapter has been expounding. Today's church would be so much healthier and happier if the lessons were learned. The apostle's teaching clearly denies the claim that any of the gifts can be ours if only we have the faith to claim them and exercise them. In that case, verses 29–30 would be irrelevant. It also denies the argument that *all* Spirit-filled Christians must exhibit one particular gift (usually tongues) as proof of their new birth. *Do all speak with tongues?* Paul asks, without any hint of an exhortation that all should, any more than all should, or could, be apostles. Clearly, they did not and do not, so that the contrary teaching that concentrates on tongues as the necessary sign of the new life, is injurious to the body of Christ and destructive of its God-given unity.

In a climate where there continues to be a widespread ignorance about spiritual gifts, and which is often characterized by wild claims and sweeping judgements, we need chapter 12 as a model of good teaching and practice. It is vital to see that the *charismata* are God's gifts, in both their diversity and equality. They are designed to express unity, to build up the body and to provide the church with the much-needed resources by which she lives out her confession that 'Jesus is Lord'. That sort of community will be characterized above all by one supreme virtue to which the apostle now turns, namely, love.

34

A Still More Excellent Way

And I will show you a still more excellent way. ¹*If I speak in the tongues of men and of angels, but have not love, I am a noisy gong or a clanging cymbal.* ²*And if I have prophetic powers, and understand all mysteries and all knowledge, and if I have all faith, so as to remove mountains, but have not love, I am nothing.* ³*If I give away all I have, and if I deliver up my body to be burned, but have not love, I gain nothing.*

⁴*Love is patient and kind; love does not envy or boast; it is not arrogant* ⁵*or rude. It does not insist on its own way; it is not irritable or resentful;* ⁶*it does not rejoice at wrongdoing, but rejoices with the truth.* ⁷*Love bears all things, believes all things, hopes all things, endures all things* (1 Cor. 13:1–7).

The instruction with which chapter 12 ends (12:31a) is balanced by the opening statement of chapter 14. The same verb is used on both occasions. Literally translated they read, 'Earnestly desire the higher gifts' (*charismata*), and 'Earnestly desire the spiritual gifts (*pneumatika*). In between stands one of the most well-known and greatly loved passages of the whole Bible, read at countless marriage services, used on innumerable state and other occasions, and included in many anthologies of great literature. It is an amazing composition in its own right, but all the more so when we see it in its context. For this great poem about *agape* is actually a pastoral corrective to the deluded and wandering congregation at Corinth. They are dearly loved by Christ and by his apostle, but Paul is deeply concerned for them lest all their apparent spiritual vitality and enthusiasm should add up, in the end, to one large zero. This chapter is a model, therefore of *how* spiritual gifts are to be exercised within the Christian community and it builds on the teaching we have just studied about the value and inter-dependence of every part of the body of Christ. The *more excellent way* is also the indispensable way, for without love the gifts will be pursued and used selfishly and selectively, resulting in an over-estimation of some, the denigration of others, and the ultimate division of the church. To exercise them in love means doing so with care, honour, and respect for others and, above all, with the overall aim of building up and maturing others to the maximum effect. Those gifts that have that outcome are those most to be desired, but even these are worse than useless if they are not exercised in love.

1. WHY LOVE MATTERS (verses 1–3)

It is clear that the first paragraph is constructed very carefully, as most commentators point out. The verses list the various evidences of the Spirit's presence and power in the church, as witnessed by various gifts and activities. The progression is from tongues to martyrdom, from the lesser to the greater. In this way the whole congregation, whatever their individual gifts might be, is encouraged to affirm Paul's conclusion that it is only love that can validate the exercise of any of them. The suggestion has also been made that in verse 1, Paul focuses on the gifts which were especially valued by the Corinthians; in verse 2, he concentrates on those which he himself esteemed the most, and in verse 3, on those which the surrounding pagan culture would most admire. If that is so, it shows again that he is concerned to leave no stone unturned. Without love, there is nothing. As their apostle and example (11:1), Paul adopts the first person singular to make his points; he identifies himself with his readers and refuses to see himself in any way different from them.

He begins with *the tongues of men and of angels*, a gift much prized in the Corinthian church, it seems, and one that he himself exercises 'more than all of you', as he later points out (14:18). He is not denying its authenticity or down valuing it in any way. Calvin, and many following him, suggests that this gift refers to human languages miraculously given by God and is the counterpart to the miracle of hearing the gospel in one's own tongue, as experienced by the crowds who listened to Spirit-filled believers on the Day of Pentecost, in Jerusalem (*Acts* 2:7–11). Others suggest that that is the explanation of the 'tongues of men', but that the 'tongues of angels' indicate ecstatic speech, corresponding to no known earthly language, in which the mind is 'unfruitful' (14:14) while the Spirit prays. It could also be a way of expressing a superlative, as if the sentence read: 'No matter how wonderfully developed and impressive my use of the gift of tongues might be.' In a city of pagan worship where religious ecstasy was hugely valued as a sign of great godliness, this might well have been Paul's target. And in that case, the second part of the verse might be a reference to the practice of the pagan temple. Tongues, without love, make me *a noisy gong or a clanging cymbal* (verse 1). The exercise of the gift even in the most impressive way has no more value than the hollow gong or the tinny cymbals struck in the pagan temples, to wake the gods up, to call their attention, or to drive away evil spirits – all being but meaningless noise. Paul is both very bold in his challenge and very abrupt in his dismissal of something that his readers valued so highly. But if the gift was being exercised without love, he is ruthless in his condemnation. And the situation in the church revealed that this was precisely the case.

However, Paul will not allow them to ignore his strictures on the grounds that he is prejudiced against them or against a particular gift, and so, as a second example, he applies exactly the same argument to the gift that he views as the most beneficial for the church (see 14:1,3). *And if I have prophetic powers and understand all mysteries and all knowledge* (verse 2a). The language indicates that he is imagining the use of the gift to a superlative degree, so that *all* of God's secrets and knowledge are revealed, understood and passed on by the 'prophet'. Of course, that is not actually possible (see *Deut.* 29:29), but even if it were, without love it would be nothing. The comment has been made that it might be speaking God's Word but it would not be in God's tone of voice. Indeed, there is a sense in which truth without love ceases to be fully truth, since it represents God's self-revelation without reference to God's nature, for 'God is love' (*1 John* 4:8 and see *Eph.* 4:15–16). The prophet who ministers in love will want to build up his hearers. He will be marked by humility and compassion rather than arrogance and assertiveness. The former is a sign of divine grace, the latter a mark of nothingness.

Here, Paul links with prophecy *all faith, so as to remove mountains* (verse 2b), and uses the terminology that the Lord Jesus himself first made use of (see *Matt.* 21:21). Mountain-moving faith is expressed in prayer and leads to what seems to be the impossible actually happening. Surely that would be a sign of great spirituality? Not necessarily, is Paul's reply. If such faith is motivated by personal glory or kudos, rather than love, then in God's sight that person is nothing. Here is a real challenge to today's desire for miracles, both within and outside the church. Christians can long for them in order to be noticed, to be vindicated and successful, or just for the sheer excitement of it all. But love is the only indicator of eternal value.

Finally, Paul turns to those external marks of religious conviction that the pagan would always value highly. *If I give away all I have, and if I deliver up my body to be burnt* (verse 3a). Surely this is the ultimate proof of reality. Apparently not. Dividing up property to share it with others can be heartless. Giving to those in need may be done in order to acquire merit, or attract attention, but without love nothing is gained. Even martyrdom would be without value if it was endured without love. All these activities could be merely external, but God is always concerned with the heart. The point is that one could include any spiritual gift, activity or service in these verses and the proposition would always remain true. Only love matters, and without love there can be nothing of value. The message therefore is plain. The spiritual life of an individual, or of a congregation, is measured not by gifts or busy activity, not by size and impact, not by commitment to sound doctrine or keenness to experience God's power, but by love. Like the Corinthians, we find that very hard to accept. It is not the gifts that are being criticized here, but the individuals who exercise them without love. The lesson we all have to learn is that the existence and use of spiritual gifts are not in themselves the mark of genuine spirituality. It is only the controlling presence and motivation of love that denotes the presence of God's Spirit, because biblical spirituality is all about the self-giving love of Christ in his atoning sacrifice for sinners.

2. WHAT LOVE LOOKS LIKE (verses 4–7)

These verses are often labelled a hymn to love, or a portrait of love, but one of the striking characteristics of the passage is that it is so strong on the negatives – what love is not. This is because the love of Christ is the polar opposite of our sinful, self-centred human nature, and also because this is a corrective passage to the particular denials of love on show in the church at Corinth. Instead of reading this as a purple prose passage, we should see it as a purple face passage, as seen on the faces of the congregation as their embarrassment and shame would have increased when they first heard this apostolic indictment of their loveless practice.

The best way to feel the force of what Paul is saying is to unpack the content of true Christian love revealed in these verses, and then compare these qualities to what we have seen of the Corinthian congregation in the rest of the letter. *Love is patient*, or more literally 'long-suffering', bearing up with whatever it takes to go on serving Christ and his body. *Love is kind,* which is the positive side of the coin, actively doing good to those who do you harm. It *does not envy* because it does not think itself inferior to others or wish that it was someone else, or had their gifts or opportunities. Love is glad to receive God's good gifts and to use them to strengthen others and glorify the Giver. It does not *boast,* or brag about itself, or about what it has or has achieved. Love is self-effacing, not superior and brash. *It is not arrogant.* The word was used in 8:1 where knowledge was contrasted with love, and where the contrast was drawn between being 'puffed up' and building others up. Proud Christians are self-confident in their knowledge, by which they can put others down. Loving Christians long to build others up.

It is not . . . rude, in the sense of not behaving towards others in an unChristlike way, taking advantage of them or riding roughshod over them. When a gift or ministry is lacking in sensitivity toward others, when there is a refusal to listen to others or to learn from them, that is a sure indication that self is on the throne, not the crucified Saviour. *It does not insist on its own.* Yet how often churches have been torn apart over the issue of spiritual gifts, because someone was determined to have his own little empire. Sometimes a gifted Christian refuses to accept the leadership given by God to his church. Instead of loving it and praying it into better shape he is determined to be up-front, to have his say and his way. Such behaviour is often dressed up in 'spiritual' clothes, of course, and presented in plausible language. 'We must have freedom to exercise our gifts, to develop a deeper spirituality, to move on into new areas.' But it is self-seeking, for however gifted the individual, it is not love's way to divide a church and spoil God's work. Gifts are given to build up God's church, not a human's ego. *It is not irritable,* or provoked. Loving people are not touchy. Love has a long fuse. *It is not . . . resentful,* yet, how often we are. Disagreements deepen into grievances, and bitterness hardens grievances into hostility. It is a monstrous denial of the gospel when believers in the same congregation will not speak to each other because of some wrong in the past, real or imagined, that has been indelibly recorded and revisited on a regular basis. Where would we be if God were to treat us like that? Love wipes the slate clean, because Jesus did so, by his cross. Wherever there has been division over gifts there has to be a full and unconditional reconciliation if ever these gifts are to be exercised rightly in love.

Love *does not rejoice at wrongdoing, but rejoices with the truth* (verse 6). The evil referred to here would seem to be *un*truthfulness. Why ever would a Christian delight in that? He or she might do so in order to be censorious, or superior, or both; or perhaps in order to gloat over the faults of others, in blind self-righteousness, imagining oneself to be better than them. It is not a distinctive of love to be always tracking down and pointing out what is wrong in others' lives. It wants to rejoice in what is right, because love's delight is in the God who is love. So, *love bears all things, believes all things, hopes all things, endures all things* (verse 7). This does not mean that love is naïve or gullible but, as Calvin expresses it: 'Love would rather be deceived by its gentleness of heart than injure a brother by suspicion. It is always ready to think the best, to put the most favourable construction on anything.' That is why love never ceases to hope for God's best in every life and every situation. No hardship, reversal or rebuff can ever stop love from loving. That is why love will ultimately triumph; it never fails. It is the greatest force in the universe, because God is love. Nothing can overcome love, because nothing can overcome God.

But before we leave this wonderful passage, we must return once more to Corinth and remind ourselves of its context. How did Paul's readers measure up to this foundational statement of the nature of square-one Christianity – love? Their faces (and perhaps ours too) were very red. Think of how the apostle has had to describe them already. They were 'of the flesh . . . infants in Christ', because 'there is jealousy and strife among you' (3:1–3). They were 'puffed up in favour of one man against another' (4:6). 'Some are arrogant', brash and boastful in speech (4:18–20). There was immorality in the church, 'of a kind that is not tolerated even among pagans . . . and you are arrogant' (5:1–2). They were taking their disputes against one another to the pagan courts for judgement, holding on to grievances; keeping a record of wrongs; brother going to law against brother. All this indicated that it was 'already a defeat for you' (6:1–7). They were puffed up by knowledge and by forcing this knowledge upon their weaker brothers they were compromising their consciences and causing them to stumble (8:1–13). They were abusing the Lord's Table, not valuing one another as members together of the one body (11:17–22), despising the less advantaged and looking down on them as not worth bothering about (12:21–26).

Put all that alongside chapter 13 and you will understand why Paul had to write it. Their behaviour record was the polar opposite of Christian love. All their gifts and experiences, all their wisdom and knowledge, were therefore reduced to zero, because the church was not characterized by love. It was a stinging rebuke to the Corinthian values, and simply testifies to their immaturity: 'infants in Christ'. What would Paul say to the divided congregations of the twenty-first century? Would he not tell us also to grow up?

35

Love Never Ends

⁸Love never ends. As for prophecies, they will pass away; as for tongues, they will cease; as for knowledge, it will pass away. ⁹For we know in part and we prophesy in part, ¹⁰but when the perfect comes, the partial will pass away. ¹¹When I was a child, I spoke like a child, I thought like a child, I reasoned like a child. When I became a man, I gave up childish ways. ¹²For now we see in a mirror dimly, but then face to face. Now I know in part; then I shall know fully, even as I have been fully known.
¹³So now faith, hope, and love abide, these three; but the greatest of these is love (1 Cor. 13:8–13).

In this concluding paragraph, Paul crowns his argument by widening his perspective to include the eternal realms. The primary importance of Christian love is established by reference to its everlasting character. *Love never ends.* The apostle is thinking again of the gifts which were so greatly valued among his readers – *prophecies . . . tongues . . . knowledge*, but only to affirm their temporal, transient nature. *They will cease . . . pass away* (verse 8). They are valuable gifts, but only in the perspective of this world with all its imperfections and impermanence. To elevate them, therefore, in our scale of values above what is eternal, is to make a huge error of judgement. If all our energies are engaged in our present experiences and use of spiritual gifts, without recognizing the priority of love, we are investing in time rather than in eternity.

For we know in part and we prophesy in part (verse 9). The word translated *in part* occurs again in verse 10 where it is translated as *the partial*, which disappears when perfection, or completeness, comes. Therefore whatever gifts of knowledge God may give his people in this world and whatever ability to speak out his truth in prophecy, they will always be less than complete and only partial. This is part of what it means to be God's people living in mortal bodies, in a fallen world. We have not yet arrived at home. We are on pilgrimage to our heavenly city, where we shall see the King in all his glory and then we shall be changed into his likeness (see *1 John* 3:2). Here we live in shadow-land, in the temporary and the transient, in a world that is itself destined to be replaced by new heavens and a new earth. Paul will re-visit this theme in his second letter with its great Christian affirmation: 'We look not to the things that are seen but to the things that are unseen. For the things that are seen are transient, but the things that are unseen are eternal' (*2 Cor.* 4:18). Present prophecy and knowledge are only a pale foreshadowing, a partial and temporary substitute for the full and complete knowledge we shall have *when the perfect comes.*

To help us understand this profoundly important reality, Paul uses two contrasting images from the area of everyday experience. In verse 11, he compares childhood with adulthood, and in verse 12, the reflection in a mirror with the reality it represents. He has already exhorted the Corinthians on several occasions to grow up, but that is not so much his point here. Rather, he is saying that however much we may mature in Christian character and behaviour in this life, as indeed we should, yet, at best, it will be only a childhood, compared with our full adult status of complete maturity in heaven. Childish language, thought and reasoning are entirely appropriate to children. But they are not the permanent state. Children are in process, in transit to adulthood, and while the figure of Peter Pan (the boy who never grew up) has some attraction in a fairy-tale, in real life its equivalent would be an unmitigated tragedy. *When I became a man, I gave up childish ways* (verse 11b). But the tragedy unfolding in Corinth is that the Christians are continuing to hold on to their childish ways, settling for immaturity rather than adulthood, because of their insistence on majoring on the transient gifts of time rather than the eternal values of love. Their bickering and jealousies, their pride and spite, their factions and divisions all belong to the nursery and are totally inappropriate in those who should be adult. Children at the nursery stage have no perspective on the adult life that lies ahead of them, but when it arrives, holding on to childish ways will not be an option. The Corinthians seem to have forgotten the realities of perfection in heaven in their squabbles about their transient, earthly gifts. They were living as if there was no life beyond the nursery.

The second picture reinforces the same idea. *Now we see in a mirror dimly, but then face to face* (verse 12a). The reference to seeing Christ face to face clearly connects the argument to the *parousia*, the second coming of Christ, when he will bring in his eternal kingdom in all its fullness. It is at this point that the reflection is replaced with the reality, and gifts will no longer be needed. Perfection removes all the imperfect precursors. 'Face to face' seeing removes all our misconceptions and poor understanding. The distortions of the reflections seen in a metal mirror are replaced by flawless knowledge. *Then I shall know fully, even as I have been fully known* (verse 12b). God's knowledge of me is already perfect and complete, Paul states, and on the last day my knowledge of him will be equally full, by his grace. The wise Christian lives in the light of these eternal certainties and permanent eternal values, not in transient earthly experiences, and such a life involves being committed to love.

The final verse both summarizes and clinches the argument. *So now faith, hope, and love abide. But the greatest of these is love* (verse 13). The 'now' is probably intended to refer to our present state of imperfection, in which we see only imperfectly and where faith, hope and love are all greatly needed. But there is an important sense in which they will not all last forever. Faith is no longer needed when the reality is fully apprehended. Hope is no longer in existence when what was hoped for has transpired. But love never ends. The business of heaven is to love God to perfection and to love all those who are around his throne. Love is the currency of the eternal kingdom and so it will never be superseded. How partial our best knowledge and richest experiences on earth will appear by comparison! The supreme reason, however, for the eternality of love is that it is the expression of the character of the eternal God. It is not appropriate to speak of God having faith or exercising hope, for he knows everything and understands the end from the beginning. He is not bound by our temporal constraints or our limited capacities. Yet it is entirely appropriate to speak of God loving and, more than that, to recognize that his very nature is love. That is why love is *the greatest of these* and *a still more excellent way*. Even now, faith, hope and love matter much more than gifts and ministries, since what we are is more important than what we do, but love will last for ever.

36

Speaking Intelligible Words

¹Pursue love, and earnestly desire the spiritual gifts, especially that you may prophesy. ²For one who speaks in a tongue speaks not to men but to God; for no one understands him, but he utters mysteries in the Spirit. ³On the other hand, the one who prophesies speaks to people for their upbuilding and encouragement and consolation. ⁴The one who speaks in a tongue builds up himself, but the one who prophesies builds up the church. ⁵Now I want you all to speak in tongues, but even more to prophesy. The one who prophesies is greater than the one who speaks in tongues, unless someone interprets, so that the church may be built up.

⁶Now, brothers, if I come to you speaking in tongues, how will I benefit you unless I bring you some revelation or knowledge or prophecy or teaching? ⁷If even lifeless instruments, such as the flute or the harp, do not give distinct notes, how will anyone know what is played? ⁸And if the bugle gives an indistinct sound, who will get ready for battle? ⁹So with yourselves, if with your tongue you utter speech that is not intelligible, how will anyone know what is said? For you will be speaking into the air. ¹⁰There are doubtless many different languages in the world, and none is without meaning, ¹¹but if I do not know the meaning of the language, I will be a foreigner to the speaker and the speaker a foreigner to me. ¹²So with yourselves, since you are eager for manifestations of the Spirit, strive to excel in building up the church.

¹³Therefore, one who speaks in a tongue should pray for the power to interpret. ¹⁴For if I pray in a tongue, my spirit prays but my mind is unfruitful. ¹⁵What am I to do? I will pray with my spirit, but I will pray with my mind also; I will sing praise with my spirit, but I will sing with my mind also. ¹⁶Otherwise, if you give thanks with your spirit, how can anyone in the position of an outsider say "Amen" to your thanksgiving when he does not know what you are saying? [17]For you may be giving thanks well enough, but the other person is not being built up. [18]I thank God that I speak in tongues more than all of you. [19]Nevertheless, in church I would rather speak five words with my mind in order to instruct others, than ten thousand words in a tongue (1 Cor. 14:1–19).

With the opening of this new chapter, Paul returns to the theme of the exercise of spiritual gifts within the Corinthian congregation. It was clearly a highly contentious issue, as indeed it continues to be in many churches today, so that the teaching of chapter 13 about the priority of love is now seen to be the central ingredient of Paul's treatment of the whole matter. Whatever gifts individuals may have, what is of primary importance is *how* they are used. It is as though the apostle is loath to leave this emphasis, with his opening command, *Pursue love*. But he quickly links it to the business in hand by showing that it is not contrary, but essential, to his next exhortation, namely *earnestly desire the spiritual gifts* (verse 1). The two belong together. Here, what were earlier described as *charismata*, gifts of grace, are termed *pneumatika*, gifts of the Spirit, but the two are, of course, the same. With the introduction of the additional phrase *especially that you may prophesy*, Paul launches in to the next part of his agenda, which is to correct the over-valuation of tongues in the congregation at Corinth and to establish the superiority and need of the gift of prophecy.

1. PROPHECY AND TONGUES COMPARED (verse 2–5)

The use of '*For*' at the start of verse 2 alerts us to the fact that Paul is going to justify his elevation of prophecy as the most desired gift, in comparison with tongues, which seems to have been the gift the Corinthians most desired and elevated. The word translated 'tongue' (*glossa*) has a wide range of meanings including the tongue, speech, talk or language. Several commentators have pointed out that every time the term is used in the chapter it could equally well be translated 'language', without any loss of meaning or clarity. Their point is that it does not have to signify ecstatic speech. The speaker is not in a trance but consciously self-controlled. However, the essence of the spiritual gift is the utterance of sounds (words) the meaning of which the speaker does not understand. Thus, the speaker *speaks not to men but to God, for no one understands him* (verse 2). Paul's concern is for the congregation, who listen to these utterances, that they will derive no benefit from them because they have no idea of the meaning of the sounds, as with any unlearned foreign language. Therefore, the speaker *utters mysteries in the Spirit* (verse 2b) and only God understands them. Since the purpose of speech is to convey meaning, they are speaking to God, rather than to men. This has rightly led many to recognise that uninterpreted tongues are for private, rather than public, use. The experience of those who use the gift is of a heightened capacity to praise and pray to God beyond their normal ability in their native language. Although the speaker does not understand the meaning, he knows that he is speaking to God.

On the other hand, the one who prophesies speaks to people (verse 3). This is Paul's first point of contrast, stressing the intelligibility of the prophetic message to the hearers, which automatically ensures that it is much more beneficial to the church. We must always keep his corrective purpose in mind. However, intelligibility is only the first point. Verses 3 and 4 provide further arguments for the superiority of prophecy based on what it achieves in those who hear and receive its message. It speaks for *upbuilding and encouragement and consolation* (verse 3) so that *the one who prophesies builds up the church* (verse 4). The other-focused spirituality of the cross again dictates Paul's values. While he is very happy for every one at Corinth to speak in tongues (verse 5) he would rather they prophesied because the edification of the church is what matters most and that will only happen when God's word is spoken intelligibly, in the power of God's Spirit. Therefore, *the one who prophesies is greater than the one who speaks in tongues, unless someone interprets* (verse 5). With this, the contrast is complete.

It is significant to learn also from this paragraph just how the church is to be edified, or built up. The essence of prophecy is not predictive of the future so much as revelatory of the mind and will of God. The prophet speaks God's authoritative word to the congregation. Much discussion has been generated over the issue of how God's prophetic word is heard and received today. Clearly, if it is the means by which a congregation is 'built up, encouraged and consoled' it is much needed. Some have claimed to be the channels of direct, authoritative revelation to the contemporary church, with varying results. church history has many examples of such claims that, sadly, have been the cause of much division and eventual disappointment. False prophets are an equally present reality. To claim to speak on behalf of God is no proof of the truth of the claim. Sometimes the utterances of a 'prophet' have been collected, published and given initially an authority alongside that of Scripture, but as time passes such 'words' tend to usurp and downgrade the authority of Scripture, for the simple reason that the word of the contemporary prophet will always seem more immediate and relevant and therefore more attractive than that of the Bible. Soon the 'prophet' is paid more attention than the 66 books of canonical Scripture and, all too often, a new cult or sect is born.

If we agree that the Bible is God's clear, authoritative word, spoken in specific historical contexts, but unchanging in its truth because it is revelatory of our unchanging God, then 'prophecy' today will be the authoritative proclamation of that life-giving truth in the power of the Holy Spirit. The opening verses of Hebrews teach us that, in Christ, God has spoken his final word to man and completed his finished work for man, so that we do not expect any further revelation. Nothing said by any contemporary 'prophet' has the quality or authority to be bound into our Bible as a sixty-seventh book. Indeed, any so-called prophecies must be tested by Scripture and should not be accepted as true unless they are in accord with the perfect and completed revelation. That is why the church has always seen itself as living in 'the last days'. There is only one momentous event remaining for God's salvation-plan to be completed – the return of the Lord Jesus Christ in power and glory. No further revelation is either needed or provided, for you cannot add to completeness. The contemporary church will be edified only in so far as the attested and assured word of Scripture is proclaimed, with all its relevance, in the Spirit's power, as this is the only sure and abiding Word of God.

Support for such a view is also provided by Paul's comments in Ephesians where he refers to the apostles and prophets as the 'foundation' of the church, 'Christ Jesus himself being the chief cornerstone' (*Eph.* 2:20). Before the canon of Scripture was complete the apostles and prophets were given as the channels of gospel revelation, upon whose foundation the churches were built. Ephesians 3:4–5 describes the mystery of Christ in the gospel, 'as it has now been revealed to his holy apostles and prophets by the Spirit'. These are clearly New Testament prophets, for the next verse refers to the 'mystery' of the gospel through which Jews and Gentiles are 'members of the same body'. If the apostles and prophets were foundation gifts, then the continuing gifts seem to be those listed immediately after them in Ephesians 4:11 – 'evangelists' (preaching the apostolic gospel) and 'pastors and teachers' (proclaiming prophetically the biblical revelation of God). Powerful biblical preaching is still God's great means of building up his church.

2. PROPHECY IS SUPERIOR TO TONGUES (verses 6–12)

Paul continues to pursue his emphasis that the content of a message is the criterion by which a gift's usefulness is to be assessed, within the context of the church. The Corinthians seem to have used the display of the gift and its obvious supernatural origin as their criteria, but neither of these has a beneficial effect. Personalizing his argument, Paul makes the point that his own speech would only benefit them, when he came to the congregation in Corinth, if *I bring you some revelation or knowledge or prophecy or teaching* (verse 6). The argument is illustrated by an example from the world of music. A tune can only be recognized, and identified as a tune, if its notes are distinct (verse 7). No one will get ready to go into battle unless the trumpet call is heard and its message understood (verse 8). *So with yourselves*, Paul argues. When they gather together as a church, if their time is occupied with uninterpreted tongues, *how will anyone know what is said? For you will be speaking into the air* (verse 9). It would be just the same, in terms of its value, as listening to a speaker in a foreign language of which I have no knowledge (verses 10–11). Again, he repeats, *So with yourselves* (verse 12a). If they are going to be keen to use and develop their spiritual gifts, they should major on those that edify and excel in those (verse 12).

Congregational meetings are therefore to be judged not by their excitement levels but by the content of the message proclaimed.

Words of truth strengthen faith, encourage action and equip God's people to serve him and to serve his world. They confirm what is right and correct what is wrong. But they do all this, not by magic, but by their content. If Paul had come to Corinth speaking in tongues but not preaching the gospel of Christ crucified, there would never have been a church. The way by which a church comes to birth will be the way by which it grows strong and thrives. And just as Paul was motivated by love for the people of Corinth before they ever came to faith in Christ, so now they must be motivated by love for one another in the way they conduct their meetings. To allow meaningless speech, or mindless repetition of empty mantras, to dominate their times together is to cease to love and care for one another as they should. To insist on using particular gifts in public, such as tongues, that have no beneficial effect, is a serious dereliction of their Christian duty of love to one another. They might as well be strangers and foreigners to one another. Those who 'pursue love' will excel in gifts that strengthen and encourage the whole body, not in outpourings that confuse or alienate. Once again, love is the vital test of how the gifts are used.

3. THE IMPORTANCE OF INTERPRETATION (verses 13–19)

By this time the tongues-speakers at Corinth may have been feeling very deflated and imagining that their gift was of little or no value at all. Paul is concerned therefore to identify with them and he does so by testifying to his own use of the gift of tongues, which he sees as a gift from God to be received and used with thanksgiving. *I thank God that I speak in tongues more than all of you* (verse 18). This statement ensures that they realize that he is not undervaluing or dismissing one of God's gracious gifts. In the last verse of the chapter he will reiterate that his purpose is not to forbid speaking in tongues, but to regulate it. He wants to keep it in its proper context and not to give to it an exaggerated role or importance. Following his main point that the edification of the congregation is the criterion by which the use of any gifts in the assembly is to be ordered, the logical deduction is that any tongues-speaker who uses the gift in public *should pray for the power to interpret* (verse 13). That is the only way in which the utterance can be of any use to his fellow worshippers.

Verses 14–15 explore in a little more detail what is happening when Paul prays or sings *with my spirit*. A distinction is drawn between the spirit and the mind. In the use of tongues, whether in prayer or song, Paul sees his human spirit as active under the influence of the Holy Spirit, but describes the mind as *unfruitful*. That is probably exactly how the pagan religions would have regarded ecstatic utterance. With the basic dualism of spirit and body so entrenched in Greek thinking, their inclination was to believe that the more out of body and mind the devotee became – the more wholly given over to the spirit in religious ecstasy – the deeper and more to be admired was the experience. After all, the pure spirit was imprisoned throughout its existence in the body, of which the mind was a part, sealed up in an envelope of clay from which it longed to escape. Whenever therefore an ecstatic spiritual experience could overcome the down-drag of physicality, there was given a taste of immortality. Many of the Corinthians seem to have transported this sort of thinking, quite uncritically, into their new Christian life-style, and this would explain why they were so taken up with *glossolalia*. The effect of Paul's teaching would be to move them in a totally opposite direction.

Tongues-speaking may be 'spiritual' in that it is a gift of the Spirit, but it does not engage the mind, and if the mind is not engaged no one else can be edified. Those who do not understand, because they do not know what is being said, cannot add their *Amen*, even though the thanksgiving is of the finest spiritual quality. *You may be giving thanks well enough, but the other person is not being built up* (verses 16–17). This loving concern for his brothers is what leads Paul to his conclusion that *in church I would rather speak five words with my mind in order to instruct others than ten thousand words in a tongue* (verse 19). This, we must remember, is an assessment of a gift in which he excels all the Corinthians, who were themselves so eager to see it exercised in public. About its private use, Paul has no quibble, but in public ('in church') his astonishing assessment of the relative value of unintelligible to intelligible speech is 1 to 2,000. It is 2,000 times more important for prophecy to be heard in the church, than for uninterpreted tongues. If only this view had been adhered to, how many churches today would have been saved from the pain and distress of unnecessary division?

37

A Fitting and Orderly Way

[20] *Brothers, do not be children in your thinking. Be infants in evil, but in your thinking be mature.* [21] *In the Law it is written, "By people of strange tongues and by the lips of foreigners will I speak to this people, and even then they will not listen to me, says the Lord."* [22] *Thus tongues are a sign not for believers but for unbelievers, while prophecy is a sign not for unbelievers but for believers.* [23] *If, therefore, the whole church comes together and all speak in tongues, and outsiders or unbelievers enter, will they not say that you are out of your minds?* [24] *But if all prophesy, and an unbeliever or outsider enters, he is convicted by all, he is called to account by all,* [25] *the secrets of his heart are disclosed, and so, falling on his face, he will worship God and declare that God is really among you.*

[26] *What then, brothers? When you come together, each one has a hymn, a lesson, a revelation, a tongue, or an interpretation. Let all things be done for building up.* [27] *If any speak in a tongue, let there be only two or at most three, and each in turn, and let someone interpret.* [28] *But if there is no one to interpret, let each of them keep silent in church and speak to himself and to God.* [29] *Let two or three prophets speak, and let the others weigh what is said.* [30] *If a revelation is made to another sitting there, let the first be silent.* [31] *For you can all prophesy one by one, so that all may learn and all be encouraged,* [32] *and the spirits of prophets are subject to prophets.* [33] *For God is not a God of confusion but of peace.*

As in all the churches of the saints, [34] *the women should keep silent in the churches. For they are not permitted to speak, but should be in submission, as the Law also says.* [35] *If there is anything they desire to learn, let them ask their husbands at home. For it is shameful for a woman to speak in church. ³⁶Or was it from you that the word of God came? Or are you the only ones it has reached? ³⁷If anyone thinks that he is a prophet, or spiritual, he should acknowledge that the things I am writing to you are a command of the Lord. ³⁸If anyone does not recognize this, he is not recognized. ³⁹So, my brothers, earnestly desire to prophesy, and do not forbid speaking in tongues. ⁴⁰But all things should be done decently and in order* (1 Cor. 14:20–40).

The tone of this second half of the chapter is warm and firm, relational and uncompromising at the same time. Twice (in verses 20 and 26), Paul addresses his readers as *brothers*, building on the family unity they enjoy through Christ and in the gospel. He wants to encourage them to move beyond their present limitations into a deeper and richer maturity. In verse 39 he calls them *my brothers*, expressing his personal affection for them, but he will not yield on his principles and in the same context he warns that any who choose to ignore his teaching will themselves be ignored (verse 38). In this, he is, as ever, the model pastor, not allowing his personal warmth and love for them to compromise the clarity of his instruction. In fact, the proof of his love is that he will not let the church continue its slide into pagan-conditioned compromise. There is a battle on for the heart of this giddy congregation, and it is a measure of the apostle's love for them that whilst all he says to them is spoken in love, yet he will not be swayed from speaking the truth (see also *Eph.* 4:14–16). Once again, the emphasis continues to be on the public meetings and the impact they are having on those who attend them, whether they are Christians or not.

1. LOOKING OUT FOR THE UNBELIEVER (verses 20–25)

Within their family relationship of brotherhood, Paul begins by delivering quite a stunning rebuke. *Do not be children in your thinking.* From the evidence of this letter it is clear that many of the Corinthians did not consider themselves to be spiritually immature. Their spectacular gifts tempted them to think that they were spectacular people, to the extent that some of them were quite happy to criticize Paul's ministry as unimpressive and below par for a trendy, sharp-edged place like Corinth. But throughout the letter Paul has been presenting evidence of their childishness, not in order to score points over them, but to change their lives. When they so easily lose their grip on the gospel of the cross with its call to self-sacrificing love; drift into divisive factions; tolerate immoral and unethical behaviour; and even use God's good gifts to boost their personal status, the charge of immaturity is proven beyond all reasonable doubt.

Paul's demand is that they must grow up, and so verse 20 stresses that the area in which change must come is in their minds, or thinking. Those very minds that were unfruitful (verse 14) now have to be informed by God's word. There may be an acceptable naiveté, or infancy, with regard to evil. Christians do not need to delve into every kind of evil in order to repudiate it. For example, they did not have to attend a pagan orgy in a Corinthian temple in order to understand why they should not attend a pagan orgy! There are plenty of contemporary parallels in today's culture, where a little more Christian innocence might not come amiss. *Be infants in evil, but* (and it is a very important 'but') *in your thinking be mature* (verse 20). The battle is always for the mind. Children are not profound thinkers; they do not yet possess the mental abilities. They love movement, noise, anything exciting and unusual. But what is appropriate for childhood is not so in adult life. 'Grow up!' is Paul's message to them and to us.

Many Christians today have a childish mentality, impressed by sensation and spectacle, swayed by manipulative music, susceptible to sentiment and suggestion. They would rather be made to feel than to think. They prefer their emotions to be stirred, rather than their thinking to be changed. Nursery rhymes are appropriate to the nursery, but God's church is the place for growing up, not for arrested development. True to his point, Paul now begins to stretch his readers' thinking, starting with a quotation from Isaiah 28:11–12 that he describes as written *in the Law,* his short-hand term for the Old Testament (verse 21). The Lord says that he will speak to his people, Israel, in foreign languages, which they cannot understand, *and even then they will not listen to me.* It is a strange quotation at first reading, because it seems as if God is sending unintelligible messages and then rebuking Israel for not listening to him, even though it was impossible for them to understand the words declared.

When we put the quotation in its original context however, we discover that it was a prophesy of judgement. When Isaiah was called, he was warned by God that his message would be rejected by his contemporaries. His ministry would actually make their hearts calloused, their ears dull, and their eyes blind (*Isa.* 6:10). That is exactly what happened and by chapter 28, in the two verses preceding the one quoted by Paul, we find the people mocking Isaiah and accusing him of bringing a message suitable only for the nursery. 'Who is he trying to teach? To whom is he explaining his message? To children weaned from their milk, to those just taken from the breast?' Then they parody his message and reduce it to the level of a nursery rhyme – 'line upon line, line upon line' (see *Isa.* 28:9–10). It is in response to this determined unbelief and flagrant rejection of his word by unbelieving Israel, that God declared his word of judgement, quoted here. They had not listened to his word through Isaiah in their own language that they *could* understand, so he would send the invading armies of Assyria, speaking a language they did not comprehend, to bring his judgement upon their unbelief and sweep them away. In its context, therefore, the unknown tongues were not God's blessing to a faithful congregation, but his sharp, corrective judgement on their unbelief.

Paul now applies this principle to unbelievers who find themselves in a Christian meeting, at Corinth, or anywhere else. The believers who wanted to major on tongues would have argued, almost certainly, that this sign of the supernatural would be the overwhelming evidence to their unbelieving friends, of the reality of God and of his presence among his people. Paul's view is different. *Thus tongues are a sign not for believers but for unbelievers* (verse 22a). He agrees that they are a sign, but in a negative, not a positive way, because, as in Isaiah 28, they are a sign of judgement. Verse 23 traces the thought through. The unbelievers come in and discover that the whole church is gathered together and everyone is speaking in tongues which they cannot comprehend. How are they going to react? They will not understand anything of the gospel through what they hear, since it is totally unintelligible to them, so they will learn nothing about 'Jesus Christ and him crucified', or about God's great offer of grace and mercy to them in the gospel. To them the God of these Christians is totally incomprehensible and so they reject him; they remain in their unbelief and ultimately incur his judgement. The 'sign' for them is not one of life or truth, but one of judgement. Moreover, they will be seriously deterred from ever coming back, because, Paul says, *will they not say that you are out of your minds?* So instead of them finding Christ and new life, they find madness and incomprehensibility, and the God of the gospel is maligned, for though the day of his wrath will certainly come, today is a day of salvation. The sign of tongues has simply confirmed them in their unbelief.

While prophecy is a sign not for unbelievers but for believers (verse 22b) so Paul now turns the coin over to examine the alternative. The gift of prophecy is designed to benefit the church, to build up the believers, as we saw in 14:3–4. It is not specifically addressed to unbelievers, but if they come into a meeting where prophecy is central, their reaction is likely to be very different. For now the non-Christian can understand the message, because the language is recognizable and familiar. The meaning is clear. Although the gift is intended primarily for the church, yet as the unbeliever 'overhears' the content of God's self-revelation in the prophecy, it may have a profound effect on him. *He is convicted by all, he is called to account by all*, since each prophetic contribution will bring God's truth to bear upon his life. In such a meaningful presentation, the Spirit's work in the unbeliever is 'to convict the world of guilt in regard to sin and righteousness and judgement' (*John* 16:8). The gift that is nourishing believers then impacts the unbeliever's mind through the truth, and *the secrets of his heart are disclosed, and so, falling down on his face, he will worship God and declare that God is really among you* (verse 25).

The point is clear. It is prophecy, not tongues, which can move the unbeliever from unbelief to faith, from ignorance to the true knowledge of the living God. The evidences of the reality of God and of his indisputable presence among his people is not in the gift of tongues, but in the powerful proclamation of prophecy; not in ecstatic confusion, but in meaningful communication. To think otherwise is naïve and childish. If the congregation persists in pleasing itself, without any love or thought for the unbeliever, its 'spirituality' is infantile. Grown up Christians order their meetings so that God's power is at work as his word is expounded.

2. NOURISHING THE BELIEVERS (verse 26–40)

This final section of the chapter has been subject to even more scrutiny than the first part over recent years, because it is a unique description of what a congregational meeting may have been like in the Early church. All sorts of projections have been drawn from it with implications, positive and negative, for corporate worship in the contemporary church. But in assessing the validity of these implications it is important to keep in mind the corrective nature of the context. Rather than writing a prescription for all Christian meetings everywhere, at all times, Paul is placing a firm hand on the tiller of a boat that he fears is heading for the rocks, out of control. An equally important consideration, however, is that it is not difficult to have order in a cemetery! The problems at Corinth were the problems of life, as produced by the work of the Holy Spirit in a very pagan city. The challenge to us is how much we know the reality of his ministry breathing through our own patterns and routines. In a day when much emphasis is placed on changing structures, this passage, by its emphasis on submission to God and seeking his will rather than our own, remains a powerful corrective to bureaucratic control as well as to undisciplined chaos.

In the context of the letter, we have noted Paul's strongly recurring emphasis on each member of Christ's body having their part to play. Verse 26 now takes the application of that principle into the organization of the congregational meetings. He first describes their normal procedure. *Each one has a hymn, a lesson, a revelation, a tongue or an interpretation.* The way seems to have been open for many to make their contribution to the meeting, but problems have arisen over the length of the meetings due to self-indulgence. The clear implication is that selfish gift-centredness was turning the meetings into something of a free-for-all, or *confusion* (verse 33). While some monopolized the time for the use of their gifts, others were eased out so that virtually no contribution from them was possible. Rather like the situation with the Lord's Supper in chapter 11, it appears that some were dominating whilst others were becoming discouraged and despairing. Once again, the maturity-principle of working for the good of others – the priority of love – is the remedy stressed by Paul. *Let all things be done for building up.* The aim is not to take part, but to build one another up – the word, literally, is 'edification'. It is for edification that the church gathers together, and edification is what we ought to take away from all our meetings.

Immediately he has re-stated the principle, Paul applies it to the tongues-speakers, who were clearly the chief 'offenders'. The rules are perfectly clear. Repeating the earlier teaching of the chapter, Paul emphasizes that the most important rule is: *let someone interpret* (verse 27b). If this does not happen then tongues must be ruled out of the public meeting altogether. There are not to be more than three such speakers, at the very most, and they are not to speak together but *one by one*. The description of verse 23 where everyone was speaking in tongues at the same time, is probably an indication of what the situation was like in Corinth, namely, one of sheer self-indulgence. Verse 28 pre-empts an objection a tongues-speaker might make to Paul's regulative principles. The speaker can *keep silent in church*. He is not under an irresistible influence of the Spirit, over which he has no control, as a pagan medium might be. He can choose not to speak and he should do so, if it has not been established that there is an interpreter present; otherwise the church will be damaged rather than edified. Nor does the instruction that he should *speak to himself and to God* allow him to exercise his gift under his breath, or in a stage whisper, as a mark of superior piety – keeping quiet means exactly that.

Next, Paul turns to prophecy, as he has done by way of contrast throughout this chapter. Here, however, the practical procedure is remarkably similar. Again, *let two or three prophets speak* (verse 29a) while the *others*, probably the other prophets, but ultimately the whole congregation, *weigh what is said*. The prophets would be recognized by their regular use of the gift and the benefit the church had received from them, but the emphasis is on their function rather than their status. The point is that the prophetic utterance is to be 'weighed', or tested with discrimination, to ensure that the congregation is not being led astray. If a spontaneous divine revelation was given to another, then it should be heard at once and the original speaker should give way (verse 30). *For you can all prophesy one by one* (verse 31) probably indicates that they were not making way for one another and that several prophets were speaking at the same time, refusing to give way. As with the tongues-speakers, there is no exception allowed to this ordered pattern by claiming some irresistible spiritual compulsion, forcing the prophet to break out. *The spirits of prophets are subject to prophets* (verse 32). This is not some uncontrollable frenzy or ecstatic disorder. The prophet retains control of himself and where prophetic messages are given, one by one, in their turn, *all may learn and all be encouraged*. In this way, the prophets, who speak for God, reflect the character of the God whom they claim to represent – *not a God of disorder but of peace* (verse 33a).

In his last corrective statement, Paul turns to the women in the congregational meeting. *As in all the churches of the saints, the women should keep silent in the churches* (verse 34). He is keen to disabuse the Corinthians of the idea that they have some superior spiritual authority to make up their own rules as they go along, or to carve out their own distinctive niche in such matters. The note will be repeated in verse 36, as it was in 4:17. There is no room for opt-out clauses at Corinth in any of these instructions. They are principles that should be followed in every congregation. 'Is Christ divided?' (1:13).

At first sight this looks like a blanket prohibition on women speaking at any time, in any congregational meeting. But that is impossible to square with 11:5 where clearly women are praying and prophesying, in the congregational context. Arguments that Paul is inconsistent, or that this is a later interpretation, must be rejected, since they make the ability of the interpreter the measure and arbiter of God's truth. Others suggest that the word 'women' should be translated 'wives', because of the reference to their husbands, but the same word is used in 11:5. Still others suggest that they were undisciplined, noisy chatterers during the meetings, and that this was a particularly Corinthian problem, but Paul stresses that this is a rule for all the churches. So what does he mean? The rest of verse 34 and verse 35 help us to work it out.

They *should be in submission* and *if there is anything they desire to learn, let them ask their husbands at home*. The immediate context is the weighing of prophecies and these verses are best understood in terms of this activity. The law to which Paul appeals would be the principle of male headship, established at creation and recorded in Genesis 2:20–24. From this the apostle derives a creation pattern of the respective male and female roles, both within marriage and in the church, that is usually termed male 'headship'. If the women were to participate in weighing the prophecies they would usurp the male leadership role in the teaching of the church, since weighing the prophecies implies more authority than giving the prophecies in the first place. The women would then be in authority over the church, over their own and other people's husbands, and not in submission. If they had any problems concerning the prophecies being delivered then the proper course of action was for them to talk it over with their husbands at home, not to intervene verbally in the church, challenging or seizing the authority of the leaders, and so refusing to be submissive. It is in these circumstances that *it is shameful for a woman to speak in the church* (verse 35).

In verses 36–38, Paul anticipates the objections that such instruction may well bring. The Corinthians might claim the freedom to follow their own practice irrespective of Paul's strictures. But what he is teaching is *the word of God* and it did not originate with them, but with God himself. Moreover, they are members of a universal church, not just a local congregation, and they are not at liberty to turn their backs upon other congregations and to go their own way (verse 36). Others may question Paul's authority and claim superior prophetic gifts of revelation to overrule the apostle's teaching. Paul's response is that a true prophet or spiritually gifted person will readily *acknowledge that the things I am writing to you are a command from the Lord* (verse 37). This is not just advice. It has dominical authority. Earlier, in 12:28, we have been taught that, 'God has appointed ... *first* apostles.' Apostolic authority therefore overrules all other gifts and claims to revelation. Prophecy may well be revelatory (14:30) but it will not differ from, let alone undermine, the authority of the revelation already given. The mark of the truly spiritual person will be to recognize the Lord's authority in what Paul has written. If he ignores it, he demonstrates that he himself is ignorant and not worth recognizing (verse 38).

By way of summary, at the end of this long unit, Paul reiterates the primacy of prophecy, but does not forbid or rule out tongues. What concerns him most, however, is the way in which these gifts are used in the public meetings of the church. Because the character of the God who is being worshipped is that of peace and order (verse 33), *all things should be done decently and in order* (verse 40). That is in direct contrast to the chaos of the pagan temples in Corinth with their noise and frenzy; with no one knowing what would happen next and no structure, control, or discrimination. Insofar as those criteria had been imported into the church at Corinth, they were proof of the church's immaturity and ignorance. Paul's gracious, but uncompromising, message is, 'Brothers, grow up!' When even the use of spiritual gifts has been made subject to the self-sacrificing love of the cross, then, certainly, maturity will result.

38

Hold Firmly to the Word

*¹Now I would remind you, brothers, of the gospel I preached to
you, which you received, in which you stand, ²and by which you
are being saved, if you hold fast to the word I preached to you –
unless you believed in vain. ³For I delivered to you as of first
importance what I also received: that Christ died for our sins in
accordance with the Scriptures, ⁴that he was buried, that he was
raised on the third day in accordance with the Scriptures, ⁵and
that he appeared to Cephas, then to the twelve. ⁶Then he
appeared to more than five hundred brothers at one time, most
of whom are still alive, though some have fallen asleep. ⁷Then
he appeared to James, then to all the apostles. ⁸Last of all, as to
one untimely born, he appeared also to me.*

*⁹For I am the least of the apostles, unworthy to be called an
apostle, because I persecuted the church of God. ¹⁰But by the grace
of God I am what I am, and his grace toward me was not in vain.
On the contrary, I worked harder than any of them, though it was
not I, but the grace of God that is with me. ¹¹Whether then it was
I or they, so we preach and so you believed* (1 Cor. 15:1–11).

This is a magnificent chapter, a masterly argument, rich in
teaching, and full of assurance and hope for the future. It is a
fitting climax to the letter, beginning with a reminder of the essentials
of the gospel that the Corinthians had believed, and moving on to
the ultimate victory of Christ over all the hostile forces ranged against
God and his people. We have come to realize that true biblical
'spirituality', which the letter teaches and the apostle exemplifies,
is cross-shaped, finding its focus and dynamic in 'Jesus Christ and

him crucified' (2:2). The only way to be his disciple is to follow in the path of self-sacrificing love. But the climax of the story of the cross is the resurrection. Indeed, without that demonstration of his triumph, we could have no assurance of Christ's victory. But because of the empty tomb and the risen Lord, everything has been changed. It is now possible for Christians on earth to live the life-style of the cross, because of, and through, the power of his resurrection.

Before we look at the verses in more detail, it is worth taking a brief overview of the chapter as a whole. After stating the centrality of the resurrection of Jesus to the apostolic gospel (verses 1–4) and presenting a summary of the evidence proving it to be historical fact (verses 5–11), Paul turns to tackle the issue that was bothering the Corinthians, in that 'some of you say that there is no resurrection of the dead'. He begins by exploring what such a view implies for the whole gospel enterprise (verses 12–20), namely its destruction, because it denies all that believers have experienced of the risen Christ. Then he examines how Christ's resurrection impacts not only upon our status before God now, but also our future hope of glory. By comparing Christ with Adam – the representative heads of two orders of humanity – he demonstrates that Christ's victory is shared with his people (verses 21–28) and that they live in this life, therefore, as citizens of the eternal kingdom (verses 29–34). The implications of eternal life with respect to the believer's physical resurrection are then explored by means of other analogies between 'natural' and 'spiritual' bodies (verses 35–49). The chapter ends with a triumphant exultation in the certainty of the believer's ultimate participation with Christ in all the fruits of his victory, when death is swallowed up in immortality (verses 50–58). Such convictions and assurances were never more needed among God's people than today.

1. CHRIST'S RESURRECTION – BASIC TO THE GOSPEL (verses 1–4)

At the end of chapter 14, Paul has argued that the Corinthians have no separate identity from all the other churches of Christ. They are not at liberty to change, either by addition or subtraction, the apostolic teaching that has been received from the Lord himself. There is only one gospel, which must be consistently believed and constantly proclaimed. This is the link in thought to the first verses of chapter 15, where Paul reminds his readers that his relationship with them and their very existence as a church is totally dependent on the message he preached, *which you received, in which you stand.* The importance of holding firmly to this preached Word is obvious. Because it is the Word of God, divinely revealed, it is the only authoritative declaration of the way of salvation: *By which you are being saved* (verse 2). They are not saved by any other 'gospel', for all other claims are false, and belief in them will ultimately only lead to being lost. To be saved requires the believer to *hold fast to the word,* that is, to go on believing and living out the gospel. *Unless you believed in vain* (verse 2b). Paul raises the possibility that a profession of belief may be made, only for it to be revealed later as empty, or useless, because it proved to be only temporary. It is a warning to his readers not to rely on past profession alone but to demonstrate their perseverance by continuing to hold firmly to the apostolic message. That is how the church in Corinth began and how they must continue.

We are reminded next, in verses 3 and 4, of the content of that saving good news. The phrase, *For I delivered to you as of first importance what I also received* (verse 3a), stresses that Paul was simply the channel, not the initiator, of the message he preached. He himself had been arrested by the risen Christ (9:1) as he was travelling to Damascus to destroy the infant church. He had received a personal commission to preach, as an apostle of Christ, and during his period of preparation in Arabia he did not consult with the other apostles, only visiting Jerusalem after three years. This is explained in Galatians, where he affirms, 'that the gospel that was preached by me is not man's gospel. For I did not receive it from any man, nor was I taught it, but I received it through a revelation of Jesus Christ' (*Gal.* 1:11–12). He is making the same point here, emphasizing that what is *of first importance* is God's judgement and not his. The gospel that brought the church in Corinth to the birth was not a human, albeit apostolic, tradition, but God's revealed Truth, grounded in historical reality.

Christ died for our sins is the starting point, though the additional phrase *in accordance with the Scriptures* alerts us to the realization that the cross of Christ is the fulfilment of many Old Testament promises and prophecies. In this short sentence, we understand both the event and the divine explanation. The Christ who died had no need to die, for he was and is the eternal Son of the Father. Yet he freely gave his life to pay the price of our sin, and so we are forgiven and saved. *He was buried* (verse 4) is again an historical fact. His burial confirmed the reality of his death. There is an empty tomb to explain, and the Christian claim is one of resurrection, not resuscitation. *He was raised on the third day*, as he himself foretold, and the Old Testament prophecies predicted (see, for example, *Psa.* 16:9–11). Here too, with the reference to the third day, the emphasis is on the historical fact. Just as surely as he died and was buried, he rose and is alive forevermore.

Without the death of the Lord Jesus there would be no atoning sacrifice, no satisfaction of God's wrath, no penalty paid, no justification, forgiveness or reconciliation. But without his resurrection there would be no guarantee of these realities, no victory over sin and death, no conquest of the devil, no eternal life. Easter joy is the confirmation of all these gospel realities in the affirmation: 'The Lord is risen'.

2. CHRIST'S RESURRECTION – BASED ON SOLID EVIDENCE (verses 5–11)

The historical evidence for the resurrection of Christ has always been a main strand of Christian apologetics. The experience of one man, Frank Morrison, was similar to many. He set out to disprove the resurrection but was so convinced by the evidence that he came to faith himself and wrote the best-selling book '*Who Moved the Stone?*' recounting his experience. The case had rested firstly, on the empty tomb, with its unanswerable challenge as to what had happened to Christ's body if it was not raised, but secondly, on the appearances of the risen Lord, which is what Paul focuses on here. His overall purpose, in this context, is to demonstrate the historical reality of the resurrection of Jesus in order to deliver a knock-down blow to those Corinthians who were sceptical about the whole idea of resurrection.

In verses 5–8, the post-resurrection appearances of Christ (or some of them) are recorded. The list is not exhaustive, and Paul probably confines himself to those that were so well-known to the whole church that their witness was especially authoritative. Beginning with, *he appeared to Cephas*, as Peter was known in Corinth (1:12; 9:5), he broadens out to *the twelve*, the inner group of disciples, minus Judas Iscariot, who having witnessed Christ's life and death became, as a group, and some individually, witnesses of his resurrection. These accounts are familiar to us from the gospels, but verse 6 introduces new evidence. *He appeared to more than five hundred brothers at the same time.* This probably refers to the Galilean appearance referred to in Matthew 28:10, 'Go and tell my brothers to go to Galilee, and there they will see me', though Matthew 28:16 refers specifically only to 'the eleven disciples'. The indications are that there were many more followers of Christ resident in Galilee than the 120 in Jerusalem during Pentecost (*Acts* 1:15). Paul's addition, *most of whom are still alive, though some have fallen asleep* (verse 6), seems to invite any sceptics to check out the eye-witness testimony for themselves, and is a mark of his confident certainty. James (verse 7), listed apart from the apostles, is the brother of Jesus, who was an unbeliever for so long before the resurrection (*John* 7:5) but who was found amongst the group of disciples after the ascension (*Acts* 1:14) and later became the leader of the Jerusalem church. The various appearances are probably listed in chronological order here, so that the occasion '*to all the apostles*' refers to the day of Christ's ascension. It is followed by the post-ascension appearance to Saul of Tarsus, *last of all, as to one untimely born* (verse 8b). This last phrase is almost certainly a reference to the violent nature of Paul's new birth, snatched away from his persecuting zeal.

Indeed, this becomes the focus of verses 9–11. Paul's transformation, from the fanatical Pharisee to the apostle to the Gentiles, still amazes and overwhelms him. *The least of the apostles* feels that he is not worthy even of that title when he considers his past record, *because I persecuted the church of God* (verse 9). And yet, his is a wonderful story of God's grace at work through this very gospel that was preached to the Corinthians. Through the resurrection appearance to Paul, by which he was called to take the gospel to the nations, we are brought full-circle to the existence of the church in Corinth, which is itself therefore a proof of the resurrection. How can its members now start to question the reality of the resurrection? Only a risen Christ could have confronted and transformed Paul, in the way that he did, so that his life also became a confirmation of the reality of God's grace. It is *by the grace of God I am what I am* (verse 10a). Moreover, that grace not only saved Paul but also empowered him, so that he even exceeded the labours of other apostles in the work of preaching this glorious gospel. The risen Lord still turns enemies into disciples and calls them to his service, irrespective of their personal unworthiness. Paul stood united with all the apostles in proclaiming the same message of grace through Christ crucified and risen. It is in that same apostolic line that both the Corinthian church and its successors today are to keep standing (verse 11).

39

If Christ Has Not Been Raised ...

¹²Now if Christ is proclaimed as raised from the dead, how can some of you say that there is no resurrection of the dead? ¹³But if there is no resurrection of the dead, then not even Christ has been raised. ¹⁴And if Christ has not been raised, then our preaching is in vain and your faith is in vain. ¹⁵We are even found to be misrepresenting God, because we testified about God that he raised Christ, whom he did not raise if it is true that the dead are not raised. ¹⁶For if the dead are not raised, not even Christ has been raised. ¹⁷And if Christ has not been raised, your faith is futile and you are still in your sins. ¹⁸Then those also who have fallen asleep in Christ have perished. ¹⁹If in this life only we have hoped in Christ, we are of all people most to be pitied. ²⁰But in fact Christ has been raised from the dead, the firstfruits of those who have fallen asleep (1 Cor. 15:12–20).

After such ringing declarations of the certainty of Christ's resurrection and of the fact that this is the message that the Corinthians believed and that had brought them to the birth, the question of verse 12 comes as a devastating blow. *How can some of you say that there is no resurrection of the dead?* We have to stop and ask what on earth was going on in the Corinthian church that such a fundamental gospel belief could be so sceptically rejected. Paul's question in verse 12 is not, however, an expression of disbelief or frustration: 'How on earth can you be so foolish!' It is, rather, a logical deduction, expressing the fact that if the resurrection of Christ really happened, as it did, then no one can argue philosophically that resurrection is an impossibility.

1. REASONS FOR UNBELIEF

There are two possible reasons underlying this false Corinthian thinking. In Paul's last letter, written probably ten or twelve years later to Timothy, he will speak of Hymenaeus and Philetus, who said 'that the resurrection has already happened' (*2 Tim.* 2:18). This amounted to a denial of the physical resurrection, probably on the grounds that they were already experiencing the full blessing of the gospel, triumphant over sin, disease, and all of Satan's works in this world. These two may well have had their prototypes at Corinth, especially as Paul stresses later in this chapter that 'flesh and blood cannot inherit the kingdom of God' (verse 50), and that 'we shall all be changed' (verse 51), so that any triumphalist claim to be already in heaven and not to need the resurrection is shown to be false. It may be, however, that the traditional Greek division or dualism between body and spirit lies behind their attitude. They believed, perhaps, in the isolated fact of Jesus' return to life after his crucifixion, but did not see that this unique event had any resurrection implications for Christians. As taught by Plato, standard Greek thinking accepted the immortality of the soul, which was degraded by carnal desires and the vicissitudes of life during its imprisonment in the body. If death freed the soul to return to its original state of purity, then the idea of physical resurrection was horrific. A pure soul would want to escape from physicality. So Paul argues that God made both matter and spirit, and that our humanity blends both together. Regeneration is not just renewal of the soul but of the whole person, so that resurrection is a vital part of the Christian's future. The eternal state is not a mere continuance of a disembodied soul, it involves a new 'spiritual' body, suitable for the new environment of heaven. Whichever of these equally possible explanations lies behind this disastrous error in Corinthian thinking, Paul's riposte is sharply argued and without compromise. We need to follow his argument through.

2. IMPLICATIONS OF UNBELIEF

He begins, in verse 13, by stating that a blanket denial of the possibility of resurrection inevitably carries with it the denial of Christ's resurrection. If it cannot happen, then it did not happen to

Christ. Several implications are then noted. Firstly, *our preaching is in vain and your faith is in vain* (verse 14), because the message proclaimed and the belief it generated would both be founded on fiction – a religious notion – rather than on historical reality. The point is obvious, but devastating. The sceptics cannot choose to remove this stone from the edifice of their Christian faith and hope to keep the rest of the building intact. The whole structure would crumble, because there would be no guarantee that anything Christ was or did had lasted beyond his death; there would be no evidence that his sacrifice had been accepted by God, or that life beyond death exists. The stakes are already very high.

Next, *we are even found to be misrepresenting God* (verse 15). The universal apostolic testimony is that God raised Christ from the dead, but if that is not true, the apostles are liars and the foundation stones of the church are found to be totally false. They cannot be honest, sincere men; they are charlatans. Their word cannot be trusted and it is no good believing anything they say. Relentlessly, Paul drives the point home (verses 15b–16) as he forces his readers away from any compromise or fudge, and to face the question, 'Did Christ rise, or not?' There are only two possibilities. Of course, a 'middle way' is still very popular with people who would like to hold on to the aspects of the Christian faith that are more attractive to them without having to believe anything as supernatural as physical resurrection. They speak of a 'spiritual resurrection', though to first-century minds the phrase would have been a contradiction in terms. What they mean is that the memory of Christ has continued; his ideals live on and people still seek to govern their lives by his teaching, so that in these ways he is still alive and with us. It is the concept that 'John Brown's body lies a-mouldering in the grave, but his soul goes marching on!' Paul's arguments are designed to demolish all such compromises because he knows that if they are allowed to continue unchecked they will ultimately demolish the church and the gospel.

Furthermore, *if Christ has not been raised, your faith is futile and you are still in your sins* (verse 17). Faith's validity is tested by the reality of its object. It is not just faith for faith's sake, but faith in the crucified Christ that produces forgiveness of sins, and faith in the risen Christ that creates newness of life. A dead Christ means no forgiveness, no deliverance from sin's penalty at the hand of God's wrath, and no power over sin's tyranny in our everyday experience. Moreover, if there is no forgiveness of sins, then there is no way in which any human being can be ready to meet God or to live with God, beyond this world. Our guilt is so great that we could never atone for our faults even if we had a thousand lives to live. Only a perfect representative and substitute for our rebellious human wills and actions could open up the way to God. Furthermore, a dead Jesus means that *those also who have fallen asleep in Christ have perished* (verse 18). Death and sin are partners: if sin persists, without being forgiven, then death triumphs. All the Christians who died in the faith of Christ, falling asleep in the body but believing that they would wake in God's presence, in eternal life, would have been deluded. The focus of their hope was the life of the world to come, but this is a mere illusion if Christ was not raised. Thus Christians are twice losers, renouncing the life-style of a rebellious world and for a heaven that does not exist. *If in this life only we have hoped in Christ, we are of all people most to be pitied* (verse 19). What Paul means is that to undergo suffering for Christ now is nonsensical if there is no eternal reality. We are to be pitied because we are deluded and cheated. Indeed, if their present experience is all that the gospel has to offer, then not much has been gained, given that its message emphasizes our continuing propensity to sin, our weakness and our vulnerability.

Paul really wants his readers to feel the force of his 'all or nothing' argument. The resurrection is a key battleground evangelistically, because if you do not believe it happened there is no logical reason to accept God's grace in the gospel and to submit to Christ as Lord. But if it *did* happen, then his claims are proven, and everything else in Christian discipleship flows from this fundamental reality. Paul ends this section, therefore, with the resounding confidence of verse 20. After taking us through a scenario where there is no faith, no truth, no forgiveness and no hope of eternal life, because there is no resurrection, Paul now asserts, *but in fact Christ has been raised from the dead, the firstfruits of those who have fallen asleep* (verse 20).

This verse acts as a bridge between the historical fact of the resurrection and the personal expectation of the resurrection's outworking in every believer's individual experience. The link is made by the use of the term 'firstfruits'. Reverting to Old Testament imagery,

Paul recalls the provisions made in Leviticus for the annual ritual of the firstfruits. A representative sheaf of the first grain to be harvested was to be brought to the priest for him to wave it 'before the LORD, so that you may be accepted' (*Lev.* 23:11). After seven weeks from the Sabbath after the presentation of the wave offering, or the firstfruits, – that is, on the fiftieth day – an offering of new grain was to be presented. Two loaves of fine flour, baked with yeast were to be presented as a wave offering of 'firstfruits to the LORD' (*Lev.* 23:17). These were a token of the harvest that was to come and a joyful thanksgiving to the Lord for his faithfulness in providing another year's crops. On this analogy therefore, the resurrection of Christ is the firstfruits of the resurrection of all of his redeemed people, who have *fallen asleep* in him. Firstfruits was a celebration and a guarantee of the full harvest yet to come, and was expressive of God's faithfulness to his promises (for example, *Gen.* 8:22). Christ's bodily resurrection is seen, therefore, as having huge implications, not only for the future declaration and assurance of the gospel of sins forgiven and eternal life, but also for the hope of those who are saved, centred on their own physical resurrection, that he will 'transform our lowly bodies to be like his glorious body' (*Phil.* 3:21).

40

Everything Under Christ

²¹For as by a man came death, by a man has come also the resurrection of the dead. ²²For as in Adam all die, so also in Christ shall all be made alive. ²³But each in his own order: Christ the firstfruits, then at his coming those who belong to Christ. ²⁴Then comes the end, when he delivers the kingdom to God the Father after destroying every rule and every authority and power. ²⁵For he must reign until he has put all his enemies under his feet. ²⁶The last enemy to be destroyed is death. ²⁷For " God has put all things in subjection under his feet." But when it says, "all things are put in subjection," it is plain that he is excepted who put all things in subjection under him. ²⁸When all things are subjected to him, then the Son himself will also be subjected to him who put all things in subjection under him, that God may be all in all. ²⁹Otherwise, what do people mean by being baptized on behalf of the dead?

If the dead are not raised at all, why are people baptized on their behalf? ³⁰Why am I in danger every hour? ³¹I protest, brothers, by my pride in you, which I have in Christ Jesus our Lord, I die every day! ³²What do I gain if, humanly speaking, I fought with beasts at Ephesus? If the dead are not raised, "Let us eat and drink, for tomorrow we die." ³³Do not be deceived: "Bad company ruins good morals." ³⁴Wake up from your drunken stupor, as is right, and do not go on sinning. For some have no knowledge of God. I say this to your shame (1 Cor. 15:21–34).

The continuing and widening implications of Christ's resurrection are the subject matter of this breathtaking section.

The argument of the 'firstfruits', in verse 20, carries with it a strong note of inevitability, which also provides certainty. Once the first grain has been offered, the process of ripening harvest will inevitably develop and no human intervention can stop it. The full harvest is sure to appear. So, Christ's resurrection sets in motion the inevitable process by which all of God's ransomed people will be raised with him at the end.

1. THE LONG-TERM VIEW (verses 21–28)

In verse 21 we are introduced to the contrast, developed in other places in Paul's writing (especially *Rom.* 5:12–21), made between Adam and Christ, as representative human beings whose actions have a major impact on the whole of the human race. *By a man came death* is Paul's shorthand for the Genesis 3 account of the Fall of mankind from the state of innocence in the garden to the sinful corruption of human nature due to disobedience. Adam's sin infected the whole human race, so that ever since every human being has been born 'in sin' with a sinful human nature that constantly demonstrates itself in acts of sinful rebellion against God – every human being that is, except Christ. Since death is the wage paid for sin (*Rom.* 6:23), only a man who was sinless, and so not subject to the penalty of sin, would be able to deal with the problem of sin's curse. If there is to be life out of death and beyond the grave, then it must be that *by a man has come also the resurrection of the dead* (verse 21b).

The logic of this explanation is then spelt out in verse 22. *For as in Adam all die, so also in Christ shall all be made alive.* The two categories of human nature are to be carefully distinguished in this verse. Every human being is 'in Adam' and therefore subject to death, but it is only for those who are 'in Christ' that there is life. Paul is not here speaking of the general resurrection of the dead, at the final judgement, which the Lord Jesus spoke of in John 5:28–29, when every individual will appear before God. That is an awesome reality, but all who are 'in Christ' will not be subject to God's condemnation on that day. They have already 'passed from death to life' (*John* 5:24) through faith in Christ and therefore share in all the benefits of being united to him, including the eternal life of the resurrection. The inevitability of the death-process initiated by Adam's rebellion and

LET'S STUDY 1 CORINTHIANS

carried on by our own, is now reversed, and replaced by the inevitability of eternal life through Christ's obedience. Christians are raised from the dead to share in the risen life of their risen Lord.

With the start of verse 23, *but each in his own order*, Paul seems to be anticipating a possible objection. How can you be so sure of something you have not seen or experienced personally? After all, Christians 'in Christ' still die and we do not see them 'made alive' as yet. So, Paul reminds his readers that this is a process; a process that is certainly begun, and inevitably proceeding, but as yet is far from complete. It is not yet the time for Christians to receive their resurrection bodies. *Christ the firstfruits* has started the process and nothing can undo that, but its fulfilment in resurrection will be for *those who belong to Christ*, only *at his coming*. Obviously, not all the details are spelt out here, but in Paul's earlier first letter to the Thessalonians, the chronology is made clearer. At his second coming, Christ 'will bring with him those who have fallen asleep' and they will be reunited with their resurrection bodies, since 'the dead in Christ will rise first'. Those believers still alive on earth will then be transformed and 'caught up together with them in the clouds to meet the Lord in the air' (see *1 Thess.* 4:13–18). This is the moment at which the church in heaven and the church on earth will be given their resurrection bodies, raised with Christ.

Then comes the end. With his people resurrected and secure in his presence, the final scenes of the cosmic drama will be played out, as Jesus Christ is revealed as King of kings and Lord of lords, taking his power to reign in sovereign authority eternally. This is described in verse 24 as *destroying every rule and every authority and power*, by which Paul means all the powers, human or spiritual, which are hostile to God's rule and opposed to his sovereignty. Every opposition to Christ's total rule is to be liquidated, *for he must reign* (as he does now and always will) *until he has put all his enemies under his feet* (verse 25). This is a direct quotation of Psalm 110:1 in which the Lord God promises his anointed one (the Messiah) total sovereignty in mighty victory over all his foes. Death is the last great enemy because it continues throughout history until the Lord of life appears at his second coming, but at that moment death itself will be destroyed. Then the firstfruits will culminate in the full harvest as his people are raised in their resurrection bodies, eternally alive in the heavenly kingdom. When death is destroyed, then life has no further enemies and nothing any longer exists that can oppose or hinder God's eternal plan from its absolute fulfilment. The times will have reached their completion and God's great plan will come to its culmination 'to bring all things in heaven and on earth together under one head, even Christ' (see *Eph.* 1:9–10). In this great, climactic moment another Old Testament promise will be fulfilled: 'You have put all things under his feet' (*Psa.* 8:6). In context, this refers to 'man', and in its fulfilment it is the 'proper man', Christ Jesus, who assumes that rule and regains that lost authority. He has already accomplished all this through his death and resurrection. All that we wait for is the day of his revelation or 'unveiling', when his plans are finally executed.

But there is one further important strand of teaching to note from this passage. In commenting on the quotation from Psalm 8:6, Paul perhaps rather surprisingly and, we might think almost unnecessarily, reminds us that when everything is put under Christ's feet, *it is plain that he is excepted who put all things in subjection under him* (verse 27). What does he mean? It takes us back to an earlier phrase in verse 24 where the coming end is described as *when he* [Christ] *delivers over the kingdom to God the Father.* Within this passage the final victory over all the hostile powers and the establishment of God's eternal rule is attributed both to the Father and to the Son. Jesus Christ destroys all his enemies, but the Father puts all things under his feet. This is not to be read as implying any division between the persons of the Trinity, or to suggest that the Son is inferior to the Father, in any respect. The equality of the three persons, Father, Son and Holy Spirit, in the one Godhead is an absolute in the Bible's teaching about the Trinity. But we saw back in 3:22–23 and 11:3 that there is a differentiation of function or role, in the great outworking of God's salvation plan, so that Paul could say there, 'the head of Christ is God'. The same idea is present here. The Father sent the Son into the world to carry out the great plan of salvation, through his perfect deity and humanity. With that plan complete, the kingdom will then have come in all its fullness, so that the Son will be able to present his finished work, his completed task, to the Father, whose will he has perfectly carried out. At this point, *the Son himself will also be subjected to him who put all things in subjection under him* (verse 28). He will hand the kingdom over to the Father, who had handed over everything to him.

The end point is then defined – *that God may be all in all*. Such a consummation almost defies description, but we can know that it means that there will be no area of created existence where God's will is anything other than totally sovereign, where all resistance has been quelled and all enemies destroyed. With this totality will come perfect unity. Everything that hurts and harms, by division, will be gone and the perfect unity of the three Persons of the undivided Trinity will be expressed in their sovereign rule of love, over a perfectly united, resurrected people, in a perfectly appointed universe, a new heavens and a new earth which are the home of righteousness (see *2 Pet.* 3:11–13).

2. THE SHORT-TERM IMPLICATIONS (verses 29–34)

Suddenly, with something of a bump, we are returned from this vision of eternal glory to a very earthly problem, the terms of which baffle every Bible scholar. *Otherwise, what do people mean by being baptized on behalf of the dead?* All our warning bells start to ring. What is Paul talking about? He does not seem to be commending or rebuking the practice, but to what is he referring? The present tense certainly seems to indicate that it was happening in Corinth, but what the particular practice and its issues were is probably impossible to decide. Indeed, Gordon Fee suggests that there are 40 different solutions available!

What we can do, however, is to see how the verse supports and develops the apostle's overall argument. He is picking up the threads from verses 12–19 again, as he continues to work out the implications of saying *there is no resurrection*. Not only will the eternal splendours of verses 23 to 28 lose all foundation and certainty – the greatest long-term perspective of all will be destroyed – but the whole of life's priorities in the here and now will also be invalidated. *What will those do who are baptized for the dead*, if they have to be brought to realize that there is no resurrection? Why go through with such a practice, *if the dead are not raised at all?* (verse 29b). The most obvious meaning seems to be either that people were being baptized for dead believers, who had not been baptized during their earthly lives, or being baptized on behalf of unbelievers, perhaps in the hope that this would be of benefit to them for salvation. Several commentators draw attention to the fact that baptism seems to have been very important in Corinthian thinking, in that Paul drew attention to it as early as chapter 1:13–17. This might possibly indicate that to the Corinthians there was some spiritual kudos to be gained according to the identity of the person who had baptized you, and this may have led to an increase of the party spirit that was lining up behind the rival leaders. Paul plays it all down, not even remembering fully whom he had baptized and affirming 'Christ did not send me to baptize but to preach the gospel' (1:17). However, to return to the main point being made, the clear teaching is that without the reality of the resurrection none of these actions would have any significance at all.

Nor would the nature of the daily life-style that Paul had chosen to live have any significance. In this next section, we re-visit an emphasis from the earlier part of the letter, where the persecution and suffering Paul had endured as a faithful apostle of Christ was seen to reflect the spirituality of the cross much more clearly than the Corinthians' divisive triumphalism (see 4:8–16). In verse 30, '*Why am I in danger every hour?*', and in verse 31, '*I die every day*', the same thought is being expressed. This must mean that he faces possible death during every day that he lives and in case that should seem an exaggeration, he insists, *I protest, brothers*. But he endures this sort of sacrificial life-style, with all its dangers and uncertainties, because he is living in the present with his gaze firmly fixed on eternity. The thing that gives him the greatest satisfaction is that they are Christians who have arrived at *eternal* life through his sacrificial work. If however there is no resurrection, there is not the slightest point in it all. *What do I gain if, humanly speaking, I fought with beasts at Ephesus?* (verse 32). Of course, if individuals are not being saved through this mission, not being raised from the dead to live forever in God's eternal kingdom, then the answer is: nothing. If he shared the same time-bound perspectives common to unbelieving humanity then to risk the physical suffering and dangers that are his daily lot would be utterly pointless and futile. Indeed, life itself would be futile. The only coherent world-view without the resurrection would be: *Let us eat and drink, for tomorrow we die.*

That is how unbelievers live, and Paul warns the Corinthian Christians that if they persist in their unbelief about the resurrection, that is where they too will inevitably drift. They are being *deceived* by the sceptics – the *bad company* of verse 33. The proverb quoted is frequently experienced in life. We become like those with whom we habitually spend time. Therefore, if they were to give room to those who denied the resurrection, they would be corrupted by them into heresy and lose their *good morals*, grounded in God's truth. Verse 34 is a strong and uncompromising conclusion. To deny the resurrection is both senseless and sinful. They need to think through the implications of the false teaching that they seem so ready to embrace and to work out the logic of what no resurrection would imply. They need to revisit the powerful historical evidence that proves that Christ is indeed risen from the dead. They need to recognize the sinfulness of denying that there is a resurrection, because of the wilful and determined unbelief of such an act, and to repent. To fail to respond to the sceptics, in these ways, will only compound their spiritual ignorance. Denial of the resurrection clearly shows that they do not know God's great and gracious purposes, which he brought to completion in the death and resurrection of his Son, Jesus, nor do they appreciate the end-point of total fulfilment to which the whole complex of human history is irresistibly moving. To be ignorant of these realities is to deprive oneself of both motivation to live a godly life in the present, and also the certainty of the believer's glorious future in a resurrected body in the eternal kingdom of God. This great doctrinal passage therefore is also an urgent wake-up call.

Raised a Spiritual Body

[35] But someone will ask, "How are the dead raised? With what kind of body do they come?" [36] You foolish person! What you sow does not come to life unless it dies. [37] And what you sow is not the body that is to be, but a bare kernel, perhaps of wheat or of some other grain. [38] But God gives it a body as he has chosen, and to each kind of seed its own body. [39] For not all flesh is the same, but there is one kind for humans, another for animals, another for birds, and another for fish. [40] There are heavenly bodies and earthly bodies, but the glory of the heavenly is of one kind, and the glory of the earthly is of another. [41] There is one glory of the sun, and another glory of the moon, and another glory of the stars; for star differs from star in glory. [42] So is it with the resurrection of the dead. What is sown is perishable; what is raised is imperishable. [43] It is sown in dishonour; it is raised in glory. It is sown in weakness; it is raised in power. [44] It is sown a natural body; it is raised a spiritual body.

If there is a natural body, there is also a spiritual body. [45] Thus it is written, "The first man Adam became a living being"; the last Adam became a life-giving spirit. [46] But it is not the spiritual that is first but the natural, and then the spiritual. [47] The first man was from the earth, a man of dust; the second man is from heaven. [48] As was the man of dust, so also are those who are of the dust, and as is the man of heaven, so also are those who are of heaven. [49] Just as we have borne the image of the man of dust, we shall also bear the image of the man of heaven (1 Cor. 15:35–49).

D o you sometimes question how the resurrection of the dead can ever happen? Living in such a materialist age as ours, where only what is perceived by the senses is held to be 'real', we can surely identify with Paul's Corinthian questioner, when he asks, *How are the dead raised? With what kind of body will they come?* (verse 35). How can bodies that have been buried, drowned or cremated, hundreds or even thousands, of years ago, or even just yesterday, be reconstituted and raised? The question is not senseless; it is a very natural one to ask. So when Paul comments, *You foolish person!* (verse 36) he is not dismissing the problem as unworthy of his consideration. Indeed, he is going to take the next thirteen verses to answer it, at some length. His rebuke is intended for the attitude that lay behind the question as posed by some of the Corinthian 'wise men'. Like the sceptics of our own time, they were using the difficulty of understanding how it could happen, to ridicule the idea that it ever could happen at all. That *is* foolishness, because it leads to accepting only what our finite reason can fathom, and ultimately to denying the infinity of God and all supernatural demonstrations of his absolute authority and power. Paul's reasoning is based on his awareness that God's creation – his temporal and eternal worlds – is infinitely more wonderful than our present senses can ever begin to appreciate or understand. We must not limit God either to what we have already seen or experienced, or to what we think we can understand. But we have to start with those things in order to begin to comprehend what lies beyond them. So, in answering his questioner, Paul begins with the natural world that we do know, and draws from it two illustrations of a principle that is to be applied to the world that we do not yet know.

1. SEEDS AND PLANTS (verses 36–38)

In his first illustration, Paul establishes two points from the commonplace experience of planting seeds in the ground and waiting for the plant to germinate, to flower and to fruit. The first is in verse 36: *What you sow does not come to life unless it dies.* His point is that you cannot provide for next year's harvest, by taking this year's full-grown stalks and replanting them in the ground. But once they have died, then the seeds that they have produced may be used. If we knew nothing about the process of the annual cycle of seedtime and harvest as given by God in his miraculous provision of sustenance for life on earth (*Gen.* 8:22), it would seem the height of folly to take those seeds and bury them in the dark, cold earth. Who could imagine that the apparently inert bulbs that are buried in the earth all winter will produce the flowers of springtime? What is buried seems totally unconnected to what will appear. Yet, as the Lord Jesus himself taught us, 'Unless a grain of wheat falls into the earth and dies, it remains alone; but if it dies, it bears much fruit' (*John* 12:24). Death is the condition of rebirth, albeit in a totally different form from the original seed.

And Paul's second point is expressed in verses 37–38. *And what you sow is not the body that is to be, but a bare seed.* That much is very obvious to any gardener or farmer. But what actually happens? *But God gives it a body as he has chosen, and to each kind of seed its own body* (verse 38). The plant which emerges has a direct continuity with the seed which has died and been buried. You do not plant an apple seed and see a plum tree grow. Plant life is organised by God in such a way that though the general principle of planting and fruiting is the same in all, each individual specimen has its own distinctive body. But when that body is full-grown it would appear to bear no relationship at all to what was planted months earlier. There is an amazing difference, as well as a hidden continuity. What achieves the 'miracle' is the purpose and power of the divine initiative in all this – *But God* (verse 38a).

Now, says Paul, this is the key for beginning to understand the mysteries of the resurrection. As he will state later (verse 53), we cannot enter the life of the resurrection in our mortal, earthly bodies. For those believers still alive when Christ returns, their bodies will be changed, in an instant. But for the great majority of believers the body must die and decay. Death is the inevitable gateway to life immortal. The earthly body will be sown like a seed and our flesh will decay. However, just as the plant is both different from the seed and also continuous with it, so the resurrection body will be completely new and yet totally connected to the seed which was sown. God brings from the dead seed a truly new life-form, with its own personal distinctiveness. It is this thought that leads the apostle to explore his second illustration that focuses on the differences between the life-forms God has made, the emphasis being on their individuality and distinction.

2. THE VARIETY OF CREATION (verses 39–41)

Paul starts with the observation that *not all flesh is the same*. This is important since it begins to undermine the scepticism that denies the resurrection because it is so different from anything we see or experience at present. What we *do* see in this world is already hugely varied. In considering just the animal life of our planet one cannot but be struck by its almost infinite variety (verse 39). Similarly, when we think of the inanimate creation, whether in the heavens or on earth, we see the infinite variety of ways in which God is able to organise the physical constituents of the created order so as to produce our environment of such complexity and magnificence. No wonder the word that keeps occurring in these verses is *glory* (*doxa*)! The point is that if we find it hard to imagine that God can raise up his people in new resurrection bodies, we have not been looking round sufficiently at his glory manifested in the present creation. Compare human flesh with that of a butterfly – both created by God. Compare the blazing summer sun with the peaceful light of the moon, or with the scintillating beauty of the stars (verse 41). Think of the majestic glory of a mountain range, or the restless pounding of the ocean breaking on the shore. Focus in on the individual and unique complexity of each snowflake, or the tiniest alpine flower. They are all totally different from each other, and yet each is created and sustained by the one sovereign Creator. Learn from the variety within the creation that we *can* see, something of the wonders of that new creation that we are *yet* to see. Does this not prove that the resources of this unimaginably glorious God are totally without limit? He is infinite in power to accomplish his purposes. So why limit God with foolish questions about how dead bodies can possibly be reconstituted? In biblical thinking, atheism is the height of folly (*Psa.* 14:1), and to persist in doubting the reality of the resurrection is totally foolish. It is not so much an intellectual difficulty as wilful unbelief.

3. AND OF THE NEW CREATION (verses 42–44)

Once the illustrations have been presented, the argument is pressed home. *So is it with the resurrection of the dead* (verse 42a). Our resurrection bodies will be different from our present mortal bodies, because they need to be adapted to a different kind of existence. Therefore, in the contrasts that follow, the emphasis is entirely on the superiority in every way of that which is to come, over that which we currently experience. This has the dual effect of both explaining more about the nature of the resurrection and also of motivating us to look forward to it.

What is sown is perishable; what is raised is imperishable (verse 42b). It is clear that 'perishability' is a distinctive characteristic of the human body. By nature we are subject to decay, and that process which we experience throughout life does not end at death. The body that is *sown* in the grave continues to decay, and though it can be delayed, the process is ultimately inevitable. But the body that will be raised has the very quality that could never be true of an earthly body – it is *imperishable*. This is a different kind of glory, an order of magnificence beyond our present comprehension. *It is sown in dishonour, it is raised in glory* (verse 43a). The word translated 'dishonour' is used to indicate loss of rights, as, for example, rights of citizenship. To be a 'stateless' person is to have no right of permanent abode, to be a permanent alien and stranger. Christians are familiar with this description of our present life in this world (see *1 Pet.* 1:1–2 and *Heb.* 13:14). There is a sense in which all of our Christian experience in this world is one of alienation and of expectation of our heavenly dwelling. As Paul will write later in Philippians 3:20–21, 'But our citizenship is in heaven, and from it we await a Saviour, the Lord Jesus Christ, who will transform our lowly body to be like his glorious body, by the power that enables him even to subject all things to himself.' Whatever glories and honours this world may bestow on a Christian, or an unbeliever, they are all left at the grave, buried with that perishable dead body about which there is nothing glorious. But it will be very different on the resurrection morning, for just as Christ was raised from the dead through the glory of the Father, so all who are united to him, by faith, will be raised in glory, with new bodies, of which his own resurrection body is the certain prototype (see *Rom.* 6:4).

It is sown in weakness; it is raised in power (verse 43b). However strong a person may be, our bodies are fragile and weak. Human life hangs on the thinnest of threads and a dead body is an eloquent symbol of total human weakness; it is utterly powerless. But the resurrection body transcends all such limitations. It will be full of divine power and the ability to live forever in the presence of its eternal Creator. *It is sown a natural body; it is raised a spiritual body* (verse 44). Here, in the final contrast, Paul's vocabulary and focus becomes specifically Corinthian, as he picks up terms which have been used elsewhere in the letter and which were among the 'buzz' words of the congregation he is addressing. The natural (*psychikos*) body is compared with the spiritual (*pneumatikos*) body. The former describes our present experience, the latter that which is yet to be. But some of the Corinthians were describing themselves as 'spiritual' already. Indeed, Paul has himself used this very contrast, back in 2:14–16, between the unbeliever who 'does not accept the things of the Spirit of God' and the 'spiritual man' who has 'the mind of Christ'. There is no doubt that in this world believers already begin to experience the blessings of the age to come, through their union with Christ. But while there is much that can be known now, Paul's concern is to guard against a false spirituality that wants to pretend that *all* the blessings of the world to come are available in the present. If some of the Corinthians were claiming to be fully 'spiritual' already and so to have already experienced the resurrection, Paul's response is that they can only enter into the full 'pneumatikos' existence when this natural body has been 'sown' in death, just as the Lord Jesus' natural human body had been; crucified and buried in Joseph's tomb, before he was raised in power. They have no choice but to follow in Christ's pattern: the pattern of the spirituality of the cross here and now, the life of self-sacrificing love, leading through the experience of death to the glories of heaven and of the resurrection life. 'They suffer with their Lord below; they reign with him above.'

The 'natural body' belongs to this world of material reality – time, space and sense. It was created for life in that environment and is perfectly suited by the Creator for that role, so that there is nothing inferior or inadequate about it. But it is quite useless for the life of the world to come. That environment needs a 'spiritual body'. This description does not refer to a non-physical reality, as though the body was composed only of spirit. If that was the case, how could it be called a body? It has nothing to do with disembodied spirits existing in a shadowy after-world; but everything to do with a physical body existing in a different order, in the new heavens and the new earth. God, who is able to order every particle of his creation to accomplish his will, is perfectly capable of producing a new body which has continuity of identity with the natural body of this world, but which is imperishable, glorious, powerful and perfectly suited to the spiritual existence of the heavenly Jerusalem – the life of the world to come. *If there is a natural body, there is also a spiritual body* (verse 44b). It is human personhood which passes through death to the resurrection and which, perfected into the likeness of Christ, will live for ever in a perfect 'spiritual' body, recognizable in its continuity (as was the risen Jesus) and yet transformed in its newness.

4. THE UNDERLYING THEOLOGY (verses 45–49)

The contrast between the natural and the spiritual takes us back to the other contrast developed earlier in the chapter (verses 21–22), between Adam and Christ. Quoting from the creation account in Genesis 2:7: *The first man Adam became a living being*, Paul reminds us implicitly that this was the result of a direct and decisive act of God, as he breathed into Adam's nostrils the breath of life. In this way, Adam became the father of the human race, created for life in God's world. From him we all inherit the same bodily characteristics, and with them the same fallen sinful nature. In contrast, and by a similar decisive act of God, *the last Adam became a life-giving spirit* (verse 45). As the head of a new humanity, Jesus Christ not only has life but gives life (spiritual life) to the sons and daughters of Adam. 'For as the Father raises the dead and gives them life, so also the Son gives life to whom he will . . . For as the Father has life in himself, so he has granted the Son also to have life in himself' (*John 5:21–26*). Again, Paul stresses God's order of events. *But it is not the spiritual that is first but the natural, and then the spiritual* (verse 46). The one leads to the other. The apprenticeship of cross-bearing is necessary as a preparation for glory. For Christians therefore to pretend to some sort of super-spirituality in this life, claiming that the natural body and the life we live in it do not matter, is to distort the divine order. The same error lies at the root of the pretence that we can have the full glories and triumphs of heaven here on earth, if only we can generate sufficient 'faith'. These are serious misunderstandings.

The origins of Adam and Christ are as different as the lives into which they lead their people. Adam, the *man of dust*, is *from the earth*, whose likeness we bear in our physical life in this world. Christ is *the man of heaven*, through whom we share the eternal, spiritual life of his eternal kingdom. The theology of our identification with these two representative heads lies at the heart of the certainty that characterizes Paul's words. *Just as we have borne the image of the man of dust*, through our physical birth and life in this world, *we shall also bear the image of the man of heaven* (verse 49), through our spiritual rebirth, culminating in our resurrection bodies. There is no doubt that our earthly life, even at its best, is marked by our Adamic weakness, sin, impotence and failure. But just as certain is the assurance that we are going to be transformed into the likeness of Christ when we are raised to eternal life. Every believer will be an original, unique individual, and yet every believer will bear Christ's likeness fully, because we are fully in Christ.

42

We Will Be Changed

⁵⁰I tell you this, brothers: flesh and blood cannot inherit the kingdom of God, nor does the perishable inherit the imperishable. ⁵¹Behold! I tell you a mystery. We shall not all sleep, but we shall all be changed, ⁵²in a moment, in the twinkling of an eye, at the last trumpet. For the trumpet will sound, and the dead will be raised imperishable, and we shall be changed. ⁵³For this perishable body must put on the imperishable, and this mortal body must put on immortality. ⁵⁴When the perishable puts on the imperishable, and the mortal puts on immortality, then shall come to pass the saying that is written: "Death is swallowed up in victory."

⁵⁵"O death, where is your victory?
O death, where is your sting?"

⁵⁶The sting of death is sin, and the power of sin is the law. ⁵⁷But thanks be to God, who gives us the victory through our Lord Jesus Christ.

⁵⁸Therefore, my beloved brothers, be steadfast, immovable, always abounding in the work of the Lord, knowing that in the Lord your labour is not in vain (1 Cor. 15:50–58).

This last magnificent section of a mountain-peak chapter begins with a ringing declaration, summarizing the apostle's argument up to this point, and maintaining the absolute necessity of the resurrection. *Flesh and blood cannot inherit the kingdom of God, nor does the perishable inherit the imperishable* (verse 50). There can be little doubt that Paul's opponents in Corinth saw the physical and spiritual in direct contrast, if not conflict, with each other. The more obviously supernatural gifts, such as tongues, were most highly valued in the congregation precisely because they were evidence of a spiritual reality beyond the merely physical. If these gifts were a foretaste of the world to come, and of true spirituality, then it seemed as if the body must be the chief hindrance to the realization of heaven. They could choose to deny the body, or indulge the body, but neither affected the spiritual reality of seeking to escape from the body, in order to set the immortal soul free from its prison-house of clay. Clearly, all such views were only so many compromises with the philosophical ideas of Greek culture. The apostle has consistently sought to correct them during the course of the letter. But in verse 50, he does affirm that major changes have to take place before the life of the kingdom of God can be experienced and enjoyed in its fullness.

What must have brought the Corinthians up sharply was Paul's insistence that the body is essential to the life of the world to come. Far from the body being left behind and forgotten at the end of time, Paul's teaching is that it will be redeemed and transformed. His detailed argument accompanied by the vocabulary of glory and splendour has dismissed any wrong notions that he is talking about corpses being resuscitated. His theology is rooted in the whole revelation of God, from Genesis onwards, in which the created order is shown to be good, since it is the expression of the mind and will of the Creator, who is perfection. Certainly it is true that through the disobedience and rebellion that constituted the Fall, the image of God in humankind has been marred, and the whole creation has shared in the curse which resulted (see *Gen.* 3:17–19 and *Rom.* 8:19–25). But the New Testament's teaching is that all creation, including our human bodies, is involved in Christ's redemptive purposes and work, so that although there will be judgement and destruction of everything that offends God's righteous character, yet according to his promise we are waiting for new heavens and a new earth in which righteousness dwells' (*2 Pet.* 3:13). It is in view of that new environment of a redeemed creation, that the changes Paul now focuses on must take place, in each one of Christ's redeemed people.

1. A WINDOW ON THE FUTURE (verses 51–57)

Behold! I tell you a mystery. This semi-technical term in the apostolic vocabulary signifies a secret that God has chosen to reveal, which could never have been guessed at, let alone understood, unless God had disclosed it. This is entirely in accord with the argument of the chapter that it is a foolish mistake to judge what God will do by our present perceptions or thinking power. The curtain that veils the future will be lifted, as the final piece of the jigsaw is put into position. *We shall not all sleep, but we shall all be changed* (verse 51b). The reference is clearly to a specific future event, a moment in time which we might describe as marking the end of time as we know it, and the beginning of eternity.

The use of the term *sleep* is an important ingredient of the revealed secret, just as the use of the verb 'sown' was, earlier (verses 42–44). Christians have traditionally referred to death as 'sleep', partly because it is the bodily state we know which is most akin to death, but more importantly because it includes within it the idea of waking. If you are asleep and not going to wake up, then you are unarguably dead! But death for the believer is sleep, at least from the point of view of the inactive, perishable body. The spirit, however, has departed to be with Christ, which is 'far better' (*Phil.* 1:23), 'away from the body and at home with the Lord' (*2 Cor.* 5:8). However, on the resurrection morning the body will awake and be reunited with its departed spirit, in all the glorious transformation of the new creation and so 'the dead in Christ will rise first'. After that the living believers, who have not slept, will also be changed into his likeness and be caught up together with the saints of every generation 'to meet the Lord in the air' (see *1 Thess.* 4:16–17). This is when the harvest of resurrection life will be seen springing up from all the seeds that have been sown as Christians have been buried or cremated down the centuries. It is for this reason that churchyards were often called 'God's acre' – the piece of land where his seeds of perishable bodies have been planted, in sure and certain hope of the resurrection to eternal life of all who have put their trust in Christ. All that was sown in perishability will now be raised to inherit the imperishable kingdom.

This instantaneous and totally miraculous transformation reveals the limitless power and sovereign authority of the only living and true God. The majesty of *the last trumpet* signifies a rule and authority that no one can delay or thwart. The origin of the phrase lies in the words of the Lord Jesus himself, when he spoke of the angels of God being sent out 'with a loud trumpet call, and they will gather his elect from the four winds, from one end of the heavens to the other' (*Matt.* 24:31). *The dead will be raised imperishable,* (never to die again) *and we* (Paul is speaking on behalf of all living believers at that climactic moment) *shall be changed* (verse 52). The exact nature of that change is explained in the next two verses. The perishable body preserves a degree of continuity in that it *puts on the imperishable, and the mortal puts on immortality*. Both those believers who have died, and those who are still alive at Christ's coming, are thus totally transformed and receive their resurrection bodies to enable them to live in the new order.

The full implications of this sudden, irreversible and miraculous transformation are spelt out at the end of verse 54, when the promise of Isaiah 25:8 is now, at last, brought to fulfilment. 'He will swallow up death forever'. The context of the original is interesting. It comes within the section in Isaiah (chapters 24–27) that deals with the eternal realities: God's universal judgement of humankind; his glorious victory over evil; and his eternal rule over all, in the heavenly city. The glories of heaven are prefigured in the metaphor of the most lavish banquet imaginable, prepared by the Lord on his holy mountain, for the peoples of the world. This image is developed in the wedding banquet parables of Jesus, and comes to its biblical climax in Revelation 19:9, with the wedding feast of the Lamb. Associated with this great celebration is the death of death itself, which is 'the veil that spread over all nations' (*Isa.* 25:7). This, of course, is exactly what the resurrection of the Lord Jesus proclaims. Death no longer has any power over him. Resurrection is a conquest of death and spells its total defeat. What Christ's resurrection has proclaimed as the firstfruits (verses 20, 23) is now accomplished by the harvest of all his resurrected people, and death's destruction is sealed, as God had always promised (verse 55, quoting *Hos.* 13:14).

Once again, Paul is concerned to spell out the theological reasoning behind these world-shattering assertions. Power has been given to death because of the universal problem of human sin. It is because of this that death is able to rule, as a tyrant, over the whole human race. We find the principle at the very earliest point of the biblical record. God instructs Adam, 'But of the tree of the knowledge of good and evil you shall not eat, for in the day that you eat of it you shall surely die' (*Gen.* 2:17). The long story of human mortality stems from that moment of disobedience. As Paul himself expresses it, the wage that sin pays is death (*Rom.* 6:23) and that is always so because *the power of sin is the law*. It is by the law of God, which is itself the expression of God's perfect righteousness, that sin is defined, and we are pronounced guilty. Indeed, such is the perversity of human nature that the law which is holy and just actually provokes our further rebellion against God, as we resist his commands and refuse to submit to his rule in our lives. Physical death is the entrance gate to that spiritual death of separation from God, under his righteous judgement and wrath, for all eternity. Death could never be conquered by sinners, since we are all born, by nature, under its tyranny; we are guilty by nature and by practice, condemned to be cut off for ever from God.

But, *thanks be to God*, the last Adam became a life-giving spirit! (verse 45). And his victory, as the perfect sinless man, over all the hostile powers that were ranged against him and us, proclaims forgiveness, freedom and newness of life to all who are united to him by faith. *Who gives us the victory through our Lord Jesus Christ.* On the cross, dying as our representative and substitute, Jesus Christ, the sinless Son of God, offered his perfect life of obedience to the Father in the place of our rebellious hearts and wills, carried our punishment and made atonement for our sins. He conquered our death by drawing sin's sting and satisfying the law's just demands, and in so doing opened the kingdom of heaven to all believers.

> He hell, in hell, laid low.
> Made sin, he sin o'erthrew.
> Bowed to the grave, destroyed it so,
> And death, by dying, slew.

God has given to us the victory of eternal life, through what the Lord Jesus accomplished for us in his cross and resurrection, when he 'was delivered up for our trespasses and raised for our justification (*Rom.* 4:25). The empty tomb and the risen Lord, with which this chapter began, are the ultimate proof of the fact that Christ's victory is total and final. All our enemies – the law, sin and death – are conquered forever. It needs no second fight because there are no second foes. No wonder the logic catches fire in these concluding sentences! No wonder Paul bursts into praise and thanksgiving, as he considers the scale of this victory and the immeasurable benefits that flow from it to every one of God's redeemed people! Yet none of this would be so, he has reminded his foolish Corinthian readers, if there is no resurrection from the dead (verses 12–18). What a wonderful assurance to know instead, in the words of the ancient Easter greeting, that: 'The Lord is risen; he is risen indeed!'

2. WISDOM FOR THE PRESENT (verses 58)

The certainty of this glorious future must animate and motivate the believer to live here and now in the light of eternity. *Therefore*, says Paul, in the light of all that lies ahead of us, apply all its implications to your present discipleship and service. We are not to live in the future, becoming detached from the present world in an insulated super-spiritual environment of unreality. We are to live now, but always in the light of the future, as citizens of heaven but fully engaged in the Master's service in this world. Just a moment's reflection shows us how totally different our outlook on life in this world will be, when we realize that death is a defeated foe, its sting has been pulled, and the experience of the ending of life here is 'but the gate to life immortal'. There is then nothing to fear in death, and every reason to devote our energies in this world towards gaining our eternal reward.

This is the motivation that lies behind Paul's closing commands: *be steadfast, immovable*. Because God's final plans are clear and settled and because nothing can shake them, we are to be equally immovable, firmly rooted in the Person and work of our crucified, risen, ascended and coming King, and not allowing ourselves to be blown off course, or uprooted, by whatever hurricanes of scepticism and unbelief we may encounter. The risen Lord will return. He will bring every son and daughter home to glory. We shall be changed into his likeness – all of us. We shall live with him forever. Such assurances will govern all our attitudes to life in the present, if once we make them our own. And the mark of such faith is active, cross-focused service for the Lord.

Always abounding in the work of the Lord, knowing that in the Lord your labour is not in vain (verse 58). At one level this is a very obvious deduction from all that has preceded it, but what a constant challenge it also provides. Think of those two words *always* and *abounding*. What a goal they provide for us to aim for. Now is the time for work and labour, and as time is the only one of God's gifts that is continually decreasing, we cannot afford to be anything other than purposefully centred on the Lord's work. Such activity is *not in vain*, because it has eternal value and reward. It is the longest-term investment possible and it yields eternal dividends (cf. 9:24–27). The theme of the letter is that true spirituality centres on the self-sacrificing love of the crucified Saviour, and that we are called to tread the same pathway. Here is the ultimate incentive to sacrificial service, such as Paul constantly demonstrated. The outcome of all the suffering, work, and labour is the victory of the resurrection and the everlasting life that Christ has purchased for us. It is because we cannot lose, that nothing we do in the work of this gracious, victorious Lord can ever be in vain.

43

If the Lord Permits

¹Now concerning the collection for the saints: as I directed the churches of Galatia, so you also are to do. ²On the first day of every week, each of you is to put something aside and store it up, as he may prosper, so that there will be no collecting when I come. ³And when I arrive, I will send those whom you accredit by letter to carry your gift to Jerusalem. ⁴If it seems advisable that I should go also, they will accompany me.

⁵I will visit you after passing through Macedonia, for I intend to pass through Macedonia, ⁶and perhaps I will stay with you or even spend the winter, so that you may help me on my journey, wherever I go. ⁷For I do not want to see you now just in passing. I hope to spend some time with you, if the Lord permits. ⁸But I will stay in Ephesus until Pentecost, ⁹for a wide door for effective work has opened to me, and there are many adversaries.

¹⁰When Timothy comes, see that you put him at ease among you, for he is doing the work of the Lord, as I am. ¹¹So let no one despise him. Help him on his way in peace, that he may return to me, for I am expecting him with the brothers. ¹²Now concerning our brother Apollos, I strongly urged him to visit you with the other brothers, but it was not at all his will to come now. He will come when he has opportunity (1 Cor. 16:1–12).

This last chapter begins, as did chapters 7, 8 and 12, with the now familiar phrase: '*Now concerning*', indicating again that Paul is taking up an issue that the church in Corinth had raised with him, in their earlier correspondence. This time it concerns the collection Paul was making '*for the saints*', especially, as we know from elsewhere in his writings, for the believers in the Jerusalem church.

1. REGULAR GIVING (verses 1–4)

These few verses provide a fascinating insight into the way in which Paul's itinerant ministry helped to unite together the churches of the Gentile mission, both with one another, and with the original Christian congregation in Jerusalem. There has been some speculation as to why the Jerusalem church was suffering poverty at that time. Acts 2:45 tells us that from the day of Pentecost onwards they were 'selling their possessions and belongings and distributing the proceeds to all, as any had need'. Did the supplies run out? Or was their poverty caused by the scattering due to persecution, recorded in Acts 8:1, or perhaps by the famine referred to in Acts 11:28–29? We cannot be certain of the cause, but we do know that Paul made it something of a crusade among the Gentile churches of Galatia and Macedonia to remember their Jewish brothers and sisters in their need, since he had agreed with the Jerusalem leaders to 'remember the poor, the very thing I was eager to do' (*Gal.* 2:10). That same obligation he now presses upon the Corinthian church.

Paul's instruction is that their giving should be regular and proportionate to their income (verse 2). He does not want to witness a panic-stricken 'whip-round' when he arrives, as that would be more likely to indicate a face-saving exercise, rather than genuine love. Much better to give on a weekly basis, *put ... aside* a suitable sum of money and *store it up,* so that when the apostle comes funds will be collected and readily available. This is a mark of continuous commitment, not haphazard concern. Interestingly, Paul does not expand on the phrase *as he may prosper,* in any sort of detail, and so does not lay down a prescribed proportion or figure. In his second letter, he will tell the Corinthians that 'God loves a cheerful giver', which he defines as a heart generosity, 'not reluctantly or under compulsion' (*2 Cor.* 9:7). But he never takes the opportunity to tell the Corinthians to tithe, as we might have expected. The New Testament emphasis on generous giving militates against the idea of a percentage levy, since some would be able to give much more than 10% and others may for a time not even be able to give that.

This is not a matter of legislation, but of the individual conscience before God, and there are numerous incentives to sow generously in order to reap a generous harvest (e.g. *2 Cor.* 9:6).

It is also important that the money contributed should be properly administered, and that those who have given it should have every confidence that it has been used for the original purpose for which it was given. Verse 3 explains how Paul intends this to happen. He will not take it to Jerusalem himself, but he will provide a letter of introduction to the leaders of the church there, to be carried by delegates from the church in Corinth, approved by the sending congregation. Clearly, they will choose men whom they can trust to carry the mission through faithfully and an added benefit will be the personal contact between individuals within the two churches. Paul may accompany them (verse 4) if the time and circumstances seem appropriate, but his main concern seems to be to establish brotherly fellowship between the congregations. This may be another example of his concern to draw the Corinthian church away from its increasing isolationism and to recall it to its rightful place amongst all the congregations of the saints. Such principles are still applicable to church life today.

2. TRAVEL PLANS (verses 5–9)

This little paragraph provides a significant window on to the way the apostle thought about his ministry and the plans he had in mind. There is an outline scheme in view, dictated partly by the comparative difficulty of travel in winter and partly by the needs and circumstances of the congregations for whom he felt a special responsibility and care. Verse 8 indicates that he is writing the current letter from Ephesus, probably during the winter or early spring, since he plans to stay on there until Pentecost. *A wide door for effective work has opened to me* (verse 9) and we know from Acts 19 that this was his longest period of settled ministry in any one place, and a time during which the word of the Lord spread from Ephesus throughout the whole province of Asia Minor. Luke's account also tells us of the opposition he frequently encountered – *there are many adversaries* – but the two experiences of great opportunities matched by fierce opposition are the common experience of gospel workers down through the centuries. The opponents could not stop Paul, and they should not stop us, as we stand in the only valid apostolic succession, that of gospel proclamation.

However, Paul has some future plans to re-visit Corinth, not by the most direct sea-route across the Aegean, but by the land-route, calling in on the churches of Macedonia (Thessalonica, Philippi and Berea) on the way. His estimate is that this will take him all the summer, so that he may need to *spend the winter* with them in Corinth, *so that you can help me on my journey, wherever I go* (verse 6b). Clearly, the further destination beyond Corinth is unknown at this stage, but Paul has had to come to a judgement that a shorter, earlier visit would not be appropriate for the Corinthians, which is probably the reason why he had written such a detailed letter. The letter prepares the way for a longer visit when he will be able to deal in greater depth with these issues about which he has been so concerned. *I hope to spend some time with you* (verse 7). The pressing current needs and opportunities of Ephesus have led to his decision that he must focus his labours in that city for the time being.

One is struck both by the flexibility of these plans and also by the apostle's deep dependence on God's sovereign overruling and direction. *Perhaps I will stay with you . . . I hope to spend some time . . . if the Lord permits* (verses 6–7). Here is a man who is aware of his own responsibility to use his time for the maximum effectiveness in the work of the Lord, but recognizes also that he is simply a tool in the Master's hands, and that it is the Lord's work, not his. His plans are being formulated, but they are all put at God's disposal, since he is clearly dependent on God opening doors for ministry and wants only to work where God directs him. In our generation of full diaries and fixed schedules, increasingly far ahead, we would surely do well to recover something of the New Testament's perspective of God's ordering of all our steps, making our plans dependent on God's overruling, and accepting James's corrective that since 'you do not know what will happen tomorrow . . . you ought to say, "If the Lord wills, we will live and do this or that" ' (*James* 4:14–15).

3. FELLOW WORKERS (verses 10–12)

It looks as though Timothy will be visiting Corinth, as Paul's agent, before the apostle himself arrives (verse 10 and 4:17). Paul seems to be quite apprehensive about the treatment Timothy may receive at the hands of his Corinthian detractors, and it seems that Timothy may also have had his misgivings about entering the lions' den. They are to *put him at ease among you* (verse 10) and to ensure that his visit is not the cause of any personal fear while he is with them, *for he is doing the work of the Lord, as I am* (verse 10b), and just as they should be, if they heed the injunction of 15:58. Paul's point is that to refuse to receive Timothy will be to oppose themselves to the Lord's work carried on through their apostle and his 'son', and so to put themselves at variance with the ongoing progress of the gospel. Paul's expectation therefore is that Timothy will be well received and listened to. He will 'remind you of my ways in Christ' (4:17b). They are to respond to his teaching and *help him on his way in peace*, to return to Paul (verse 11b) with his reports and news. This will have to be how their problems are dealt with for the time being, and Paul's personal visit will follow within the year.

Our brother Apollos (verse 12) is, however, quite a different matter. We recall from the opening chapters how some in Corinth seem to have been setting Apollos up in opposition to Paul. The apostle is concerned always to destroy this perception. He views himself and Apollos as planter and waterer in the same field (3:6–8) and here he affirms his brotherhood with him. But Apollos is his own man. For whatever reason *it was not at all his will* to accede to Paul's urgent request that he should join the Timothy delegation to Corinth. *He will come when he has opportunity*, but the time is not yet ripe. Part of Paul's concern may be to point out that he is not in any way trying to prevent Apollos from re-visiting Corinth in some forlorn attempt to shore up his own influence as against that of Apollos. They may interpret Apollos' non-appearance in that way and the Apollos 'party' may be disappointed, or even offended, but that is not the truth of the situation. The rivalry between Paul and Apollos is the product of the Corinthian factions, not of the two men themselves. Even though they have disagreed about their travel plans, they are still united in the work of the Lord. How good it would be if today's disagreements among Christian leaders over non-essentials could deepen rather than threaten their gospel unity!

44

Let All Be Done in Love

*[13]Be watchful, stand firm in the faith, act like men, be strong.
[14]Let all that you do be done in love.*

*[15]Now I urge you, brothers – you know that the household of
Stephanas were the first converts in Achaia, and that they have
devoted themselves to the service of the saints – [16]be subject to
such as these, and to every fellow worker and labourer. [17]I rejoice
at the coming of Stephanas and Fortunatus and Achaicus,
because they have made up for your absence, [18]for they refreshed
my spirit as well as yours. Give recognition to such men.*

*[19]The churches of Asia send you greetings. Aquila and Prisca,
together with the church in their house, send you hearty greetings
in the Lord. [20]All the brothers send you greetings. Greet one another
with a holy kiss. [21]I, Paul, write this greeting with my own hand.
[22]If anyone has no love for the Lord, let him be accursed. Our Lord,
come! [23]The grace of the Lord Jesus be with you. [24]My love be
with you all in Christ Jesus. Amen (1 Cor. 16:13–24).*

As the letter draws to its conclusion, the apostle reiterates its
burden one last time in a series of crisp exhortations. These
exhortations indicate the practical action he wants to see his readers
take, in response to all the teaching he has been giving them.

1. RECALL TO PRIORITIES (verses 13–14)

Be watchful is a note which has been sounded many times throughout
the letter. It speaks of an alertness to the dangers which are
threatening the continued health and existence of the church, and a

willingness to take the necessary action to ameliorate the situation. The danger is that the unreality of the super-spiritual stance of some in the church will generate a false sense of security and well-being, which will blind the leadership to the perils they are facing. Triumphalist attitudes will obscure the yawning gap between profession and reality that the apostle has identified. This note of urgency is sounded both because the enemies of the gospel are numerous, subtle and hard to identify, and also because in the resurrection of Christ, God has inaugurated the process of the end of all things (the *eschaton*), and the time is short. The Lord Jesus himself taught all of us, as his people, to be watchful, since we 'do not know when the master of the house will come' (*Mark* 13:32–37). The same challenges face us in our contemporary context. False teachers still arise within the church, distorting God's truth and gathering a following of personal disciples (see *Acts* 20:29–31) to boost their egos and support their cause. Lack of vigilance is still a major cause of defection from the pure gospel of Christ and so it remains a primary duty of under-shepherds, but also of every individual member of God's flock, to be alert and resist error.

Stand firm in the faith is clearly the corollary of such vigilance. Wrong thinking and teaching can only be identified when the truth is clearly understood and believed. So it is always of primary importance in any congregation that 'the faith' must be taught and learned, as without that solid foundation it will be impossible to 'stand firm'. At the beginning of chapter 15, we saw that it was 'the gospel . . . in which you stand' (15:1), the good news of Christ crucified and risen (15:3–4), and now again, we are reminded that there is no other solid foundation on which to build. If the Corinthian Christians really are moving away from 'Jesus Christ and him crucified' (2:2) the church is committing spiritual suicide. It cannot stand on any other basis, 'for no one can lay a foundation other than that which is laid, which is Jesus Christ' (3:11). There should be no surprise at the collapse of Christianity in the western world over the past century or more in that the main denominations have consistently refused to stand firm on Christ crucified and risen. Nor should there be any surprise that where that foundation is faithfully laid and built upon, all around the world, the church is growing apace.

Act like men, Paul continues, or, as in the stirring translation of 1611, 'Quit you like men'. Again this is a note we have already heard sounded in the letter. Back in 3:1, Paul has had to rebuke them, as 'infants in Christ,' for still not being ready for solid food. Their quarrelling and jealousies are symptoms of arrested spiritual development, suitable only for the nursery, indisputable evidence of chronic immaturity. Towards the end of the long section on spiritual gifts, the same exhortation occurs. 'Brothers, do not be children in your thinking. Be infants in evil, but in your thinking be mature' (14:20). 'Grow up' has been a consistent message all the way through the epistle. And the mark of the grown-up spiritual man is courage. He stands firm on the foundation of Christ and the gospel, knowing the convictions God has given him and being prepared to defend those convictions at whatever cost. He is not dependent on the approval of others, as children are, nor constantly seeking to be centre-stage, another child-like trait. He is prepared to plough a lone furrow in loyalty to Christ, whether others approve or not, and whether they understand or not. Such men of gospel courage (of both sexes!) are always needed in the church of Christ, gracious but unyielding, their consciences captive to the Word of God.

Be strong is an exhortation only possible to fulfil through the strength which God supplies, in and through the gospel, and by the power of the indwelling Holy Spirit. Such strength does not reside in any Christian by nature, but it is indisputable evidence of the work of God in us when we are empowered to do what is right without fear or favour. This strength is all about confidence in God and his truth, and it results in initiatives of righteousness and carries them through to a conclusion. Lack of this strength had produced the divisive factions in Corinth; the tolerance of gross sin within the church (5:1–5); the lawsuits between believers (6:1–8); and the abusive behaviour at the Lord's Table (11:17–22). No one seems to have been prepared to stand up against these things, and all too often the same charge could be laid against our own congregations and leaderships. Meekness is not the same thing as weakness. Love does not preclude strength. Of course, the way in which such abuses are identified and corrected is vitally important, but the current danger is that in the name of tolerance and a desire not to offend, destructive abuses are allowed to thrive in local churches and very few seem strong enough, in Christ and in the truth, to be able to deal with both issues and personalities.

Let all that you do be done in love is therefore a suitable conclusion to this series of exhortations, and also to the letter as a whole. Chapter 13 stands out as one of its mountain peaks, calling us to 'the most excellent way', reminding us of the values that led the Lord Jesus to his cross, and describing the qualities of true discipleship. There were plenty of people in Corinth who behaved with love towards their favoured leader but not towards the others leaders or their followers. They were partial and prejudiced toward many of their fellow believers in a way that true Christian love (*agape*) cannot possibly be. That was why the marks of division afflicted the body in Corinth and from that lack of love all the other defeats and difficulties, demerits and diseases, flowed. A panacea is a universal remedy or cure, and these days we do not really believe in them; we have been cheated by false claims too many times. But love is God's panacea for all our human ills. Just think of the changes that would take place in your own church, in your own relationships, perhaps within your own family or marriage, if love were the distinguishing character of everything we Christians did. This remains the uncompromising message of 1 Corinthians to the church in every generation, across the world.

2. FELLOWSHIP LINKS (verses 15–20)

Paul now turns to *the household of Stephanas* whom he describes as *the first converts in Achaia*. He has mentioned them before as having been among those he baptized in Corinth (1:16), but it is not their personal relationship to him as their father in the faith that Paul is concerned to highlight here, rather the proof of the genuineness of their response to the message he preached. Paul wants the Corinthians to be assured that the message Stephanas and his household believed was the true and only authentic, saving gospel, so that they all might continue to believe and embrace it without any changes or dilution. The proof he adduces is that *they have devoted themselves to the service of the saints* (verse 15). We learn from verse 17 that *Stephanas and Fortunatus and Achaicus* have been present with Paul in Ephesus, presumably having brought the letter from the congregation in

Corinth, to which this letter is his reply. Paul is concerned that the church should have every confidence in their messengers, *because they have made up for your absence, for they refreshed my spirit* (verse 17–18). It seems that they are about to return to Corinth, conveying Paul's reply, which he is very conscious may not be well received by some of the church's factions. He does not want Stephanas and his group to be rejected by his opponents just because his reply is un-favourable to many of their attitudes and positions. So, twice he commends these returning members to the church as fine examples of faithful gospel workers. *Now I urge you, brothers . . . be subject to such as these, and to every fellow worker and labourer* (verse 16). Again, verse 18 ends, *Give recognition to such men.*

Paul's concern is to show that they have not become 'his' men. They are gospel men, just as he is, and as every member of the congregation should be. Their devotion to gospel service is con-clusive proof of that. Some of the super-spiritual members, who were looking for a more sophisticated wisdom and a greater demonstration of power than Paul seemed able to supply, might well have despised them for the ordinariness of their practical Christian love. They were not 'spiritual' enough. But the implied rebuke of verse 17b indicates that they provided what the 'super-spirituals' did not, in the way of practical help and refreshment to Paul and his circle. Their example of 'service' and 'refreshment' is the very embodiment of love that the letter has been advocating, and everyone in Corinth should acknowledge this and emulate their example.

Verses 19–20 convey greetings from *the churches of Asia* – these are probably churches that lay in the vicinity of Paul's ministerial base at Ephesus – and from *Aquila and Priscilla* along with their home-based congregation. Acts 18:18–19 tells us that these two had met Paul when he arrived in Corinth, where they had settled when the Jews had been expelled from Rome by the decree of the Emperor, Claudius. As a fellow-Jew and a fellow-tentmaker, Paul had stayed and worked with this Christian couple who then accompanied him when he left Corinth and travelled by sea to Ephesus. It was they who met Apollos in the synagogue at Ephesus and 'explained to him the way of God more adequately', encouraging him to travel on to Corinth where 'he greatly helped' the believers (*Acts* 18:24–28). Paul is concerned to do all that he can to strengthen these links of brotherly love and friendship both between the congregations and between individuals. There are no barriers between the believers at Ephesus and those in Corinth and so the whole church sends greetings, symbolized by *a holy kiss* (verse 20), and indicating in a culturally acceptable way the bonds of mutual love and respect which exist among God's people. It is a kiss of peace and friendship. If Christians are unable to exchange such a kiss, it indicates that something is badly wrong in their fellowship. Verse 14 has been forgotten.

3. A FINAL PERSONAL NOTE (verses 21–24)

Paul now picks up the stylus, to inscribe his own personal greeting to the congregation founded through his ministry, *with my own hand* (verse 21). This is a guarantee of the genuineness of the letter, like a personal signature, because even at this early stage in church history false letters were apparently circulating, supposed to have Pauline authorship (see *2 Thess.* 2:2). It is also a more personal way of signing off and the apostle is keen to do what he can to rebuild the personal relationship with the members of the congregation, especially those who are dissatisfied with his message and leadership.

The greeting, however, is startling in its final confrontation of the issues that have been addressed throughout the letter. *If anyone has no love for the Lord, let him be accursed* (verse 22). The Lord Jesus has again and again been shown to be the centre and foundation of the whole Christian faith and therefore of Paul's entire missionary enterprise. This was his main thrust at the very beginning, in that the first ten verses of the letter each contain a reference to the Lord Jesus Christ – more often than not his full title – indicating that every strand of Christian belief and practice finds its origin and significance in him. The same thrust is here again at the very end. 'Is Christ divided?' is the haunting question of 1:13. The only possible answer, 'No', requires therefore a unity of love among his people, for one another and for the lost world. This is the supreme evidence of a genuine love for the Lord. The pronounced anathema surely continues to search deeply the heart of every reader of this letter. To love the Lord is the only authentic response to the gospel of the cross. It is the heart and soul of all genuine Christian profession and experience.

Perhaps the test of the reality of that love is the degree of sincere longing with which the one-word Aramaic prayer, 'Maranatha', is uttered from each individual heart. *O Lord, come!* When we really love someone, we long to see them, to be reunited with them, never to be separated from them. Our love for the Lord Jesus is expressed therefore in the joyful, prayerful expectation of his return. Such an expectation will not allow us to put our roots down in the culture of Corinth, or in any other costly location, but keep us living for the heavenly realities and the resurrection morning. Verse 22 is not an apostolic excommunication of any individual. It is a profound and searching challenge of all. Only God knows the heart, and Paul is content to express the essential test of real Christian faith and to leave the outcome between God and the individual's heart. The tension persists all the way to the end. The choice belongs to every one of us.

Then the letter ends, not with the curse, but with a blessing of grace and love (verses 23–24). Grace is the great characteristic of the ruler who came to be our rescuer. It flows from the Lord Jesus to everyone whose heart is open to receive it. And because Paul's heart has been mastered by that grace, his love flows out to *you in Christ Jesus*, in Corinth. It is a striking ending that illustrates and enacts the message of love with which the letter pulsates. Paul's love is not just directed to some of the congregation, to those who agree with him, or receive Timothy, or honour Stephanas. If they are in Christ Jesus then Paul loves them, warts and all, with all their squabbles and childishness, their pride and prejudice. For he loves them as Christ loved Saul of Tarsus when he captured his heart on the Damascus Road, and as that same Christ loved and still loves the pagans and sinners of Corinth, with all the patience and long-suffering, compassion and self-sacrifice that sent him to the cross, in the manifestation of the power and wisdom of God. In the end, the final words of the gospel are love and grace. That is the way of the cross. That is the way of ultimate victory. That is the mark of true spirituality. That is the heart of the gospel.

Group Study Guide

SCHEME FOR GROUP BIBLE STUDY
(Covers 26 Weeks; before each study read the passage indicated and the chapters from this book shown below.)

	STUDY PASSAGE	CHAPTERS
1.	1 Corinthians 1:1–9	1–2
2.	1 Corinthians 1:10–17	3
3.	1 Corinthians 1:18–2:5	4–5
4.	1 Corinthians 2:6–16	6–7
5.	1 Corinthians 3:1–15	8–9
6.	1 Corinthians 3:16–4:5	10–11
7.	1 Corinthians 4:6–21	12–13
8.	1 Corinthians 5:1–13	14–15
9.	1 Corinthians 6:1–11	16
10.	1 Corinthians 6:12–20	17
11.	1 Corinthians 7:1–16	18–19
12.	1 Corinthians 7:17–40	20–21
13.	1 Corinthians 8:1–13	22–23
14.	1 Corinthians 9:1–23	24–25
15.	1 Corinthians 9:24–10:5	26
16.	1 Corinthians 10:6–22	27–28
17.	1 Corinthians 10:23–11:1	29
18.	1 Corinthians 11:2–16	30
19.	1 Corinthians 11:17–34	31
20.	1 Corinthians 12:1–31	32–33
21.	1 Corinthians 13:1–13	34–35

Study Passage	Chapters
22. 1 Corinthians 14:1–40	36–37
23. 1 Corinthians 15:1–11	38
24. 1 Corinthians 15:12–34	39–40
25. 1 Corinthians 15:35–58	41–42
26. 1 Corinthians 16:1–24	43–44

This Study Guide has been prepared for group Bible study, but it can also be used individually. Those who use it on their own may find it helpful to keep a note of their responses in a notebook.

The way in which group Bible studies are led can greatly enhance their value. A well-conducted study will appear as though it has been easy to lead, but that is usually because the leader has worked hard and planned well. Clear aims are essential.

AIMS

In all Bible study, individual or corporate, we have several aims:

1. To gain an understanding of the original meaning of the particular passage of Scripture;

2. To apply this to ourselves and our own situation;

3. To develop some specific ways of putting the biblical teaching into practice.

2 Timothy 3:16–17 provides a helpful structure. Paul says that Scripture is useful for:

(i) teaching us;

(ii) rebuking us;

(iii) correcting, or changing us;

(iv) training us in righteousness.

Consequently, in studying any passage of Scripture, we should always have in mind these questions:

What does this passage teach us (about God, ourselves, etc.)?

Does it rebuke us in some way?

How can its teaching transform us?

What equipment does it give us for serving Christ?

[288]

In fact, these four questions alone would provide a safe guide in any Bible study.

PRINCIPLES

In group Bible study we meet in order to learn about God's Word and ways 'with all the saints' (*Eph.* 3:18). But our own experience, as well as Scripture, tells us that the saints are not always what they *are* called to be in every situation – including group Bible study! Leaders ordinarily have to work hard and prepare well if the work of the group is to be spiritually profitable. The following guidelines for leaders may help to make this a reality.

Preparation:

1. Study and understand the passage yourself. The better prepared and more sure of the direction of the study you are, the more likely it is that the group will have a beneficial and enjoyable study.
Ask: What are the main things this passage is saying? How can this be made clear? This is not the same question as the more common 'What does this passage "say to you"?', which expects a reaction rather than an exposition of the passage. Be clear about that distinction yourself, and work at making it clear in the group study.

2. On the basis of your own study form a clear idea *before* the group meets of (i) the main theme(s) of the passage which should be opened out for discussion, and (ii) some general conclusions the group ought to reach as a result of the study. Here the questions which arise from 2 Timothy 3:16–17 should act as our guide.

3. The guidelines and questions which follow may help to provide a general framework for each discussion; leaders should use them as starting places which can be further developed. It is usually helpful to have a specific goal or theme in mind for group discussion, and one is suggested for each study. But even more important than tracing a single theme is understanding the teaching and the implications of the passage.

Leading the Group:

1. Announce the passage and theme for the study, and begin with prayer. In group studies it may be helpful to invite a different person to lead in prayer each time you meet.

2. Introduce the passage and theme, briefly reminding people of its outline and highlighting the content of each subsidiary section.

3. Lead the group through the discussion questions. Use your own if you are comfortable in doing so; those provided may be used, developing them with your own points. As discussion proceeds, continue to encourage the group first of all to discuss the significance of the passage (teaching) and only then its application (meaning for us). It may be helpful to write important points and applications on a board by way of summary as well as visual aid.

4. At the end of each meeting, remind members of the group of their assignments for the next meeting, and encourage them to come prepared. Be sufficiently prepared as the leader to give specific assignments to individuals, or even couples or groups, to come with specific contributions.

5. Remember that you are the leader of the group! Encourage clear contributions, and do not be embarrassed to ask someone to explain what they have said more fully or to help them to do so ('Do you mean . . . ?').

Most groups include the 'over-talkative', the 'over-silent' and the 'red-herring raisers'! Leaders must control the first, encourage the second and redirect the third! Each leader will develop his or her own most natural way of doing that; but it will be helpful to think out what that is before the occasion arises! The first two groups can be helped by some judicious direction of questions to specific individuals or even groups (for example, 'Jane, you know something about this from personal experience . . .'); the third by redirecting the discussion to the passage itself ('That is an interesting point, but isn't it true that this passage really concentrates on . . . ?'). It may be helpful to break the group up into smaller groups sometimes, giving each subgroup specific points to discuss and to report back on. A wise arranging of these smaller groups may also help each member to participate.

More important than any techniques we may develop is the help of the Spirit enabling us to understand and to apply the Scriptures. Have and encourage a humble, prayerful spirit.

6. Keep faith with the schedule; it is better that some of the group wished the study could have been longer than that others are inconvenienced by it stretching beyond the time limits set.

7. Close in prayer. As time permits, spend the closing minutes in corporate prayer, encouraging the group to apply what they have learned in praise and thanks, intercession and petition.

STUDY 1: 1 Corinthians 1:1–9

AIM: To appreciate the Lordship of Jesus Christ and to thank God for the blessings with which he has enriched his people.

1. Imagine you are talking to a non-Christian friend about why you are studying 1 Corinthians. Your friend thinks that Paul's writings offer just one of many possible ways of looking at the Christian life. How would you respond?

2. Christians are 'sanctified' and 'do not belong to anyone else but Christ' (chapter 1). How does this encourage you to fight against sin in your life?

3. Are you tempted to live any parts of your Christian life as a 'lone ranger'?

4. What can you do to encourage and support other Christians more?

5. The Corinthians were Christians who, in many areas, had lost their focus on Jesus. In what areas of your life do you feel your focus on Jesus has been lost?

Pray that as you read 1 Corinthians God would speak to you and put Jesus back at the centre of your life.

6. Do you find it difficult to thank God for the good things he does in the lives of other Christians? If so, why might this be?

7. Pray and thank God for the grace he has given to some other Christians you know.

8. 'Speech and knowledge' were areas of lifestyle the Corinthians struggled to honour Jesus in. How would you evaluate your living in these two areas of speech and knowledge?

9. Are you tempted to become depressed at failure in your Christian life, or caught up in a focus on present problems? What

can you do to stay focused on God's faithfulness and the future Day of Christ?

10. Thank God for the promise that he will 'sustain you to the end'.

STUDY 2: 1 Corinthians 1:10–17

AIM: To prize and promote Christian unity by focusing on the central message of the Cross.

1. Why is Paul so concerned that the church family be 'united in the same mind and judgement?'

2. What practical things can you do to help true Christian unity grow in your church? For example, is there somebody you could give an encouraging word? Do you need to say sorry to someone?

3. In what ways are you tempted to idolize Christian leaders?

4. How can you see a quest for spirituality and effective methods eclipse the message of the Cross today?

STUDY 3: 1 Corinthians 1:18–2:5

AIM: To show that God's message and methods must be the means we use to promote God's work in the church.

1. Why is it such foolishness to reject the message of the Cross?

2. Describe your understanding of the worldly wisdom our culture preaches. How is the church led by the demands this modern culture makes?

3. Why do people find it so difficult to accept that what they most urgently need is not power or wisdom but salvation?

4. Are you determined to follow the crucified Christ despite people around you viewing Christianity as foolishness?

5. Why has God not simply chosen the best looking, most popular and influential people to be in his church?

6. When do you boast in yourself rather than God?

7. 'True Christians delight in Christ' (p28). What will this delight look like in your daily life?

8. Why was Paul not trying to make his preaching the most eloquent and polished media presentation available in Corinth?

9. You meet a pastor who leads a large church who thinks that good, relevant preaching must include flashy media presentations and computer displays. He defends his approach by saying that it works really well. How could you respond?

10. Are there any areas of your life where your faith is resting in 'the wisdom of men' rather than 'in the power of God'?

11. Our culture encourages people to live in as much comfort as is reasonably possible. How does the Cross of Christ shatter this respectable approach to life?

STUDY 4: 1 Corinthians 2:6–16

AIM: To learn to thank God for the gift of his Spirit who gives us wisdom and understanding that we might know Christ in the Scriptures.

1. What is the eventual end of human wisdom that is man-centred and time-bound?

2. Why can we never work out God's wisdom for ourselves?

3. What evidence do you see in your daily life of people failing to understand God's secret wisdom?

4. How has it been made possible for you to know the thoughts of God?

5. What is the great work of the Spirit described in this passage?

6. You hear a teacher who says that in order to truly know God you must not just have the Spirit, but must also have a profound religious experience. How would you respond to this idea?

7. Why can the natural man not understand spiritual things?

8. It is impossible for the natural man to understand the things of God; how should this encourage us as we do evangelism?

STUDY 5: 1 Corinthians 3:1–15

AIM: To learn how to work together with God and in a way that will pass the scrutiny of the coming judgment.

1. Are there any areas of life where you would like to be content with spiritual childishness?

2. What evidence does Paul produce in these verses to show that the Corinthians are childish Christians drifting back to worldly thinking?

3. What evidence do you see in the church today that we regard jealousy and factions less seriously than Paul did?

4. Is there anybody with whom you have disagreed in a worldly manner, and with whom you need to be reconciled?

5. Try to explain how the Cross is the paradigm of Christian ministry. (It may be helpful to consider how the world's methods of leadership contrast with this.)

6. Are there any ministry areas that you are possessive of and have come to cherish as belonging to you rather than Jesus?

7. How should knowing that God will not compare our ministry with another person's ministry change our attitudes and thinking?

8. What is the foundation upon which a church must be built?

9. What other foundations do people try and build churches on?

10. The Corinthians' main concern is impressing the world around them; Paul's aim is surviving the coming judgment. Which of these two perspectives dominates your thinking and church life?

11. How can you lovingly encourage other people in your church to keep a focus on future-looking ministry that will survive the coming judgment?

12. How does this passage help us deal with despair that our ministry does not look that impressive?

STUDY 6: 1 Corinthians 3:16-4:5

AIM: To see and evaluate wisdom, power and Christian ministry from God's perspective.

1. How does Paul's definition of the church transcend our more worldly definitions such as the 'denomination' or 'building'?

2. Summarize the delusion the Corinthians are living under.

3. What does it mean to be a 'Christian fool'?

4. How does the positive perspective of 3:21–23 help us to stop envying the wisdom and power of the world?

5. Read Matthew 9:36–38 and pray that God would raise up workers who have this Cross-focused sacrificial ministry.

6. What does Paul say is the correct standard by which to evaluate ministry?

7. When are you tempted to judge other people's ministry?

8. How should our inability to judge our own secret motives change our thinking about our own ministry?

9. How should Paul's focus on the future judgment affect our attitude to judging ministers today?

10. Are there any areas of ministry in which you are not being faithful?

STUDY 7: 1 Corinthians 4:6–21

AIM: To learn that a powerful and fruitful Christian life is marked by self-denial and suffering for Christ's sake.

1. What is the attitude that lies at the heart of the Corinthian problem?

2. How does a love of 'extra-biblical revelation' flow from this wrong attitude?

3. How does grace liberate Christians from the tyrannies of comparison and judgementalism?

4. Why is it wrong to think that we have already received all the riches God has for us?

5. How would you explain Paul's view of the normal Christian life to an unbeliever?

6. When Paul faces suffering and hostility, how does his response reveal the amazing power of God?

7. How did God in Jesus resolve the conflict between humanity and heaven?

8. How does this provide a template for Paul's resolution of the conflict between himself and the Corinthians?

9. How does Paul's lifestyle relate to his teaching?

10. Why is it so urgent that we turn from forms of ministry and living that are focused on talk of our own power and ingenuity?

STUDY 8: 1 Corinthians 5:1–13

AIM: To view sin in the light of the Cross and to understand the need for corporate discipline to keep the body of Christ pure and holy.

1. How would a corporate church approach to sexual ethics be different to the more individualized approach we are more used to?

2. What should our reaction be to cases of sexual scandal within the church?

3. What does it mean for discipline to be an act of love?

4. What point does the illustration about leaven make?

5. How does the death of Jesus as our Passover lamb lay upon us the greatest of responsibilities to get rid of sin?

6. What are the two extremes to which the church tends to swing regarding the nature of its relationship with the culture around it?

7. Is the church today known for sexual purity and loving, firm judgment of those within it?

8. What are the effects of a hard and critical spirit in dealing with matters of discipline?

9. Does your church have guidelines on how it would deal with a matter of discipline, should the event occur?

STUDY 9: 1 Corinthians 6:1–11

AIM: To learn that the church is a family, the members of which are to love one another, and if mistreated to bear it, while seeking reconciliation within the church.

1. Why is it so wrong for Christians to get secular courts to settle their internal disagreements with each other?

2. What kind of problems in church life do we think of as legal which may in fact be spiritual?

3. Why is any court case between believers a defeat before the trial has begun?

4. Would you rather be wronged and cheated than stand by your 'rights'?

5. Why is it necessary for Paul to warn us 'not to be deceived' regarding the concrete realities of moral demands in the church?

6. How does the example of the Corinthians in verse 11 hold out great hope for us?

STUDY 10: 1 Corinthians 6:12–20

AIM: To realize that our union with Christ has very important implications for what we do with our bodies, and in particular, sexual purity.

1. What is the difference between true Christian liberty and licence?

2. Are you engaged in behaviour that is not beneficial to your Christian walk?

3. Are you engaged in behaviour that enslaves and addicts you?

4. Why is what we do with our bodies in this life so important?

5. Why is it not possible for sex without commitment to be 'loving'?

6. What situations do you need to flee from to avoid sexual immorality?

7. Why does sexual sin cause so much pain and damage to people?

8. List all the motivations Paul gives us to help us fight sexual temptation.

STUDY 11: 1 Corinthians 7:1-16

AIM: To realize our responsibilities to Christ and one another in marriage.

1. How do we respond to the accusation that Christianity is against sex?

2. What is Paul's teaching to the married Christian couple?

3. Why is it important to remember that neither marriage nor singleness is necessarily permanent?

4. Are you tempted to think that the best way to improve your godliness would be simply by a change in the external situation?

5. What is Paul's teaching to the unmarried and widows?

6. How does this differ from our surrounding culture?

7. What can you do to make single people feel more valuable in your church life?

8. What is Paul's teaching to married Christian couples?

9. Why does God regulate and make provision for the breaking of his laws?

10. What is Paul's teaching to a Christian married to a non-Christian?

STUDY 12: 1 Corinthians 7:17–40

AIM: To learn contentment with the place in life the Lord has appointed for us and to serve him in it.

1. Why does Paul urge people to stay as they are?

2. How does this contrast with the attitudes of our secular society?

3. How does a deeper appreciation of God's sovereignty help us deal with a restless longing to change our life situation?

4. What is the supreme issue which concerns Paul regarding how we live our lives? Is this our concern?

5. Are you in danger of becoming a 'slave of men' as you pursue a change in external circumstances?

6. What does it mean for a married man to live as if he is not married?

7. If you are single, are you using your gift of singleness to be devoted fully to the work of the Lord?

8. What can your church family do to encourage single and married people to use their respective gifts for the glory of God?

9. Are people in your church put under pressure either to stay single or get married?

10. Are you enjoying the liberty of being a slave to Christ in your present situation?

STUDY 13: 1 Corinthians 8:1–13

AIM: To ensure that all our conduct is guided by love and not pride.

1. How does knowledge on its own 'puff up'?

2. How does love change this situation?

3. Why can knowledge without love not lead to a person knowing God?

4. In what areas of your life are you using your knowledge in a way that is not loving?

5. How sensitive are you to young Christian converts?

6. In what kind of situations do you need to be careful not to upset a recent convert?

7. How does the Cross model for us sacrificial love and rights set aside for the benefit of others?

8. Are there any ways in which you sacrifice your freedom for the benefit of others?

STUDY 14: 1 Corinthians 9:1-23

AIM: To embrace the 'freedom' of sacrificing our rights in order to further the cause of the gospel.

1. How does Paul defend his authority?

2. What rights does Paul say that he is entitled to in his ministry?

3. Why has Paul laid these rights aside?

4. Do you care enough about the gospel not to take up material privileges to which you feel entitled?

5. How does the Cross of Jesus govern your life-style decisions?

6. Why does Paul want to be sacrificial in his ministry life-style?

7. What situations and cultural barriers do you feel uncomfortable crossing?

8. Will you become all things to all men in those situations to win some to Christ?

9. In what areas of your life can you change your attitudes and decisions so that you are living sacrificially to further the gospel?

STUDY 15: 1 Corinthians 9:24–10:5

AIM: To learn that discipline is an essential element in living the Christian life.

1.   Are you working hard and being disciplined for a crown that will fade?

2.   What will you do to win the crown that lasts for ever?

3.   In what areas do you need to work at self-discipline? How do these verses provide motivation?

4.   Are you tempted to just think that everything will work out in the end?

5.   Are you running the race in such a way as to finish well?

STUDY 16: 1 Corinthians 10:6–22

AIM: To learn from the example of others the dangers of sexual immorality and idolatry and our responsibility to pursue the way of escape from these temptations that God provides.

1.   What are the things that your heart runs after in addition to Jesus?

2.   Why is sexual immorality incompatible with single-hearted love to God?

3.   What does grumbling reveal about our heart's attitude to God?

4.   How does verse 11 help us deal with the objection that the Bible is not relevant to the modern person?

5.   What are you going to do in response to the warning of verse 12?

6.   What are the 'ways of escape' God has provided for the temptations that you face in normal life?

7.   God provides a way out of temptation (v13), what then is our responsibility?

8.   How does communion show fellowship with God and Christians?

9.   With what does idolatry bring us into fellowship?

10. Are there any areas in which you are subtly compromising and allowing idolatry a foothold in your heart?

STUDY 17: 1 Corinthians 10:23–11:1

AIM: To learn how to imitate Paul and Christ by seeking the good of others and the glory of God in everything.

1. What are the things which Paul says must control our exercise of freedom?

2. Who does your life influence? Is it an influence that builds them up?

3. In what way should our view of the world be positive?

4. In what way should our view of the world be negative?

5. How can you change your behaviour to make your presentation of the gospel to non-Christians more consistent and compelling?

STUDY 18: 1 Corinthians 11:2–16

AIM: To appreciate the distinct, yet dependent, roles of men and women in the church.

1. How should we react to Bible passages that are difficult and which have been misused in the past?

2. What does headship mean?

3. How does the Trinity act as an example of a relationship where there is both authority and equality?

4. What will it mean for a man to be under the authority of his head in church?

5. What will it mean for a woman to be under the authority of her head in church?

6. Why does Paul see a need to emphasize the interdependence of men and women in their relationships with each other?

7. How does this teaching challenge our culture and offer answers to problems people face?

STUDY 19: 1 Corinthians 11:17–34

AIM: To learn how to partake of the Lord's Supper in a worthy manner.

1. How does the behaviour of the Corinthians at the Lord's Supper contradict the reality of the Cross?

2. Do you see any of these attitudes in your church meetings?

3. How does the image of broken bread help us grasp the fact that Jesus' death was 'for us'?

4. What does it mean for the cup to remind us of God's covenant with us?

5. To what great task does our taking of the Lord's Supper commit us?

6. How do we take the Lord's Super in a worthy manner?

7. What will you do in preparation before you next take part in the Lord's Supper?

STUDY 20: 1 Corinthians 12:1–31

AIM: To grasp the implications for unity and edification of being a member of a body that has many parts.

1. What is the purpose of gifts?

2. Why is speaking unintelligibly and being uncontrolled in behaviour unloving things to do?

3. How can you seek to benefit other Christians?

4. What could be done in your church to help people use their gifts for the building up of others in unity?

5. Do you act towards other Christians as if you are part of one body?

6. How does baptism provide a basis for our unity?

7. What are the two dangers we can face as part of a church body?

8. To which danger are you most tempted?

9. Why are word gifts important?

10. Why is it impossible for the gift of tongues to be the biblical proof a person is Spirit-filled?

STUDY 21: 1 Corinthians 13:1–13

AIM: To see the crucial importance of love as the controlling motivation in all that we do in the service of Christ and his church.

1. Why is this section on love included in Paul's letter?

2. What practical difference will love make to the use of our gifts?

3. Are you more impressed by love or gifts?

4. What things other than love can motivate Christians to great (futile!) acts of service and ministry?

5. What is the mark of true spirituality?

6. Why should this passage shame and humble us?

7. Are you holding on to past hurts done to you which hinder you from exercising love?

8. How does Paul extol the greatness of love in this passage?

9. What childish attitudes do you like to hold on to?

10. How does the future of heaven spur us on to the maturity of love in this life?

STUDY 22: 1 Corinthians 14:1–40

AIM: To grasp the vitally important place the ministry of the Word has in the edification of the church.

1. How is the church most edified today, in terms of its public spoken ministry? How can we best support this in our local congregations?

2. In an age where 'spin' and 'image' are frequently regarded as more important than truth and content, how does Paul's argument in this section nerve us to be counter-cultural?

3. What evidences in our thinking as Christians today remind us that the old Greek dualism of body and spirit, physical and spiritual, secular and sacred still persist? What is the remedy?

4. How do we see Paul's pastoral ability demonstrated in this passage?

5. What will it mean for you to be an infant in evil, but mature in your thinking?

6. What does it mean for tongues to be a sign for unbelievers?

7. Do most people who 'speak in tongues' understand the phenomena in this biblical way?

8. What is so different about prophecy, that it is able to have a positive effect on people?

9. What were the problems in the Corinthian meetings that Paul sought to correct?

10. How do we see the concern for order in the corrective teaching?

11. What will it mean for a woman to 'be in submission'?

12. What will happen to anybody who ignores Paul's teaching on these matters?

13. How would you define Christian maturity from this passage?

STUDY 23: 1 Corinthians 15:1–11

AIM: To learn that we are saved by believing and continuing to believe the contents of the same gospel that Paul and his fellow apostles preached.

1. Are you holding firmly to the same gospel by which you were saved?

2. What is the content of this gospel?

3. What does it mean for Christ to die 'according to the Scriptures'?

4. What would you say to a person who believes that the resurrection of Jesus was spiritual and non-physical?

5. How has the grace of God changed you?

STUDY 24: 1 Corinthians 15:12–34

AIM: To grasp the fact of Christ's resurrection and its implications for Christian life and mission.

1. Why may the Corinthians have denied the resurrection?

2. What are the results of denying the reality of Jesus' resurrection?

3.   How does the resurrection of Jesus encourage you to suffer patiently and with confidence?

4.   Are you often tempted to forget the importance of Jesus' resurrection? Take some time now to thank God for it.

5.   What is the essence of the contrast between Adam and Christ?

6.   What are we still waiting for in the process of God's plan, as described here?

7.   How does the certain knowledge that death will be defeated give us strength to live Cross-centred lives?

8.   What things do you do in your life that shows you are living for the future rather than the present?

STUDY 25: 1 Corinthians 15:35–58

AIM: To appreciate the bodily nature of the resurrection and the great change that it will bring about.

1.   What things in daily life do you believe in that are difficult to understand?

2.   Why is it foolish to disbelieve the resurrection because it is difficult to understand?

3.   How does the analogy of a seed and a plant help us understand something of the resurrection body?

4.   How do the analogies of the sun, moon and different animals help us understand something of the resurrection body?

5.   What are the specific contrasts in verses 42–44 between the present and future life?

6. As you look to the future, do you have the certainty with which Paul wrote verse 49?

7.   On what grounds must the Christian see the physical world as good?

8.   On what grounds must the Christian see the physical world as bad?

9.   What is the great change that we look forward to after the sleep of death?

10. Our generation avoids talking about death. From 1 Corinthians 15, what sort of things can you say to your non-Christian friends that would help them face the grave?

11. Are you standing firm in life, confident in the victory that Jesus achieved on the Cross?

12. How then will you always give yourself fully to the work of the Lord?

STUDY 26: 1 Corinthians 16:1–24

AIM: To submit our lives to the Lord's will in everything out of love for him, his servants and his people.

1. Is your giving regular and proportionate to your income? What steps can you take to improve on this?

2. How does Paul's standards for giving differ from the demand for tithes?

3. Are you excited by the wide doors for effective gospel work open in our day? Are you concerned about the opposition to gospel work in our generation?

4. What can you do then to support gospel ministry through your church family?

5. How do we see Paul both planning and relying on God in these verses?

6. What are the dangers your church faces that may lure you away from a Cross-shaped life?

7. What are the exhortations Paul calls us to in the light of spiritual testing?

8. What is the evidence Stephanas' household was converted? Is this evidence to be seen in your life?

9. How has 1 Corinthians taught you what it means to 'love the Lord'?

10. How are you now going to live out a 'Cross-shaped spirituality'?